"*The Peacemaker* is an awesome and thorough tool of reference on biblical peacemaking and reconciliation that will transform the lives of Christians in the twenty-first century."

—William L. Sheals, pastor, Hopewell Missionary Baptist Church, Norcross, Georgia

"Sande weaves the theology of conflict resolution into a tapestry portraying Jesus Christ and his gospel as the only true foundation for peacemaking. . . . I highly recommend this 'new and improved' version."

—Dennis Rainey, president of FamilyLife and radio host of *FamilyLife Today*

"This generation of believers is called to authentic Christian peacemaking and reconciliation. Ken Sande shows the way in *The Peacemaker*. All pastors and Christian leaders should read this book."

—R. Albert Mohler Jr., president, Southern Baptist Theological Seminary

"The third edition of *The Peacemaker* is simply outstanding. Conflict is deeply rooted in the heart, but there is a gloriously liberating remedy, and you will hear about it in the pages of this life-changing, relationship-mending book."

—Bruce W. Green, dean, Liberty University School of Law

"A culture of gospel unity should characterize God's covenant family. *The Peacemaker* gives hope for victory in what is often a hard-fought battle for unity."

—Susan Hunt, author of *Spiritual Mothering*

"Here is wisdom both biblical and practical. You can tell it was written by a man who has lived out these principles as a lawyer in practice, and as a leader in his church. We are in his debt."

—Mark Dever, pastor, Capitol Hill Baptist Church, Washington, D.C.

"Who would have thought that Ken Sande's landmark book *The Peacemaker* could be better? This updated version is! Let your heart be shaped by this book and go out and do what the Prince of Peace called all of his children to do: make peace."

—Paul David Tripp, director, Changing Lives Ministries

"The Bible calls Christians to defend the truth, but the Bible also calls Christians to work hard at unity. Ken Sande gives us valuable, practical help in our 'fight for peace' among Christians in addition to our fight for truth."

—Ric Cannada, president, Reformed Theological Seminary

"Ken has given us a biblical and practical strategy for resolving personal conflict. While the enemy is busy trying to destroy relationships, this book will give you the strength and the strategy to make peace."

—Mac Brunson, pastor, First Baptist Church, Dallas

"*The Peacemaker* helps the believer stop seeing conflicts as obstacles and start seeing them as 'opportunities to glorify God.'"

—Peter N. Nanfelt, president, the Christian and Missionary Alliance

"*The Peacemaker* is an indispensable tool for pastors. . . . There is no need for another book on this topic to be written now that this volume exists."

—C. J. Mahaney, pastor, Covenant Life Church

"A solid, Bible-based guide to process the local church through conflict. Absolutely one of the best books I know of to minimize personal and organizational conflict."

—Gary R. Allen, national coordinator of ministerial enrichment, Assemblies of God

"*The Peacemaker* is the most thorough and comprehensive guide to resolving conflicts I have ever read. It is insightful, convicting, and biblical."

—Josh McDowell, international speaker and author

"This updated version of a well-respected book should be invaluable to Christian leaders who want to create a culture of peace in their organizations and churches."

—Bob Creson, president, Wycliffe U.S.A.

"My church, and my own pastoral leadership, have benefited immeasurably from *The Peacemaker* . . . the most comprehensive 'how to' book on the subject."

—Joel Hunter, pastor, Northland—A Church Distributed, Orlando

"For over a decade, this book has been the 'go to' guide for biblical conflict resolution. And now Ken Sande has made it even better by sharing his experiences as a conciliator, bringing us rich real-life stories and Christ-centered truth."

—Elyse Fitzpatrick, counselor and author

"In an age when conflict is more often the norm in the world and the church, a practical guide to being a peacemaker is sorely needed. Ken Sande provides that guide. It is timely. It is biblical. It is user friendly."

—Sam Casey, executive director, Christian Legal Society

"Ken refreshes the heart with winsome, biblical guidance on how to live out the gospel in human relationships. A must read for everyone—especially those in the helping professions where relationships and conflict are central concerns."

—Judy Dabler, executive director, Center for Biblical Counseling & Education

"[Sande] laces the book with examples of his experience in conciliation work. He makes a strong case for the 'must' of reconciliation, and he demonstrates the how-tos with which to arrive at peace."

—Rolf Bouma, *The Banner*

"It is rare to find a Christian lawyer who will depend so wholly on the Scriptures."

—Jay E. Adams, pastor and author

"Through the years I have read much . . . of the enormous body of literature dealing with conflict resolution and its allied problems. This treatment is the most concrete and helpful I have yet to find."

—Vernon Grounds, Denver Conservative Baptist Seminary

THE
PEACEMAKER

A BIBLICAL GUIDE TO RESOLVING
PERSONAL CONFLICT

THIRD EDITION

KEN SANDE

BakerBooks
A Division of Baker Book House Co
Grand Rapids, Michigan 49516

© 1991, 1997, 2004 by Kenneth Sande

Published by Baker Books
a division of Baker Publishing Group
P.O. Box 6287, Grand Rapids, MI 49516-6287
www.bakerbooks.com

Sixth printing, October 2006

Printed in the United States of America

Library of Congress Cataloging-in-Publication Data
Sande, Ken.
    The peacemaker : a biblical guide to resolving personal conflict / Ken Sande.—
3rd ed.
        p.   cm.
    Includes bibliographical references and indexes.
    ISBN 10: 0-8010-6485-6 (pbk.)
    ISBN 978-0-8010-6485-2 (pbk.)
    1. Reconciliation—Religious aspects—Christianity. 2. Interpersonal relations—
Religious aspects—Christianity. 3. Conflict management—Religious aspects—
Christianity. 4. Peace—Religious aspects—Christianity. I. Title.
BV4509.5 S26 2004
253.5′2—dc22   2003019166

To Corlette,
whose love and encouragement
kept me writing

and to Kris,
whose insights and common sense
added so greatly to this book

CONTENTS

What's New
in the
Third Edition?

An entirely new preface

A stronger emphasis on the gospel of Jesus Christ as the foundation for true peacemaking

More examples of resolving conflict in the family, church, and workplace

An expanded discussion about how to identify and overcome the desires in our hearts that fuel conflict

Additional insights into how to show others their wrongs by involving intermediaries, using stories and metaphors, and offering hope for change through the gospel

New ways to understand and practice forgiveness and use it as an opportunity to witness for Christ

A new appendix on how the church can develop a "culture of peace" by equipping and assisting its people to respond to conflict biblically

PREFACE

Peacemakers are people who breathe grace. They draw continually on the goodness and power of Jesus Christ, and then they bring his love, mercy, forgiveness, strength, and wisdom to the conflicts of daily life. God delights to breathe his grace through peacemakers and use them to dissipate anger, improve understanding, promote justice, and encourage repentance and reconciliation.

As a lawyer and full-time Christian conciliator, I have seen this powerful dynamic bring peace in hundreds of conflicts, including contract disputes, divorce and custody battles, personal injury actions, neighborhood feuds, and church splits. As an elder in my church, I have also watched God work through committed peacemakers to preserve and actually improve congregational unity as we wrestled through serious differences over vision, leadership roles, finances, worship style, staffing, children's education, and building programs.

As a husband and father, I have seen biblical peacemaking turn frustrating conflicts into opportunities for our family to face our sins, see our mutual need for the Savior, and grow closer to him and one another. And as a former engineer and now a parachurch ministry leader, I have observed how even the most difficult workplace issues can be resolved constructively when even one employee decides to breathe grace in the midst of conflict.

Most of us have observed that these results are not common in today's world. When people lock horns in a courtroom, a congregational meeting, the bedroom, or the workplace, relationships are often severely damaged. Conflict robs us of immeasurable time, energy, money, and opportunities in ministry or business. Worst of all, it can destroy our Christian witness. When believers are bitterly embroiled in disagreement or coldly estranged from one another, few people will pay attention when we try to talk with them about the reconciling love of Jesus Christ.

But the opposite is also true. When Christians learn to be peacemakers, they can turn conflict into an opportunity to strengthen relationships, preserve valuable resources, and make their lives a testimony to the love and power of Christ.

This book is designed to help you become this kind of peacemaker. It provides a simple yet comprehensive approach to resolving conflict. Because this approach is based solidly on God's Word, it is effective in every type of conflict. It has been used not only to resolve the normal differences of daily life, but also to stop divorces, prevent church splits, and settle multimillion dollar lawsuits. This approach to resolving conflict may be summarized in four basic principles, which I refer to as the "Four G's."

> *Glorify God* (1 Cor. 10:31). Biblical peacemaking is motivated and guided by a deep desire to bring honor to God by revealing the reconciling love and power of Jesus Christ. As we draw on his grace, follow his example, and put his teachings into practice, we can find freedom from the impulsive, self-centered decisions that make conflict worse, and bring praise to God by displaying the power of the gospel in our lives.
>
> *Get the log out of your eye* (Matt. 7:5). Attacking others only invites counterattacks. This is why Jesus teaches us to face up to our own contributions to a conflict before we focus on what others have done. When we overlook others' minor offenses and honestly admit our own faults, our opponents will often respond in kind. As tensions decrease, the way may be opened for sincere discussion, negotiation, and reconciliation.
>
> *Gently restore* (Gal. 6:1). When others fail to see their contributions to a conflict, we sometimes need to graciously show

them their fault. If they refuse to respond appropriately, Jesus calls us to involve respected friends, church leaders, or other objective individuals who can help us encourage repentance and restore peace.

Go and be reconciled (Matt. 5:24). Finally, peacemaking involves a commitment to restoring damaged relationships and negotiating just agreements. When we forgive others as Jesus has forgiven us and seek solutions that satisfy others' interests as well as our own, the debris of conflict is cleared away and the door is opened for genuine peace.

These principles were developed by Peacemaker Ministries, which was established in 1982 to equip and assist Christians and their churches to respond to conflict biblically (see appendix E). Working through a network of gifted peacemakers throughout the world, we have found that these principles transcend international and cultural boundaries. They have proven to be as needed and effective in South Korea, Australia, India, Rwanda, Bulgaria, and Peru as they are in the United States.

These principles have also proven to be universally *countercultural*. No matter what race or country we come from, none of us is naturally inclined to obey Jesus' commands to love our enemies, confess our wrongs, gently correct others, submit to our church, and forgive those who hurt us. In fact, left to our own instincts, we are disposed to do just the opposite.

Fortunately, God has provided a way for us to overcome our innate weakness as peacemakers and learn to respond to conflict constructively. His solution is the gospel, the good news that "Christ Jesus came into the world to save sinners" (1 Tim. 1:15). God sent his Son to pay the price for our sins through his death and resurrection. When we believe this and put our trust in Jesus, God forgives all our sins. Through the gospel he also enables us to learn how to resist temptation, obey his commands, and live a life that honors him.

This wonderful news can radically change the way we respond to conflict. Through the gospel, the foundational G, the Lord enables us to live out the Four G's of peacemaking. As we stand in awe of his matchless grace, we find more joy in glorifying God than in pursuing our own selfish ends. When we realize that God has mercy on those who confess their sins, our defensiveness lifts and we are able to admit our wrongs. As we accept and benefit from the way the gospel lovingly shows us our sin, we are inspired to gently correct and restore others who have done wrong. And as we rejoice in the liberating forgiveness of God, we are empowered to go and forgive others in the same way. Through the gospel, God provides both the model and motivation for peacemaking!

The Lord has also provided a powerful support system for peacemaking. It is the church. When we are unable to resolve a conflict on our own, God commands the local church to step in and bring its wisdom, resources, and authority to bear on the problem (Matt. 18:16–17; Phil. 4:2–3; 1 Cor. 6:1–8). I thank God for the many churches that are fulfilling this important responsibility so faithfully. They are teaching their people to be peacemakers, training gifted members to serve as conflict coaches and mediators, and reinstating the ministry of loving, redemptive accountability as a means to restore members who have become entangled in destructive sin. As you will see throughout this book, this kind of training and assistance from local churches has often proven to be the key to restoring relationships, averting divorce, and resolving seemingly hopeless conflicts.

Unfortunately, many believers and their churches have not yet developed the commitment and ability to respond to conflict in a gospel-centered and biblically faithful manner. This is often because they have succumbed to the relentless pressure our secular culture exerts on us to forsake the timeless truths of Scripture and adopt the relativism of our postmodern age. Although many Christians and their churches believe they have held on to God's Word as their standard for life, their responses to conflict, among other things, show that they have in fact surrendered much ground to the world. Instead of resolving differences in a distinctively biblical fashion, they often react to conflict with the same avoidance, manipulation, and control that characterize the world. In effect, both individually and congregationally, they have given in to the world's postmodern standard, which is "What feels good, sounds true, and seems beneficial *to me?*"

This self-validating and self-serving mind-set clashes head on with the divinely established and self-denying way of thinking God has revealed in Scripture. I hope this book will help you see this clash of cultures more clearly and identify some of the ways that you and your church may have been led away from a firm reliance on God and his Word, especially when it comes to resolving conflict. I also hope you will dedicate yourself to resisting this infiltration by the world and deliberately pursuing a solidly biblical approach to peacemaking, both personally and within your church. To assist you in serving your congregation in this area, I have provided in appendix F a detailed vision and practical strategy for developing a genuine "culture of peace" in your church.

The primary focus of this book, however, will be on how God can help *you* as an individual Christian throw off worldly ideas about resolving conflict and become a true peacemaker. Among other things, it will explain

How to use conflict as an opportunity to demonstrate the love and power of Jesus

When it is appropriate to overlook an offense

How to change attitudes and habits that lead to conflict

How to confess wrongs honestly and effectively

When to assert your rights

How to correct others effectively

How to forgive others and achieve genuine reconciliation

How to negotiate just and reasonable agreements

When to ask the church to intervene in a conflict

How to deal with people who refuse to be reasonable

When it is appropriate for a Christian to go to court

As you learn to draw on God's grace and deal with these issues in a biblical way, you can follow an entirely new approach to resolving conflict. Instead of reacting to disputes in a confused, defensive, or angry manner, you can learn to respond to conflict confidently and constructively. To spur you on, all of the key principles in this book are reinforced with real-life illustrations. (The names of the people and some distinguishing facts have been changed to protect the privacy of those involved.)

The more you study and apply God's peacemaking principles, the more you will see how practical and powerful they are. When used in the light of the gospel, these principles can rob conflict of its destructive tendencies and turn it into an opportunity to find lasting solutions to serious problems, to experience significant personal growth, to deepen relationships, and, best of all, to experience and demonstrate the love of God in a new and life-giving way. I hope this book will encourage this process in your life and enable you to experience the fulfillment and joy that come from being a peacemaker.

Ken Sande

PART 1

GLORIFY GOD

> *How can I please and honor God*
> *in this situation?*

So whether you eat or drink or whatever you do, do it
all for the glory of God.

1 Corinthians 10:31

Don't you try to come in!" Frank yelled through the door.
"I have a bat, and I'll hit anyone who comes in."

"Come on. Open the door, Frank!" Joe responded from the
porch. "We just want to talk."

"This is getting out of control," Jenny said as she pulled at Joe's arm.
"I think we should call our lawyer and have him talk with Frank."

"But the realtor and the buyer will be here in ten minutes! The
deal will fall apart if they can't get in to look at the house."

"It will fall apart a lot worse if Frank goes after them with a bat!
I'm going to call right now and postpone the meeting until we can
do something with Frank."

"OK, but I won't let him hold this sale up forever. You've got two days to get him out of here, Jenny, and after that I'll come back with my own bat. I'm sure John and Matt will be happy to join me."

Joe stormed over to his car and drove out of the farmyard, venting his anger by spinning a wave of gravel across the yard.

As Jenny drove back to town, she felt utterly trapped between her four brothers. Ever since their mother died, they had been fighting over the farm. Frank had been born with a disability that had kept him at home all his life. In the early years, their mother had cared for him, but as her health failed, Frank became the caregiver, rarely leaving her side. When she finally succumbed to a massive stroke, Frank's world collapsed.

Things got worse when their mother's will was read. She and their dad had established a trust many years earlier to provide for Frank. In their wills they left the farm equally to their other four children. Now that both parents were dead, Joe, John, and Matt wanted to sell the property as quickly as possible. When they told Frank, he was terrified at the prospect of moving out of the only home he had ever lived in. As he resisted the idea, heated arguments ensued, and now Frank was cornered in the lonely farmhouse.

Although Jenny needed the money from the sale as much as her brothers did, she did not like the idea of forcibly evicting Frank. The three brothers were oblivious to his fears and determined to push ahead. Jenny felt powerless to stop them.

Then she remembered that her pastor had recently attended a seminar on biblical peacemaking. A brief call to him led to a meeting that night, which resulted in an intense discussion with three of her brothers.

"Look, Pastor," Joe said, "I'm only asking that we honor Mom's wishes and follow the law. She and Dad decided years ago to set up a trust for Frank and divide the farm among the rest of us. As personal representative for her estate, it's my legal responsibility to honor her will. I know it will be a little hard on Frank to move out, but there's a nice apartment complex in town. He'll settle in there in no time."

"But it could kill him," Jenny pleaded. "Losing Mom devastated Frank. If we force him out of the house, he'll lose everything that's familiar to him. I'm afraid of what it will do to him."

"So what do we do?" Matt injected. "Just sit around until he dies years from now and then finally divide up the property? I've got two kids in college, and if Mom were here I'm sure she'd want to see the farm sold to help them out. I agree with Joe. We should honor Mom's will and follow the law."

"I appreciate your respect for your mother and for the law," said Pastor Barry, "but there's something else to consider. All of you profess to be Christians. So what is the difference between the way you are handling this conflict and the way a good atheist would handle it?"

After several moments of awkward silence, Joe finally replied, "I'm not sure I see your point."

"Let me put it another way. What is more important to you in this situation: to get your money as soon as possible, as most people would, or to demonstrate the love of Christ to your brother?"

"Oh, I see," said John, "You want us to be good little Christians who just give in to others and walk away from what's rightfully ours."

"No, that's not what I'm saying. God loves justice, and he certainly wants you to respect your parents' wishes. But there is something he wants even more: to see you treating one another in a way that shows the power of the gospel in each of your lives."

"That sounds good, Pastor," Joe replied, "but I just don't see how religion applies to this problem."

"If you really want to know, let's pray together right now and ask God to show you how you can resolve this conflict in a way that honors him *and* fulfills your parents' wishes."

God answered their prayers in a way Joe had never expected.

Three weeks later the entire extended family gathered together in the banquet room of a local restaurant. Jenny had somehow overcome Frank's fears and persuaded him to leave the house and join the family for dinner. Twelve nephews and nieces watched with rapt attention as he walked into the room and nervously sat down at one end of the table.

As the eldest son, Joe asked for everyone's attention. "Frank, our family is gathered together today to honor you. For the past ten years you devoted yourself to caring for Mom. Today we want to present you with this special plaque. It says, "To our brother, Frank, the best of all sons, who cared for our mother with selfless love and undying devotion. Your companionship filled her life with joy and delight and was a constant reminder to her of the love of God. With deepest gratitude to a wonderful brother, from Joe, John, Jenny, and Matt."

Tears welled up in Frank's eyes as Joe handed him the plaque. Before he could speak, Joe handed him an envelope.

"Frank," he went on, "in appreciation for all you did for Mom, we want to give you this gift. It is an agreement we have all signed that gives you a life estate in the farmhouse. That means you will be able to stay there as long as you live. We found a buyer who is willing to purchase the rest of the farmland. Ownership of the house will eventually pass to our children. But as long as you want to live there, we want you to know that it is your home."

As Frank clutched the envelope, the dam of emotions finally burst. Months of uncertainty and fear gave way to sobs of relief and gratitude. As Joe leaned over and hugged his brother for the first time in years, Joe's teenage son leaned toward his sister and whispered, "Maybe there is a God after all, because there's no way Dad would have done this on his own."

When someone mistreats or opposes us, our instinctive reaction is to justify ourselves and do everything we can to get our way. This selfish attitude usually leads to impulsive decisions that only make matters worse.

The gospel of Jesus Christ provides the way out of this downward spiral. When we remember what Jesus did for us on the cross, our blinding self-absorption can be replaced with a liberating desire to draw attention to the goodness and power of God. As Colossians 3:1–2 teaches, "Since, then, you have been raised with Christ, set your hearts on things above, where Christ is seated at the right hand of God. Set your minds on things above, not on earthly things."

Focusing on God is the key to resolving conflict constructively. When we remember his mercy and draw on his strength, we invariably see things more clearly and respond to conflict more wisely. In doing so, we can find far better solutions to our problems. At the same time, we can show others that there really is a God and that he delights in helping us do things we could never do on our own.

1

CONFLICT PROVIDES OPPORTUNITIES

Well done, good and faithful servant!

Matthew 25:21

I love to backpack in Montana's spectacular Beartooth Mountains. One year I ventured out in late spring with three friends. The streams were still swollen from melting snow. Ten miles into the mountains, we came to a stream where the bridge had been washed away. The water was deep and icy cold. There was one place where we might have been able to cross by leaping from rock to rock, but it would mean risking a fall into the rapids.

As we stood there trying to decide what to do, three different perspectives surfaced. One person saw the stream as a dangerous obstacle. Afraid that one of us might fall in and be swept away, he wanted to turn back and look for another trail. Another friend saw the stream as a means to show how tough he was. He wanted to wade straight across, even if that meant we would be wet and cold for a few hours. But two of us saw the stream as an interesting challenge. We studied the rocks leading to the other side and determined where we would need additional footing. Finding a fallen tree in the woods, we laid it across the largest gap between the rocks.

At this point, our two friends began to cooperate with us. Working together, we managed to get one person over to the other bank. Then two of us stood on rocks in the middle of the stream, and the packs were passed to the other side. One by one, we jumped from rock to rock, receiving support from the person ahead. Before long, we were all on the far bank, perfectly dry and exhilarated by our accomplishment.

I have found that people look at conflict in much the same way that my friends and I viewed that stream. To some, conflict is a hazard that threatens to sweep them off their feet and leave them bruised and hurting. To others, it is an obstacle that they should conquer quickly and firmly, regardless of the consequences. But some people have learned that conflict is an opportunity to solve common problems in a way that honors God and offers benefits to those involved. As you will see, the latter view can transform the way you respond to conflict.

The Slippery Slope of Conflict

There are three basic ways that people respond to conflict. These responses may be arranged on a curve that resembles a hill. On the left slope of the hill we find the *escape responses* to conflict. On

the right side are the *attack responses*. And in the center we find the *peacemaking responses*.

Imagine that this hill is covered with ice. If you go too far to the left or the right, you can lose your footing and slide down the slope. Similarly, when you experience conflict, it is easy to become defensive or antagonistic. Both responses make matters worse and can lead to more extreme reactions.

If you want to stay on top of this slippery slope, you need to do two things. First, ask God to help you resist the natural inclination to escape or attack when faced with conflict. Second, ask him to help you develop the ability to live out the gospel by using the peacemaking response that is best suited to resolving a particular conflict. Let's look at each of these responses in more detail.

Escape Responses

The three responses found on the left side of the slippery slope are called the *escape responses*. People tend to use these responses when they are more interested in avoiding a conflict than in resolving it. This attitude is common within the church, because many Christians believe that all conflict is wrong or dangerous. Thinking that Christians should always agree, or fearing that conflict will inevitably damage relationships, these people usually do one of three things to escape from conflict.

Denial. One way to escape from a conflict is to pretend that it does not exist. Or, if we cannot deny that the problem exists, we simply refuse to do what should be done to resolve a conflict properly. These responses bring only temporary relief and usually make matters worse (see Gen. 16:1–6; 1 Sam. 2:22–25).

Flight. Another way to escape from a conflict is to run away. This may include leaving the house, ending a friendship, quitting a job, filing for divorce, or changing churches. In most cases, running away only postpones a proper solution to a problem (see Gen. 16:6–8), so flight is usually a harmful way to deal with conflict. Of course, there may be times when it is appropriate to respectfully withdraw from a confusing or emotional situation *temporarily* to calm down, organize your thoughts, and pray. Flight may also be a legitimate response in seriously threatening circumstances, such as cases of physical or sexual abuse (see 1 Sam. 19:9–10). If a family is involved in such a situation, however, every reasonable effort should still be made to find trustworthy assistance and come back to seek a lasting solution to the problem. (I will discuss this in more detail in chapter 9.)

Suicide. When people lose all hope of resolving a conflict, they may seek to escape the situation (or make a desperate cry for help) by attempting to take their own lives (see 1 Sam. 31:4). Suicide is never the right way to deal with conflict. Tragically, however, suicide has become the third leading cause of death among adolescents in the United States, partly because so many children have never learned how to deal with conflict constructively.

Attack Responses

The three responses found on the right side of the slippery slope are called the *attack responses.* These responses are used by people who are more interested in winning a conflict than in preserving a relationship. This attitude is seen in people who view conflict as a contest or a chance to assert their rights, to control others, or to take advantage of their situation. Attack responses are typically used by people who are strong and self-confident. But they may also be used by those who feel weak, fearful, insecure, or vulnerable. Whatever the motive, these responses are directed at bringing as much pressure to bear on opponents as is necessary to eliminate their opposition.

Assault. Some people try to overcome an opponent by using various forms of force or intimidation, such as verbal attacks (including gossip and slander), physical violence, or efforts to damage a person financially or professionally (see Acts 6:8–15). Such conduct always makes conflicts worse.

Litigation. Another way to force people to bend to our will is to take them to court. Although some conflicts may legitimately be taken before a civil judge (see Acts 24:1–26:32; Rom. 13:1–5), lawsuits usually damage relationships and often fail to achieve complete justice. When Christians are involved on both sides, their witness can be severely damaged. This is why Christians are commanded to settle their differences within the church rather than in the civil courts (1 Cor. 6:1–8). Therefore, it is important to make every effort to settle a dispute out of court whenever possible (Matt. 5:25–26; see appendix D for further discussion).

Murder. In extreme cases, people may be so desperate to win a dispute that they will try to kill those who oppose them (see Acts 7:54–58). While most Christians would not actually kill someone, we should never forget that we stand guilty of murder in God's eyes when we harbor anger or contempt in our hearts toward others (see 1 John 3:15; Matt. 5:21–22).

There are two ways that people move into the attack zone. Some resort to an attack response the minute they encounter a conflict. Others move into this zone after they have tried unsuccessfully to escape from a conflict. When they can no longer ignore, cover up, or run away from the problem, they go to the other extreme and attack those who oppose them.

Peacemaking Responses

The six responses found on the top portion of the slippery slope are called the *peacemaking responses.* These responses are commanded by God, empowered by the gospel, and directed toward finding just and mutually agreeable solutions to conflict. Each of these responses will be discussed in detail in the following chapters, but for now we will do a brief overview.

The first three peacemaking responses may be referred to as "personal peacemaking," because they may be carried out personally and privately, just between you and the other party. The vast majority of conflicts in life should and can be resolved in one of these ways.

Overlook an offense. Many disputes are so insignificant that they should be resolved by quietly and deliberately overlooking an offense. "A man's wisdom gives him patience; it is to his glory to overlook an offense" (Prov. 19:11; see also 12:16; 17:14; Col. 3:13; 1 Peter 4:8). Overlooking an offense is a form of forgiveness and involves a deliberate decision not to talk about it, dwell on it, or let it grow into pent-up bitterness or anger.

Reconciliation. If an offense is too serious to overlook or has damaged the relationship, we need to resolve personal or relational issues through confession, loving correction, and forgiveness. "[If] your brother has something against you . . . go and be reconciled" (Matt. 5:23–24; see Prov. 28:13). "Brothers, if someone is caught in a sin, you who are spiritual should restore him gently" (Gal. 6:1; see Matt. 18:15). "Forgive as the Lord forgave you" (Col. 3:13).

Negotiation. Even if we successfully resolve *relational* issues, we may still need to work through *material* issues related to money, property, or other rights. This should be done through a cooperative bargaining process in which you and the other person seek to reach a settlement that satisfies the legitimate needs of each side. "Each of you should look not only to your own interests, but also to the interests of others" (Phil. 2:4).

When a dispute cannot be resolved through one of the personal peacemaking responses, God calls us to use one of the next three peacemaking responses, referred to as "assisted peacemaking." These responses require the involvement of other people from your church or Christian community.

Mediation. If two people cannot reach an agreement in private, they should ask one or more objective outside people to meet with them to help them communicate more effectively and explore possible solutions. "If he will not listen [to you], take one or two others along" (Matt. 18:16). These mediators may ask questions and give advice, but they have no authority to force you to accept a particular solution.

Arbitration. When you and an opponent cannot come to a voluntary agreement on a material issue, you may appoint one or more arbitrators to listen to your arguments and render a binding decision to settle the issue. In 1 Corinthians 6:1–8, Paul indicates that this is how Christians ought to resolve even their legal conflicts with one another: "If you have disputes about such matters, appoint as judges even men of little account in the church" (1 Cor. 6:4).

Accountability. If a person who professes to be a Christian refuses to be reconciled and do what is right, Jesus commands church leaders to formally intervene to hold him or her accountable to Scripture and to promote repentance, justice, and forgiveness: "If he refuses to listen [to others], tell it to the church" (Matt. 18:17). Direct church involvement is often viewed negatively among Christians today, but when it is done as Jesus instructs—lovingly, redemptively, and restoratively—it can be the key to saving relationships and bringing about justice and peace.

Interesting Trends on the Slope

The slippery slope reveals several interesting trends about our responses to conflict. As we move from the left side of the slope to the right (clockwise), our responses tend to go from being private to being public. When we fail to resolve a matter through a private response, more people must get involved as we look to mediation, arbitration, church accountability, or even litigation to settle a dispute.

Moving from left to right on the curve also involves a move from voluntary to forced solutions. In all the responses on the left side of the curve, the parties decide on their own solution. From arbitration on, others impose a result. This is usually less palatable to everyone involved.

The extreme responses to conflict also result in greater losses. Every response to conflict costs you something; you must give up one thing to gain another. Personal peacemaking responses generally produce the most "profitable" exchange; the benefits of your solution are usually worth the time and energy you invest to reach an agreement, especially from a spiritual standpoint. The further you move away from the personal peacemaking zone in either direction, the greater your costs will be, whether in time, money, effort, relationships, or a clear conscience.

There are also three noteworthy parallels between the two sides of the slippery slope. Both extremes of the spectrum result in death, either through suicide or murder, which are terrible problems in our culture. Similarly, assault and flight often come together in classic "fight or flight" behavior, both sides of which avoid dealing with the underlying causes of the conflict. Finally, litigation is often nothing more than professionally assisted denial and attack. When you enter the legal adversarial system, your attorney is expected to make you look faultless and paint your opponent as the one who is entirely responsible for the problem. This distortion of reality usually takes a devastating toll on relationships.

There are also some interesting contrasts between the various responses to conflict. First, there is a difference in focus. When I resort to an escape response, I am generally focusing on "me." I am looking for what is easy, convenient, or nonthreatening for myself. When I use an attack response, I am generally focusing on "you," blaming you and expecting you to give in and solve the problem. When I use a peacemaking response, my focus is on "us." I am aware of everyone's interests in the dispute, especially God's, and I am working toward mutual responsibility in solving a problem.

The issue of goals reveals a second difference between various responses. People who use escape responses are usually intent on "peace-faking," or making things look good even when they are not. (This is especially common in the church, where people are often more concerned about the appearance of peace than the reality of peace.) Attack responses are used by people who are prone to "peace-breaking." They are more than willing to sacrifice peace and unity to get what they want. Those who use the responses on the top of the slippery slope are committed to "peace-making" and will work long and hard to achieve true justice and genuine harmony with others.

Finally, there is a difference in results. When a person earnestly pursues the peacemaking responses to conflict, there is a greater likelihood that he or she will eventually see reconciliation. In contrast, both the escape and attack responses to conflict almost inevitably result in KYRG: *Kiss your relationship good-bye.*

The different responses to conflict and their associated dynamics were dramatically revealed in a family conflict I conciliated. I was asked to help seven adult brothers and sisters settle a dispute over whether they should keep their elderly mother in her home or place her in a retirement center. Five of the siblings were doing all they could to escape from the situation, either by pretending that the conflict did not exist or by refusing to meet with the others to talk about it. The other two attacked each other intensely and frequently, slandering one another to family and friends and fighting in court to obtain control through legal guardianship.

The first step in resolving the dispute was to help the family change the way they had been responding to the situation. The five siblings who had been trying to escape from the problem finally saw the benefits of mediation and agreed to meet together. The other two sisters grudgingly consented to mediation, but they continued to attack each other during our meetings, accusing each other of improper motives and demanding opposing solutions. Our investment of time and energy was producing no results, and relationships were suffering further damage.

I finally asked to talk with the two sisters in private. Putting the guardianship issue aside for a moment, I asked them to take a look at how they were treating one another. As we examined their attitudes and behavior in the light of a few relevant Bible passages, the Lord began to work in their hearts. The real cause of the conflict finally came to the surface. Almost twenty years earlier, one sister had said something that deeply hurt the other. The offended sister brooded over the insult, and their relationship was steadily poisoned. Consequently, they opposed each other in everything, even if it involved their mother's care.

As we continued to talk and pray, they began to deal with their feelings and actions in the light of the gospel. God softened their hearts and moved them to confess their sins and forgive each other. With tears in their eyes, they embraced each other for the first time in twenty years. They soon joined their brothers and sister and explained what had happened. Within five minutes, all seven children agreed that their mother would be happier in her own home, and in another fifteen minutes they negotiated a schedule for her care. As you can imagine, when they told her the news that evening, the reconciliation of her children brought her more joy than the decision about her living arrangement.

A Biblical View of Conflict

Many of the problems associated with the escape and attack responses to conflict can be prevented if you learn to look at and respond to conflict in a biblical way. In his Word, God has explained why conflicts occur and how we should deal with them. The more we understand and obey what he teaches, the more effective we will be in resolving disagreements with other people. The following are a few of the basic principles behind a biblical view of conflict.

Let's begin our discussion by defining conflict as *a difference in opinion or purpose that frustrates someone's goals or desires.* This definition is broad enough to include innocuous variations in taste, such as one spouse wanting to vacation in the mountains while the other prefers the waterfront, as well as hostile arguments, such as fights, quarrels, lawsuits, or church divisions.

There are four primary causes of conflict. Some disputes arise because of misunderstandings resulting from poor communication (see Josh. 22:10–34). Differences in values, goals, gifts, calling, priorities, expectations, interests, or opinions can also lead to conflict (see Acts 15:39; 1 Cor. 12:12–31). Competition over limited resources, such as time or money, is a frequent source of disputes in families, churches, and businesses (see Gen. 13:1–12). And, as we will see below, many conflicts are caused or aggravated by sinful attitudes and habits that lead to sinful words and actions (see James 4:1–2).

Conflict is not necessarily bad, however. In fact, the Bible teaches that *some* differences are natural and beneficial. Since God has created us as unique individuals, human beings will often have different opinions, convictions, desires, perspectives, and priorities. Many of these differences are not inherently right or wrong; they are simply the result of God-given diversity and personal preferences (see 1 Cor. 12:21–31). When handled properly, disagreements in these areas can stimulate productive dialogue, encourage creativity, promote helpful change, and generally make life more interesting. Therefore, although we should seek *unity* in our relationships, we should not demand *uniformity* (see Eph. 4:1–13). Instead of avoiding all conflicts or demanding that others always agree with us, we should rejoice in the diversity of God's creation and learn to accept and work with people who simply see things differently than we do (see Rom. 15:7; cf. 14:1–13).

Not all conflict is neutral or beneficial, however. The Bible teaches that many disagreements are the direct result of sinful attitudes and behavior. As James 4:1–2 tells us, "What causes fights and quarrels among you? Don't they come from your desires that battle within you? You want something but don't get it. You kill and covet, but you cannot have what you want. You quarrel and fight. . . ." When a conflict is the result of sinful desires or actions that are too serious to be overlooked, we need to avoid the temptation to escape or attack. Instead, we need to pursue one of the peacemaking responses to conflict, which can help us get to the root cause of the conflict and restore genuine peace.

Most importantly, the Bible teaches that we should see conflict neither as an inconvenience nor as an occasion to force our will on others, but rather as an opportunity to demonstrate the love and power of God in our lives. This is what Paul told the Christians in Corinth when religious, legal, and dietary disputes threatened to divide their church:

> So whether you eat or drink or whatever you do, do it all for the glory of God. Do not cause anyone to stumble, whether Jews, Greeks or the church of God—even as I try to please everybody in every way. For I am not seeking my own good but the good of many, so that they may be saved. Follow my example, as I follow the example of Christ.
>
> 1 Corinthians 10:31–11:1

This passage presents a radical view of conflict: It encourages us to look at conflict as an opportunity to glorify God, serve others, and grow to be like Christ. This perspective may seem naive and impractical at first glance, especially to someone who is presently embroiled in a dispute. As you will see, however, this view can inspire remarkably practical responses to conflict. These responses are described in detail later in this book, but an overview now will be helpful.

Glorify God

Conflict always provides an opportunity to glorify God, that is, to bring him praise and honor by showing who he is, what he is like, and what he is doing. The best way to glorify God in the midst of conflict is to depend on and draw attention to his grace, that is, the undeserved love, mercy, forgiveness, strength, and wisdom he gives to us through Jesus Christ. You can do this in several ways.

First, *you can trust God.* Instead of relying on your own ideas and abilities as you respond to people who oppose you, ask God to give you grace to depend on him and follow his ways, even if they are completely opposite to what you feel like doing (Prov. 3:5–7).

Above all, hold on tightly to the liberating promises of the gospel. Trust that Jesus has forgiven your sins, and confess them freely. Believe that he is using the pressures of conflict to help you to grow, and cooperate with him. Depend on his assurance that he is always watching over you, and stop fearing what others might do to you. Know that he delights to display his sanctifying power in your life, and attempt to do things that you could never accomplish in your own strength, such as forgiving someone who has hurt you deeply. As you trust the Lord in these "unnatural" ways, people will have the opportunity to see that God is real and praise him for his work in your life (see Acts 16:22–31).

Second, *you can obey God.* One of the most powerful ways to glorify God is to do what he commands (Matt. 5:16; John 17:4; Phil. 1:9–10). As Jesus said, "This is to my Father's glory, that you bear much fruit, showing yourselves to be my disciples" (John 15:8). Obeying God's commands without compromise honors him by showing that his ways are absolutely good, wise, and dependable. Our obedience also demonstrates that he is worthy of our deepest love and devotion. Jesus said, "If you love me, you will obey what I command. . . . Whoever has my commands and obeys them, he is the one who loves me. . . . If anyone loves me, he will obey my teaching. . . . He who does not love me will not obey my teaching. . . . the world must learn that I love the Father and that I do exactly what my Father has commanded me" (John 14:15–31; cf. 1 John 5:3 and 2 John 5–6). This repetition makes a life-changing point: If you want to honor Jesus and show that he is worthy to be loved more than anything in the world, learn his ways and obey his commands.

Third, *you can imitate God.* When the believers in Ephesus were struggling with conflict, the apostle Paul gave them this timeless advice: "Be imitators of God, therefore, as dearly loved children and live a life of love, just as Christ loved us and gave himself up for us as a fragrant offering and sacrifice to God" (Eph. 5:1–2; see 1 John 2:6). As Paul knew, imitating Jesus in the midst of conflict is the surest path to restoring peace and unity with those who oppose us (see Eph. 4:1–3). More importantly, when we live out the gospel in our lives and mirror Jesus' humility, mercy, forgiveness, and loving correction, we surprise the world and give concrete evidence of the Lord's presence and power in our lives (see Phil. 1:9–11; 1 Peter 2:12).

Fourth, *you can acknowledge God.* As God gives you grace to respond to conflict in unusual and effective ways, other people will often take notice and wonder how you do it. If you are silent, they may give you credit for the remarkable things you have done, which would rob God of his glory. Instead, use these special opportunities to breathe grace to other people by telling them that it is God who has been working in you to do things you could never do on your own (Phil. 2:13; 1 Peter 3:14–16). Then go on to share the gospel, telling them of Jesus' love for them, his saving work on the cross, and his offer to forgive their sins and free them from the attitudes and actions that lead to conflict. You may have their attention only for a moment. Make the most of it by pointing straight at Jesus and giving him all the glory.

Every time you encounter a conflict, you will inevitably show what you really think of God. If you want to show that you love him "with all your heart and with all your soul and with all your mind" (Matt. 22:37), then ask him to help you trust, obey, imitate, and acknowledge him, especially when it is difficult to do so. This behavior honors God and shows others how worthy he is of your devotion and praise.

This principle was powerfully illustrated in the apostle Peter's life. Just before Jesus ascended into heaven, he warned Peter that he would be executed for his faith. In John 21:19 we are told that "Jesus said this to indicate the kind of death by which Peter would glorify God." How would Peter glorify God by dying? He would show that God is so excellent and trustworthy and his ways are so perfect that it is better to die than to turn away from him or disobey his commands (cf. Dan. 3:1–30; 6:1–28; Acts 5:17–42; 6:8–7:60). Peter was willing to pay the highest price possible, his very life, to show how much he loved and trusted God.

Glorifying God will benefit *you* as well, especially when you are involved in a conflict. Many disputes begin or grow worse because one or both sides give in to their emotions and say or do things they later regret. When you focus on trusting, obeying, imitating, and acknowledging God, you will be less inclined to stumble in these ways. As Psalm 37:31 says, "The law of his God is in his heart; his feet do not slip."

The other benefit of a God-centered approach to conflict resolution is that it makes you less dependent on results. Even if others refuse to respond positively to your efforts to make peace, you can find comfort in the knowledge that God is pleased with your obedience. That knowledge can help you to persevere in difficult situations.

It is important to realize that if you do not glorify God when you are involved in a conflict, you will inevitably glorify someone or something else. By your actions you will show either that you have a big God or that you have a big self and big problems. To put it another way, if you do not focus on God, you will inevitably focus on yourself and your will, or on other people and the threat of their wills.

One of the best ways to keep your focus on the Lord is to continually ask yourself these questions: How can I please and honor God in this situation? In particular, how can I bring praise to Jesus by showing that he has saved me and is changing me? Seeking to please and honor God is a powerful compass for life, especially when we are faced with difficult challenges. Jesus himself was guided by these goals. He said, "I seek not to please myself but him who sent me" (John 5:30). "The one who sent me is with me; he has not left me alone, for I always do what pleases him" (John 8:29). "I have brought you glory on earth by completing the work you gave me to do" (John 17:4). King David showed the same desire when he wrote: "May the words of my mouth and the meditation of my heart be pleasing in your sight, O LORD, my Rock and my Redeemer" (Ps. 19:14).

When displaying the riches of God's love and pleasing him is more important than holding onto worldly things and pleasing yourself, it becomes increasingly natural to respond to conflict graciously, wisely, and with self-control. This approach brings glory to God and sets the stage for effective peacemaking.

Serve Others

As Paul reminded the Corinthians, conflict also provides an opportunity to serve others. This sounds absurd from a worldly perspective, because the world says, "Look out for Number One."

But Jesus says, "Love your enemies, do good to those who hate you, bless those who curse you, pray for those who mistreat you" (Luke 6:27–28). Clearly, we are *not* released from the command to love our neighbor as ourselves, even when that neighbor is hating, cursing, and mistreating us. Instead of reacting harshly or seeking revenge, God calls us to be merciful to those who offend us, just as he is merciful to us (Luke 6:36). We cannot serve others this way in our own strength. We must continually breathe in God's grace (through the study of his Word, prayer, worship, and Christian fellowship) and then breathe out his love, mercy, forgiveness, and wisdom to others through our words and actions. You can do this in several ways.

In some situations, God may use you to help an opponent understand his interests and find better solutions to his problems than he would have developed alone (Phil. 2:3–4). If you follow the principles of negotiation described in chapter 11, you can often develop creative ways to satisfy both your needs and the needs of your opponent. Instead of allowing a conflict to pit you against each other, you can learn to work together against a common problem.

In other cases, the Lord may give you an opportunity to carry your opponent's burdens by providing for his or her spiritual, emotional, or material needs (Gal. 6:2, 9–10). It may be that your conflict has little to do with actual differences between the two of you and much to do with other problems in your opponent's life. When people lash out at you, it is sometimes symptomatic of other frustrations. (This behavior is particularly common in families and close friendships.) Instead of reacting defensively, try to discern ways that you can help others deal with those problems. This does not mean you should take on their responsibilities. Rather, you should help them lift those burdens that are beyond their abilities. Such behavior brings glory to God and may soften an opponent's heart and open the way for reconciliation (see Rom. 12:20).

The Lord may also use you to help others learn where they have been wrong and need to change (Gal. 6:1–2). As we will see later, this will usually involve private correction. If that does not work, God may involve others in the church to help bring about needed repentance and change.

Conflict also provides opportunities to encourage others to trust in Jesus Christ. When you are involved in a conflict, your opponent and various bystanders will be observing you closely. If you behave in a worldly way, you will give nonbelievers yet another excuse for mocking Christians and rejecting Christ. On the other hand, if you display God's love and respond with unnatural humility, wisdom, and self-control, those who are watching you may wonder where you found the power to behave like that, which may open the door to introducing them to Christ (1 Peter 3:15–16).

Finally, serving others in the midst of conflict is a powerful way to teach and encourage others by your example. Whenever you are in conflict, there will often be many more people watching you than you realize. If you succumb to sinful emotions and lash out at your enemies, others will feel justified in doing the same. But if you respond to those who wrong you with love and self-control, many people could be inspired by your example (see 1 Cor. 4:12–13, 16; 1 Tim. 4:12; Titus 2:7). This is particularly important if you are a parent or grandparent. Your children constantly observe how you handle conflict. If you are defensive, critical, unreasonable, and impulsive, they are likely to develop the same behavior. But if you breathe grace, your children will be encouraged to imitate you. What they learn about peacemaking from you may have a profound impact on the way they handle conflict at school, in the workplace, and in their own marriages.[1]

Grow to Be like Christ

Most conflicts also provide an opportunity to grow to be more like Jesus. As Paul urged in his letter to the Corinthians, "Follow my example, as I follow the example of Christ" (1 Cor. 11:1). Paul elaborated on this opportunity when he wrote to the Christians in Rome: "And we know that in all things God works for the good of those who love him, who have been called according to his purpose. For those God foreknew he also predestined *to be conformed to the likeness of his Son,* that he might be the firstborn among many brothers" (Rom. 8:28–29, emphasis added; cf. 2 Cor. 3:18).

God's highest purpose for you is not to make you comfortable, wealthy, or happy. If you have put your faith in him, he has something far more wonderful in mind—he plans to conform you to the likeness of his Son! He began to change you the day you put your trust in him, and he will continue this process throughout your life. Conflict is one of the many tools that God will use to help you develop a more Christ-like character. To begin with, he may use conflict to remind you of your weaknesses and to encourage you to depend more on him (2 Cor. 12:7–10). The more you rely on his grace, wisdom, and power, the more you will be imitating the Lord Jesus (Luke 22:41–44).

God may also use conflict to expose sinful attitudes and habits in your life. Conflict is especially effective in breaking down appearances and revealing stubborn pride, a bitter and unforgiving heart, or a critical tongue. When you are squeezed through controversy and these sinful characteristics are brought to the surface, you will have an opportunity to recognize their existence and ask for God's help in overcoming them (Ps. 119:67).

There is more to being like Jesus than simply recognizing weaknesses and confessing sin, however. To grow, you must also draw on his grace and practice new attitudes and habits. Just as athletes develop their muscles and skills through strenuous training, you will see greater growth when you repeatedly think and behave properly in response to challenging circumstances. For example, when people provoke and frustrate you, practice love and forgiveness. When they fail to act promptly, develop patience. When you are tempted to give up on someone, exercise faithfulness. Conflict provides a rich mixture of such trials, each of which can strengthen and refine your character. As Charles Swindoll points out, "If you listen to the voices around you, you'll search for a substitute—an escape route. You'll miss the fact that each one of those problems is a God-appointed instructor ready to stretch you and challenge you and deepen your walk with him. Growth and wisdom await you at the solution of each one, the pain and mess notwithstanding."[2]

God uses conflict to stretch and challenge you in carefully tailored ways. This process is sometimes referred to as the "ABC of spiritual growth": Adversity Builds Character. As you worry less about *going* through conflict and focus more on *growing* through conflict, you will enhance that process and experience the incomparable blessing of being conformed to the likeness of Christ.

The Four G's of Peacemaking

The three opportunities of conflict give rise to four basic principles for peacemaking. The first three principles correspond one-on-one to the three opportunities (in a slightly different order), while the fourth principle encompasses all three opportunities. The four principles may be summarized in four basic questions, which we consider thoroughly in subsequent chapters:

> *Glorify God:* How can I please and honor God in this situation?
>
> *Get the log out of your own eye:* How can I show Jesus' work in me by taking responsibility for my contribution to this conflict?
>
> *Gently restore:* How can I lovingly serve others by helping them take responsibility for their contribution to this conflict?
>
> *Go and be reconciled:* How can I demonstrate the forgiveness of God and encourage a reasonable solution to this conflict?

I have used these four principles in hundreds of conflicts over the past two decades, and I have yet to encounter a situation in which they did not provide practical and effective guidance. Whether I was facing a defiant five-year-old, a split congregation, or an attorney demanding a million dollars, the Four G's have always given me a reliable track on which to run as we pursued peace.

Stewarding Conflict

Seeing conflict as an opportunity leads to an amazingly effective approach to managing conflict, which I refer to as "stewarding." This approach gives the phrase *conflict management* a unique emphasis. When Jesus talked about managing something, he was usually referring to a servant who had been entrusted by his master with certain resources and responsibilities (e.g., Luke 12:42). The Bible calls such a person a steward. A steward is not supposed to manage things for his own pleasure, convenience, or benefit. Instead, he is expected to follow his master's instructions and look out for his master's interests, even if they conflict with his own personal desires or convenience (John 12:24–26).

The concept of stewardship is especially relevant to peacemaking. Whenever you are involved in a conflict, God has given you a management opportunity. He has empowered you through the gospel and entrusted you with abilities and spiritual resources. His Word clearly explains how he wants you to manage the situation. The more faithfully you draw on his grace and follow his instructions, the more likely you are to see a constructive solution and genuine reconciliation. Faithful stewarding will also leave you with a clear conscience before God, regardless of the actions of those opposing you.

The Bible provides a detailed description of the character traits needed to manage conflict productively. Many of these qualities will be discussed later in this book, but a few of them deserve immediate attention. If you want to be an effective steward, you need to be:

Motivated. As we have seen, the gospel provides enormous motivation to respond to conflict constructively. As you continually remember and rejoice in all that the Lord has done for you, you will be inspired to overcome selfish, shortsighted attitudes and give yourself wholeheartedly to serving and honoring your Master.

Informed. As a steward, you also need to understand your Master's will (see Luke 12:47). This is not difficult, because God has written out his instructions for you. Through the Bible he provides clear and reliable guidance on how he wants you to deal with every aspect of life. The Bible is not merely a collection of religious rituals and commendable ideals. In addition to showing us how to know God personally, it provides detailed and practical instructions on how to deal with the problems that arise in daily living (2 Tim. 3:16–17). Understanding God's Word is an essential ingredient of wisdom, which is the ability to apply God's truth to life's complexities. Having wisdom does not mean that you understand all of God's ways; it means that you respond to life God's way (Deut. 29:29). The better you know the Bible, the wiser you will be and the more effectively you will deal with conflict.[3]

Strengthened. You are not alone when you are stewarding conflict: "For the eyes of the LORD range throughout the earth to strengthen those whose hearts are fully committed to him" (2 Chron. 16:9a; cf. 1 Cor. 10:13). God provides this strength to all Christians through the Holy Spirit, who plays an essential role in peacemaking. In addition to helping you understand God's will (1 Cor. 2:9–15), the Spirit will provide you with the spiritual gifts, grace, and strength you need to respond to conflict in a way that will bring honor to Christ and build up his church (Gal. 5:22–23; Eph. 3:16–21; 2 Tim. 1:7; 1 Peter 4:10–11). This help is available to you on request, which is why prayer is emphasized throughout this book.[4]

Dependent. At times, conflict can push you beyond your limits. You may have a difficult time understanding how to respond to a particular situation, or you may become so weary that you lose your determination to do what you know is right. When this happens, turn to the church and seek out spiritually mature Christians who will encourage you, give you biblically sound advice, and support your efforts to be faithful to God (Prov. 12:15; 15:22; 1 Thess. 5:10–11; Heb. 10:24–25). You won't be helped by people who are likely to tell you what they think you want to hear (2 Tim. 4:3). Therefore, be sure you turn to people who will love you enough to be honest with you. As you depend on godly advisers and submit to the counsel of the church, you can resolve many conflicts that would otherwise defeat you.

Faithful. Perhaps the most important characteristic of a steward is faithfulness: "Now it is required that those who have been given a trust must prove faithful" (1 Cor. 4:2). Faithfulness is not a matter of results; it is a matter of dependent obedience. God knows that you cannot control other people, so he will not hold you responsible for the ultimate outcome of a conflict (Rom. 12:18). What he will look at is whether you sought his strength and guidance, remembered the freedom and power you have through the gospel, and obeyed his commands and wisely used the resources he has given you. If you have depended on him and done your best to resolve a conflict in a loving and biblical manner, no matter how the situation turns out, you will have earned that marvelous commendation: "Well done, good and faithful servant!" (Matt. 25:21a).

Summary and Application

Conflict provides opportunities to glorify God, to serve others, and to grow to be like Christ. These opportunities, which are sometimes described as being faithful to God, being merciful to others, and acting justly ourselves, are commended throughout Scripture. In Micah 6:8 we are told, "He has showed you, O man, what is good. And what does the LORD require of you? To act justly and to love mercy and to walk humbly with your God." In the same way, Jesus teaches us to pay attention to "the more important matters of the law—justice, mercy and faithfulness" (Matt. 23:23). As you live out the gospel and make the Lord's priorities your priorities, you can turn every conflict into a stepping-stone to a closer relationship with God and a more fulfilling and fruitful Christian life.

If you are presently involved in a conflict, these questions will help you apply the principles presented in this chapter to your situation:

1. Briefly summarize your dispute as you perceive it, placing events in chronological order as much as possible. In particular, describe what you have done to resolve the dispute.
2. Which response to conflict (from the slippery slope diagram) have you been using to resolve this dispute? How has your response made the situation better or worse?
3. What have been your primary goals as you've tried to resolve this dispute?
4. From this point on, how could you glorify God through this conflict? Specifically, how could you please and honor God in this situation and bring praise to Jesus by showing that he has saved you and is changing you?
5. How could you serve others through this conflict?
6. How could you grow to be more like Christ through this conflict?
7. What have you been relying on for guidance in this situation: your feelings and personal opinions about what is right or the careful study and application of what is taught in the Bible? What will you rely on in the future?
8. What are you struggling with most at this time (e.g., your opponent's attacks, controlling your tongue, fear of what is going to happen, lack of support from others)?

9. How could you use the resources God has provided (the Bible, the Holy Spirit, or other Christians) to deal with these struggles?

10. If God were to evaluate this conflict after it is over, how would you like him to complete these sentences:
    "I am pleased that you did not . . ."
    "I am pleased that you . . ."

11. Go on record with the Lord by writing a prayer based on the principles taught in this chapter.

2

LIVE AT PEACE

If it is possible, as far as it depends on you, live at
peace with everyone.

Romans 12:18

God delights to make his children instruments of peace and
reconciliation in the midst of conflict. We will carry out
this challenging responsibility more effectively if we understand
why peace is so important to our heavenly Father.

The Three Dimensions of Peace

God loves peace. From Genesis to Revelation, he communicates
a deep desire to bless his people with peace and to use them to
bring peace to others. Consider these recurring themes:

1. Peace is part of God's character, for he is frequently referred
   to as "the God of peace" (see Rom. 15:33; 2 Cor. 13:11; Phil.
   4:9; Heb. 13:20; cf. Judg. 6:24).

2. Peace is one of the great blessings that God gives to those who follow him (see Lev. 26:6; Num. 6:24–26; Judg. 5:31; Ps. 29:11; 119:165; Prov. 16:7; Micah 4:1–4; Gal. 6:16).

3. God repeatedly commands his people to seek and pursue peace (see Ps. 34:14; Jer. 29:7; Rom. 14:19; 1 Cor. 7:15; 2 Cor. 13:11; Col. 3:15; 1 Thess. 5:13; Heb. 12:14). He also promises to bless those who do so (see Ps. 37:37; Prov. 12:20; Matt. 5:9; James 3:18).

4. God describes his covenant with his people in terms of peace (Num. 25:12; Isa. 54:10; Ezek. 34:25; 37:26; Mal. 2:5).

5. God taught his people to use the word *peace* (Hebrew *shalom* and Greek *eirene*) as a standard form of greeting (Judg. 6:23; 1 Sam. 16:5; Luke 24:36) and parting (1 Sam. 1:17; 2 Kings 5:19; Luke 7:50; 8:48). Nearly all of the New Testament Epistles either begin or end with a prayer for peace (Rom. 1:7; 15:13; Gal. 1:3; 2 Thess. 3:16).

Nothing reveals God's concern for peace more vividly than his decision to send his beloved Son to "guide our feet into the path of peace" (Luke 1:79; cf. Isa. 2:4). From beginning to end, Jesus' mission was one of peacemaking. Long before he was born, he was given the title "Prince of Peace" (Isa. 9:6). Throughout his ministry he was constantly preaching and giving peace (John 14:27; Eph. 2:17). As the supreme peacemaker, Jesus sacrificed his life so we could experience peace with God and with one another now and forever.

There are three dimensions to the peace that God offers to us through Christ: peace with God, peace with one another, and peace within ourselves. Many people care little about their relationships with God and other people, but they still want peace within themselves. As you will see, it is impossible to know genuine internal peace unless you also pursue peace with God and others.

Peace with God

Peace with God does not come automatically. All of us have sinned and alienated ourselves from him (Isa. 59:1–2). Instead of living the perfect lives required for enjoying fellowship with him, each of us has a record stained with sin (Rom. 3:23). As a result, we deserve to be eternally separated from God (Rom. 6:23a). That is the *bad* news.

The *good* news is that "God so loved the world that he gave his one and only Son, that whoever believes in him shall not perish but have eternal life" (John 3:16). By sacrificing himself in our place on the cross, Jesus has made it possible for us to have peace with God. The apostle Paul wrote:

> For God was pleased to have all his fullness dwell in him [Christ], and through him to reconcile to himself all things . . . by making peace through his blood, shed on the cross.
>
> Colossians 1:19–20

> Therefore, since we have been justified through faith, we have peace with God through our Lord Jesus Christ, through whom we have gained access by faith into this grace in which we now stand.
>
> Romans 5:1–2

Believing in Jesus means more than being baptized, going to church, or trying to be a good person. None of these activities can erase the sins you have already committed and will continue to commit throughout your life. Believing in Jesus means, first of all, admitting that you are a sinner and acknowledging that there is no way you can earn God's approval by your works (Rom. 3:20; Eph. 2:8–9). Second, it means believing that Jesus paid the *full* penalty for your sins when he died on the cross (Isa. 53:1–12; 1 Peter 2:24–25). In essence, believing in Jesus means trusting that he exchanged records with you at Calvary—that is, he took your sinful record on himself and paid for it in full, giving you his perfect record, which opens the way for peace with God. As you believe in Jesus, accept his gracious gift of salvation, and draw closer to him through the power of his Spirit, the study of his Word, the privilege of prayer, and the fellowship of his church, his peace can fill every part of your life.

Peace with Others

In addition to giving you peace with God, Jesus' sacrifice on the cross opened the way for you to enjoy peace with other people (Eph. 2:11–18). This peace, which is often referred to as "unity" (Ps. 133:1), is not simply the absence of conflict and strife. Unity is the presence of genuine harmony, understanding, and goodwill between people. God calls us to do all we can to "live at peace with everyone" (Rom. 12:18). This kind of peace is the direct result of obeying the second great commandment, "Love your neighbor as yourself" (Matt. 22:39). As you will see, such unity is an essential part of an effective Christian witness. The rest of this book is devoted to showing you how to pursue peace with others when conflict has disrupted your relationships.

Peace within Yourself

Through Jesus you can also experience genuine peace within yourself. Internal peace is a sense of wholeness, contentment, tranquility, order, rest, and security. Although nearly everyone longs for this kind of peace, it eludes most people. Genuine internal peace cannot be directly obtained through our own efforts; it is a gift that God gives only to those who believe in his Son and obey his commands (1 John 3:21–24). In other words, *internal peace is a by-product of righteousness.* This truth is revealed throughout Scripture:

> "You will keep in perfect peace him whose mind is steadfast, because he trusts in you" (Isa. 26:3).
> "The fruit of righteousness will be peace; the effect of righteousness will be quietness and confidence forever" (Isa. 32:17; cf. Pss. 85:10; 119:165).
> "If only you had paid attention to my commands, your peace would have been like a river, your righteousness like the waves of the sea" (Isa. 48:18).

These passages show why it is impossible to experience internal peace if you fail to pursue peace with God and peace with others.

Internal peace comes only from being reconciled to God through his Son, receiving his righteousness and the power to resist sin, and then obeying what God commands. "And this is his command: to believe in the name of his Son, Jesus Christ, and to love one another as he commanded us" (1 John 3:23). By God's design, the three dimensions of peace are inseparably joined. As one author expressed it, "Peace with God, peace with each other and peace with ourselves come in the same package."[1] Therefore, if you want to experience internal peace, you must be reconciled to God by trusting in his Son and seek harmonious relationships with those around you.

Jesus' Reputation Depends on Unity

Unity is more than a key to internal peace. It is also an essential element of your Christian witness. When peace and unity characterize your relationships with other people, you show that you are God's child and he is present and working in your life (Matt. 5:9). The converse is also true: When your life is filled with unresolved conflict and broken relationships, you will have little success in sharing the good news about Jesus' saving work on the cross. This principle is taught repeatedly throughout the New Testament.

One of the most emphatic statements on peace and unity in the Bible is found in Jesus' prayer shortly before he was arrested and taken away to be crucified. After praying for himself and for unity among his disciples (John 17:1–19), Jesus prayed for all who would someday believe in him. These words apply directly to every Christian today:

My prayer is not for [my disciples] alone. I pray also for those who will believe in me through their message, that all of them *may be one,* Father, just as you are in me and I am in you. May they also be in us so that the world may believe that you have sent me. I have given them the glory that you gave me, that they *may be one as we are one:* I in them and you in me. *May they be brought to complete unity to let the world know that you sent me and have loved them even as you have loved me.*

John 17:20–23, emphasis added

Jesus prayed these words during the final hours of his life. As death drew near, the Lord focused on a single concept he knew to be of paramount importance for all those who would believe in him. He did not pray that his followers would always be happy, that they would never suffer, or that their rights would always be defended. *Jesus prayed that his followers would get along with one another.* This was so important to him that he tied his reputation and the credibility of his message to how well his followers would display unity and oneness. Read his prayer once more and think about how important unity is to him. Is it equally important to you?

Similar words are recorded in John 13:34–35, where Jesus tells his disciples that their public witness would be closely related to the way they treated one another: "A new command I give you: Love one another. As I have loved you, so you must love one another. By this all men will know that you are my disciples, if you love one another."

The love Jesus commands us to show to one another has little to do with warm feelings; in fact, he commands us to show love even when it is the last thing in the world we feel like doing (Luke 6:27–28). The love that Jesus wants us to show for one another leaves no room for unresolved conflict:

> Love is patient, love is kind. It does not envy, it does not boast, it is not proud. It is not rude, it is not self-seeking, it is not easily angered, it keeps no record of wrongs. Love does not delight in evil but rejoices with the truth. It always protects, always trusts, always hopes, always perseveres.
>
> 1 Corinthians 13:4–7

The theme of peace and unity also occupied an important part of Jesus' Sermon on the Mount. He said, "Blessed are the peacemakers, for they will be called sons of God" (Matt. 5:9). Peacemakers provide a powerful testimony to God's presence and work in our lives. When we make peace with those who have wronged or mistreated us, others will often realize that God himself is working in and through us (1 Peter 2:12).

Later in his sermon, Jesus again urged his followers to seek peace and unity. Knowing that God will sternly judge anyone who condemns or harbors anger toward his brother (Matt. 5:21–22),

Jesus gave this command: "Therefore, if you are offering your gift at the altar and there remember that your brother has something against you, leave your gift there in front of the altar. First go and be reconciled to your brother; then come and offer your gift" (vv. 23–24).

Peace and unity are so important that Jesus commands us to seek reconciliation with a brother even ahead of worship! He teaches that we cannot love and worship God properly if we are at odds with another person and have not done everything in our power to be reconciled (1 John 4:19–21). He also reminds us that our Christian witness depends greatly on our commitment to seek peace and reconciliation with others.

I can still remember the first time I saw this principle demonstrated. When I was in law school, I brought a friend to church. Cindy was struggling in her spiritual life and disillusioned with her church. Thinking she might benefit from my church, I had invited her to worship with me one Sunday.

Moments after we took our seats, Pastor Erbele surprised everyone. He called for the attention of the congregation and asked one of the elders to come forward. Suddenly I remembered that these two men had had a heated discussion during the previous week's Sunday school class. "Oh no!" I thought. "Pastor is going to rebuke him in front of the whole church!" I was already embarrassed as my pastor continued.

"As most of you know," he said, "Kent and I had an argument during Sunday school last week. Our emotions got out of hand, and we said some things that should have been discussed in private."

As I thought of the first impression Cindy must be getting, my stomach sank. "Of all the days to bring someone to church," I thought, "why did I pick this one?" I was sure this incident would discourage Cindy and destroy her respect for my pastor.

Pastor Erbele put his arm around Kent's shoulders and went on. "We want you to know that we met later that afternoon to resolve our differences. By God's grace, we came to understand each other better, and we were fully reconciled. But we need to tell you how sorry we are for disrupting the unity of this fellowship, and we ask for your forgiveness for the poor example we gave last week."

Many eyes were filled with tears as Kent made a similar statement. Unfortunately, I was so worried about what Cindy was thinking that I missed the significance of what was happening. Making a nervous comment to Cindy, I opened the hymnal to our first song and hoped she would forget about the whole incident. The rest of the service was a blur, and before long I was driving her home. We made light conversation for a few minutes, but eventually Cindy referred to what had happened: "I still can't believe what your pastor did this morning. I've never seen a minister do something like that. Could I come back next week?"

During subsequent visits, Cindy listened intently when my pastor spoke. Having seen the power of the gospel in his life, she was eager to hear about the salvation and freedom she could experience by trusting in Jesus. Within a month, she committed her life to Christ and made our church her spiritual home.

When I brought Cindy to church that first morning, I hoped to impress her with the friendliness of my friends and the preaching of my pastor. But God had a far more effective plan in mind. He exposed the embarrassing conflict in our midst and showed that my pastor was far from perfect. And then, against this humbling backdrop of our imperfections, he revealed his grace by demonstrating the reconciling power of Jesus Christ in our midst. By moving two men to breathe grace in the midst of conflict, God brought Cindy into his kingdom.

The Enemy of Peace

Since peace and unity are essential to an effective Christian witness, you can be sure that there is someone who will do all he can to promote conflict and division among believers. Satan, whose name means "adversary," likes nothing better than to see us at odds with one another. "Your enemy the devil prowls around like a roaring lion looking for someone to devour" (1 Peter 5:8b).

Satan promotes conflict in many ways. Among other things, he tempts us so we give in to greed and dishonesty (Acts 5:3), he deceives us and misleads us (2 Tim. 2:25–26), and he takes advantage of unresolved anger (Eph. 4:26–27). Worst of all, he uses false teachers to propagate values and philosophies that encourage selfishness and stimulate controversy (1 Tim. 4:1–3). Here are some of the expressions that often reflect the devil's lies and influence:

"Look out for Number One."
"God helps those who help themselves."
"Surely God doesn't expect me to stay in an unhappy situation."
"I'll forgive you, but I won't forget."
"Don't get mad, get even."
"I deserve better than this."

Satan prefers that we do not recognize his role in our conflicts. As long as we see other people as our only adversaries and focus our attacks on them, we will give no thought to guarding against our most dangerous enemy. Both James and Peter were aware of this danger, and they warn us to actively resist Satan's schemes (James 4:7; 1 Peter 5:9). Paul gives a similar warning, reminding us that "our struggle is not against flesh and blood, but against the rulers, against the authorities, against the powers of this dark world and against the spiritual forces of evil in the heavenly realms" (Eph. 6:12). He then describes the weapons needed to withstand Satan's power: truth, righteousness, the gospel, faith, Scripture, and prayer.

Of course, it would be a serious mistake to blame all conflict on Satan. We need to take responsibility for our sins and encourage others to do the same. And we must face up to the practical problems that conflict raises and develop realistic solutions. But we should also be aware of Satan's goals and guard against his influences. By doing so, we can avoid being led astray in our efforts to restore and maintain peace.[2]

Strive like a Gladiator

The apostles understood the importance of peacemaking, and they realized that Satan will do all he can to promote conflict. The depth of their concern is revealed by the fact that *every* Epistle in the New Testament contains a command to live at peace with one another. For example:

"May the God who gives endurance and encouragement give you a spirit of unity among yourselves as you follow Christ Jesus, so that with one heart and mouth you may glorify the God and Father of our Lord Jesus Christ. Accept one another, then, just as Christ accepted you, in order to bring praise to God" (Rom. 15:5–7).

"I appeal to you, brothers, in the name of our Lord Jesus Christ, that all of you agree with one another so that there may be no divisions among you and that you may be perfectly united in mind and thought" (1 Cor. 1:10).

"The acts of the sinful nature are obvious: . . . hatred, discord, jealousy, fits of rage, selfish ambition, dissensions, factions and envy. . . . But the fruit of the Spirit is love, joy, peace" (Gal. 5:19–22).

"Bear with each other and forgive whatever grievance you may have against one another. . . . Let the peace of Christ rule in your hearts, since as members of one body you were called to peace" (Col. 3:13, 15).

"Live in peace with each other. . . . Make sure that nobody pays back wrong for wrong" (1 Thess. 5:13b–15).[3]

Paul's letter to the Ephesians focuses heavily on peacemaking. The first three chapters provide a glorious description of God's plan of salvation. In the fourth chapter, Paul begins to explain how we should respond to what Christ has done for us. Note carefully what Paul places at the top of his list of practical applications of the gospel: "As a prisoner for the Lord, then, I urge you to live a life worthy of the calling you have received. Be completely humble and gentle; be patient, bearing with one another in love. Make every effort to keep the unity of the Spirit through the bond of peace" (Eph. 4:1–3). The Greek word that is translated "make every effort" in this passage means to strive eagerly, earnestly, and diligently. It is a word that a trainer of gladiators might have used when he sent men to fight to the death in the Coliseum: "Make every effort to stay alive today!" So too must a Christian agonize for peace and unity. Obviously, token efforts and halfhearted attempts at reconciliation fall far short of what Paul had in mind.

Paul also shows that unity does not mean uniformity (Eph. 4:7–13). He reminds us that God has richly blessed his children with a wide array of gifts, talents, and callings (1 Cor. 12:12–31). Mature Christians rejoice in the diversity that God has given to his people, and they realize that believers can legitimately hold differences of opinion on "disputable matters" (Rom. 14:1). When differences rob us of harmony and peace, however, there is work to do.

Later in Ephesians, Paul uses even stronger language to emphasize the importance of harmonious relationships. He warns us that we "grieve the Holy Spirit" when we indulge in "unwholesome talk . . . bitterness, rage and anger, brawling and slander" (Eph. 4:29–31). Knowing that such conduct grieves God and quenches the work of the Holy Spirit in our lives, Paul earnestly urges us to "be kind and compassionate to one another, forgiving each other, just as in Christ God forgave you" (v. 32).

Lawsuits among Believers

God's concern for peace and unity is further emphasized by his instructions on how Christians should resolve lawsuits. When Paul learned that believers in Corinth were suing one another in secular courts, he was dismayed. Knowing that lawsuits stir up anger and damage our witness for Christ, he rebuked the Corinthians sharply:

> If any of you has a dispute with another, dare he take it before the ungodly for judgment instead of before the saints? Do you not know that the saints will judge the world? And if you are to judge the world, are you not competent to judge trivial cases? Do you not know that we will judge angels? How much more the things of this life! Therefore, if you have disputes about such matters, appoint as judges even men of little account in the church! I say this to shame you. Is it possible that there is nobody among you wise enough to judge a dispute between believers? But instead, one brother goes to law against another—and this in front of unbelievers!
>
> The very fact that you have lawsuits among you means you have been completely defeated already. Why not rather be wronged? Why not rather be cheated? Instead, you yourselves cheat and do wrong, and you do this to your brothers.
>
> 1 Corinthians 6:1–8

This is radical teaching in today's litigious and rights-oriented culture! Peace and unity among Christians is so essential to our witness for Christ that God commands us to take unresolved legal issues to the church rather than to the civil courts. Many pastors have neglected to teach regularly on this passage, so most Christians are completely unaware of this command or believe that it no longer applies. Worse yet, many churches deliberately ignore this passage and do nothing to help their members settle their legal disputes in a biblical manner. The church's failure was specifically noted in 1982 by Warren Burger, chief justice of the United States Supreme Court:

> One reason our courts have become overburdened is that Americans are increasingly turning to the courts for relief from a range of personal distresses and anxieties. Remedies for personal wrongs that once were considered the responsibility of institutions other than the courts are now boldly asserted as legal "entitlements." The courts have been expected to fill the void created by the decline of church, family and neighborhood unity.[4]

There is more than enough evidence to support this charge against the church. In my experience, there is not one church in a thousand in the United States that is committed and prepared to obey God's command to help its members resolve legal issues out of court. When legal issues arise, church leaders recoil in uncertainty. Having no alternative, tens of thousands of Christians turn away from the church every year and walk up the courthouse steps. The church's great neglect in fulfilling its traditional peacemaking responsibilities has deprived Christians of valuable assistance, contributed to the congestion of our court system, and, worst of all, damaged the church's witness for Christ.

Ironically, even though pastors usually neglect 1 Corinthians 6, there are many judges and attorneys who are calling the church to take Paul's teaching seriously. For example, associate Supreme Court justice Antonin Scalia made this observation:

> I think this passage [1 Cor. 6:1–8] has something to say about the proper Christian attitude toward civil litigation. Paul is making two points: first, he says that the mediation of a mutual friend, such

as the parish priest, should be sought before parties run off to the law courts. . . . I think we are too ready today to seek vindication or vengeance through adversary proceedings rather than peace through mediation. . . . Good Christians, just as they are slow to anger, should be slow to sue.[5]

Thank God that a justice of the United States Supreme Court reads his Bible! Justice Scalia reminds us that Paul's instructions to the Corinthians are as relevant today as they were two thousand years ago. If more pastors had such respect for this passage of Scripture, what a witness the church would have!

The command to take legal disputes to the church is not only relevant, but also highly practical and beneficial. When Paul commanded Christians to resolve their disputes in the church, he had a specific process in mind. Jesus had already established a format that Christians are to follow when they are dealing with sin and conflict, recorded in Matthew 18:15–20. This process, which will be discussed more thoroughly in chapters 7 through 9, may involve private discussions, intervention and counsel by objective advisors (mediation), or submission to a binding decision made through the church (arbitration). This approach is so wise and effective that our secular legal system is imitating it.[6]

There are many benefits to resolving conflicts in the church rather than the courts. Litigation usually increases tensions and often destroys relationships. In contrast, by bringing the gospel to bear on a conflict, the church can actively encourage forgiveness and promote reconciliation, thus preserving valuable relationships. Furthermore, a court process usually fails to deal with the underlying causes of conflict. In fact, the adversarial process, which encourages people to focus on what they have done right and what others have done wrong, often leaves the parties with a distorted view of reality. It may actually ingrain the flawed attitudes that caused the conflict in the first place.

In contrast, the church can point people to Christ and help them deal with the root causes of their problems. Once issues of sin and personal offense are resolved, the legal issues can often be settled with little additional effort. At the same time, the church can help people change harmful habits so they will experience less conflict and enjoy healthier relationships in the future.

The church can also develop more complete and effective remedies than a court. A judge is usually limited to awarding money damages, transferring property, or enforcing a contract. When a dispute is resolved within the church, the parties are encouraged to work together to develop creative solutions that resolve both material and relational issues. For example, when a church helped several brothers resolve a dispute regarding their farming operations, it encouraged the men to get their families together for dinner once a month and talk about anything but farming. That advice proved to be sound. As the bonds between various family members were strengthened through more regular personal contact, there were fewer disagreements regarding the operation of the family farm. No civil judge could have ordered these gatherings or produced this result.

The primary benefit of resolving disputes through the church is that it preserves our witness for Christ. This process prevents a public quarrel that would dishonor Christ and encourages biblical solutions and genuine reconciliation. These results bring praise to God by showing the power of the gospel: God really has delivered us from our sins, and he is actively working in us to conform us to the likeness of his Son. For these reasons alone, we should make every effort to resolve our differences outside of a courtroom.[7]

Summary and Application

The message given by Jesus and the apostles is resoundingly clear: Whether our conflicts involve minor irritations or major legal issues, God is eager to display his love and power through us as we strive to maintain peace and unity with those around us. Therefore, peacemaking is not an optional activity for a believer. If you have committed your life to Christ, he invites you to draw on his grace and commands you to seek peace with others. Token efforts will not satisfy this command; God wants you to strive earnestly, diligently, and continually to maintain harmonious relationships with those around you. Your dependence on him and obedience to this call will show the power of the gospel and enable you to enjoy the personal peace that God gives to those who faithfully follow him.

If you are presently involved in a conflict, these questions will help you apply the principles presented in this chapter:

1. Have you made peace with God by accepting Jesus Christ as your Savior, Lord, and King? If not, you can do so right now by sincerely praying this prayer: *Jesus, I know that I am a sinner, and I realize that my good deeds could never make up for my wrongs. I need your forgiveness. I believe that you died for my sins, and I want to turn away from them. I trust you now to be my Savior, and with your help I will follow you as my Lord and King, in the fellowship of your church.*

   If you have prayed this prayer, it is essential that you find fellowship with other Christians in a church where the Bible is faithfully taught and applied. This fellowship will help you to learn more about God and be strengthened in your faith.

2. Are you at peace with other people? If not, from whom are you estranged? Why?

3. Are you experiencing the kind of internal peace you desire? If not, why?

4. Has the peace and unity of the Christian community been disrupted by your dispute? How?

5. What effect might this conflict be having on the reputation of Christ?

6. Is there someone who might have something against you? What have you done to be reconciled? Do you believe that you are free to worship God, or do you need to make another effort to restore unity with that person?

7. Why and how might Satan be aggravating this dispute?

8. Have you been striving earnestly to resolve this dispute or giving only partial efforts to make peace?

9. Have you remembered the forgiveness you have in Christ and drawn on his grace to resolve this dispute, or have you been working in your own wisdom and strength? Who will you depend on from this point on?

10. Read Ephesians 4:29–32. Are you thinking, speaking, or acting in a way that might grieve the Holy Spirit?
11. Are you involved in a lawsuit? If so, what have you done to follow 1 Corinthians 6:1–8?
12. Go on record with the Lord by writing a prayer based on the principles taught in this chapter.

3

TRUST IN THE LORD AND DO GOOD

The LORD's unfailing love
surrounds the man who trusts in him.

Psalm 32:10b

The more you understand God's love and power, the easier it is to trust him. And the more you trust him, the easier it is to do his will. This is especially true when you are involved in conflict. If you believe that God is watching over you with perfect love and unlimited power, you will be able to serve him faithfully as a peacemaker, even in the most difficult circumstances. In this chapter, you will see why God is worthy of this kind of trust.

God Is Sovereign

The Bible provides many examples of people who trusted God even in the midst of terrible hardship and suffering. Our prime example is Jesus. When faced with the suffering of the cross and separation from his Father, Jesus responded to his human fears with these words: "My Father, if it is not possible for this cup to be taken away unless I drink it, may your will be done" (Matt. 26:42) and "Father, into your hands I commit my spirit" (Luke 23:46; cf. 1 Peter 2:23).

The apostle Paul responded to imprisonment, suffering, and impending execution in a similar way: "That is why I am suffering as I am. Yet I am not ashamed, because I know whom I have believed, and am convinced that he is able to guard what I have entrusted to him for that day" (2 Tim. 1:12).

One reason that Jesus and Paul trusted God so completely is that they knew he was in complete control of everything that happened in their lives. This perfect control is often referred to as "the sovereignty of God." It would take an entire book to address the implications of God's sovereignty, and even then many questions and mysteries would remain unanswered. Still, a fundamental understanding of this important doctrine is invaluable to anyone who wants to be a peacemaker.

To be sovereign means to be supreme, unlimited, and totally independent of any other influence. God alone has such power (Ps. 86:10; Isa. 46:9–10). The Bible teaches that God's dominion is so great that he has ultimate control over all things. His sovereignty extends over both creation and preservation (Ps. 135:6–7; John 1:3; Col. 1:16–17; Rev. 4:11). He rules over all governments (Prov. 21:1; Dan. 2:20–21; 4:35). He alone controls individual lives and destinies (Jer. 18:6; John 6:39; Rom. 9:15–16; 15:32; Eph. 1:11–12; James 4:15). At the same time, he watches over events as small as a sparrow's fall from a tree (Matt. 10:29).

As these and dozens of other passages show, God has ultimate control over all that happens in this world. Yet he does not exercise this power from a distance or relate to us as a mass of anonymous people. Rather, he takes personal interest in individual people and knows the smallest details of our lives (Ps. 8:3–4; 139:1–18; Prov. 16:1, 9, 33; 19:21; Matt. 10:30–31). Such loving power and attention is beyond our comprehension. When King David tried to understand the wonders of God's intimate involvement in his life, he could only conclude, "Such knowledge is too wonderful for me, too lofty for me to attain" (Ps. 139:6).

God's sovereignty is so complete that he exercises ultimate control even over painful and unjust events (Exod. 4:10–12; Job 1:6–12; 42:11; Ps. 71:20–22; Isa. 45:5–7; Lam. 3:37–38; Amos 3:6; 1 Peter 3:17). This is difficult for us to understand and accept, because we tend to judge God's actions according to our notions of what is right. Whether consciously or subconsciously, we say to ourselves, "If I were God and could control everything in the world, I wouldn't allow someone to suffer this way." Such thoughts show how little we understand and respect God. Isaiah warned, "You turn things upside down, as if the potter were thought to be like the clay! Shall what is formed say to him who formed it, 'He did not make me'? Can the pot say of the potter, 'He knows nothing'?" (Isa. 29:16).

Certainly, God takes no pleasure in what is hurtful (Ezek. 33:11), and he is never the author of sin (James 1:13–14; 1 John 1:5). Yet, for his eternal purposes, he sometimes allows suffering and permits unjust acts by men and women whom he decides not to restrain, even though he has the power to do so. Nowhere is this more vividly revealed than when the apostle Peter described the trial and execution of the Lord Jesus: "This man was handed over to you *by God's set purpose and foreknowledge;* and you, with the help of wicked men, put him to death by nailing him to the cross" (Acts 2:23, emphasis added; cf. Luke 22:42; Acts 4:27–28). Jesus did not die because God had lost control or was looking the other direction. God was fully in control at all times. He *chose* not to restrain the actions of evil men so that his plan of redemption would be fulfilled through the death and resurrection of his Son (Rom. 3:21–26). As John Piper puts it:

> People lift their hand to rebel against the Most High only to find that their rebellion is unwitting service in the wonderful designs of God. Even sin cannot frustrate the purposes of the Almighty. He himself does not commit sin, but he has decreed that there be acts that are sin—for the acts of Pilate and Herod were predestined by God's plan.[1]

Even when sinful and painful things are happening, God is somehow exercising ultimate control and working things out for his good purposes. Moreover, at the right time God administers justice and rights all wrongs. As Proverbs 16:4–5 promises, "The LORD works out everything for his own ends—even the wicked for a day of disaster. The LORD detests all the proud of heart. Be sure of this: They will not go unpunished" (cf. Ps. 33:10–11; Rom. 12:19).

The fact that God has ultimate control of all things does not release us from responsibility for our actions. He has allowed us to exercise immediate control over ourselves, and he will hold us fully accountable for the decisions we make (Matt. 12:36; Rom. 14:12). Therefore, we should never think of God's sovereignty as an excuse for our sin. Instead, knowledge of the sovereignty of God should motivate us to be even more responsible. As the passages cited above indicate, nothing in our lives happens by chance. We will never suffer trials or be involved in disputes unless God allows them and is watching over them. In other words, every conflict that comes into our lives has somehow been ordained by God. Knowing that he has personally tailored the events of our lives and is looking out for us at every moment should dramatically affect the way we respond to conflict.

God Is Good

If all we knew was that God is in control, we could have reason to fear. Indeed, if he used his power arbitrarily, sometimes for good and sometimes for evil, we would be in great danger. But this is not the case. God is good—his power is always wielded with perfect love. "One thing God has spoken, two things have I heard: that you, O God, are strong, and that you, O Lord, are loving" (Ps. 62:11–12).

The foundation for our trust in God is constructed of both power and love. He is not only in control over us; he is also *for* us! In love, he gives us life, provides for our needs, and never takes his eyes off us. As Christians, we can say with J. I. Packer:

> He knows me as a friend, one who loves me; and there is no mo-
> ment when his eye is off me, or his attention distracted from me,
> and no moment, therefore, when his care falters. This is momentous
> knowledge. There is unspeakable comfort . . . in knowing that God

is constantly taking knowledge of me in love, and watching over me for my good.[2]

The fact that God is good does not mean that he will insulate us from all suffering. Rather, it means that he will be with us in our suffering and accomplish good through it (Isa. 43:2–3). We have already seen several ways that God can use trials and difficulties for good. He often uses them to bring glory to himself by displaying his goodness, power, and faithfulness (e.g., John 9:1–5; 11:1–4; 1 Peter 1:6–7). J. I. Packer writes, "We see that he leaves us in a world of sin to be tried, tested, belaboured by troubles that threaten to crush us—in order that we may glorify him by our patience under suffering, and in order that he may display the riches of his grace and call forth new praises from us as he constantly upholds and delivers us."[3]

God also uses our trials to teach us how to minister to others when they are suffering (2 Cor. 1:3–5). Through our trials, we can set an example that will encourage others to depend on God and remain faithful to his commands (2 Cor. 1:6–11). In doing so, we are passing on the example given to us by Christ:

> If you suffer for doing good and you endure it, this is commendable before God. To this you were called, because Christ suffered for you, leaving you an example, that you should follow in his steps. . . . When they hurled their insults at him, he did not retaliate; when he suffered, he made no threats. Instead, he entrusted himself to him who judges justly. . . . So then, those who suffer according to God's will should commit themselves to their faithful Creator and continue to do good.
>
> 1 Peter 2:20, 23; 4:19[4]

By allowing us to suffer insults, conflict, and other hardships, God teaches us to rely more on him (2 Cor. 1:9; 12:7–10). When we suffer the unpleasant consequences of our sins, he is showing us our need for repentance (Ps. 119:67–71). In addition, God uses difficulties to conform us to the likeness of Christ (Rom. 8:28–29). The trials he gives us require that we practice the character qualities that will make us like our Lord. The apostles recognized and accepted this dynamic. Paul wrote, "We also rejoice in our sufferings, because we know that suffering produces perseverance; perseverance, character; and character, hope" (Rom. 5:3–4). And James elaborated, "Consider it pure joy, my brothers, whenever you face trials of many kinds, because you know that the testing of your faith develops perseverance. Perseverance must finish its work so that you may be mature and complete, not lacking anything" (James 1:2–4).

One reason that these men could face problems with such confidence is that they knew God would never give them more than they could handle. They trusted that every time he gave them a challenge, he would also give them the guidance, strength, and abilities needed to deal with it (cf. Exod. 4:11–12). As Paul promised the Corinthians, "No temptation [or trial] has seized you except what is common to man. And God is faithful; he will not let you be tempted beyond what you can bear. But when you are tempted, he will also provide a way out so that you can stand up under it" (1 Cor. 10:13). As this passage promises, God will always make available the strength and help we need to deal with the difficulties of life. It is up to us to accept and use his assistance. He also promises to provide "a way out" of our problems, and he will do this in one of two ways. Sometimes he removes the problems after they have accomplished their purpose in our lives (2 Cor. 1:3–11). At other times, he leaves the problems but gives us his strength so that we can have victory over them on a day-to-day basis, thus revealing his sustaining grace (2 Cor. 12:7–10).

Although we can be sure that God is always working for our good and the good of others, even through trials and suffering, we will not always know exactly what that good is. In many cases his ultimate purposes will not be evident for a long time. And in some situations his ways and objectives are simply too profound for us to comprehend, at least until we see God face to face (see Rom. 11:33–36). This should not diminish our confidence in him or our willingness to obey him, however. As Deuteronomy 29:29 tells us, "The secret things belong to the LORD our God, but the things revealed belong to us and to our children forever, that we may follow all the words of this law."[5]

This passage provides the key to dealing faithfully with painful and unjust situations. God may not tell us everything we *want* to know about the painful events of life, but he has already told us all we *need* to know. Therefore, instead of wasting time and energy trying to figure out things that are beyond our comprehension, we need to turn our attention to the promises and instructions that God has revealed to us through Scripture. The Bible tells us that God is both sovereign and good, so we can be sure that whatever he has brought into our lives can be used to glorify him, to benefit others, and to help us to grow. The Bible also provides clear and practical instructions on how to respond effectively to the challenges God allows in our lives. As we trust God with the "secret things," remember all he has already done for us through Christ, and focus our attention on obeying his revealed will, we will experience greater peace within ourselves (Ps. 131; Isa. 26:3) and be enabled to serve him more effectively as peacemakers (Prov. 3:5–7).[6]

The Path Has Been Marked

Trusting God does not mean that we will never have questions, doubts, or fears. We cannot simply turn off the natural thoughts and feelings that arise when we face difficult circumstances. Trusting God means that *in spite of our questions, doubts, and fears* we draw on his grace and continue to believe that he is loving, that he is in control, and that he is always working for our good. Such trust helps us to continue doing what is good and right, even in difficult circumstances.

The Bible is filled with descriptions of people who experienced all kinds of misgivings and yet continued to trust in God. For example, when Job suffered incredible hardship, he voiced many doubts and apprehensions. Even so, he eventually came to this conclusion: "I know that you can do all things; no plan of yours can be thwarted. You asked, 'Who is this that obscures my counsel without knowledge?' Surely I spoke of things I did not understand, things too wonderful for me to know" (Job 42:2–3; see 40:1–41:34).

One of my favorite Bible characters, Joseph, had a similar experience, which is described in Genesis 37–50. Because his father favored him, Joseph's brothers envied him and sold him into slavery in Egypt. Although Joseph probably struggled with times of doubt and frustration, he did not take things into his own hands. Instead, he continued to serve God faithfully (e.g., Gen. 39:9). In spite of Joseph's honesty and diligence, however, his master's wife brought false charges against him, and his master threw him into prison. Even there, Joseph continued to trust in God and faithfully served those who imprisoned him (Gen. 39:11–23).

The Lord showed kindness to Joseph, giving him great wisdom and empowering him to interpret dreams. This led Pharaoh to make Joseph prime minister of Egypt. In that position, Joseph was able to save the entire nation of Egypt, as well as his family, from starvation when famine devastated the Middle East. His brothers eventually came to him in fear, seeking forgiveness for the great wrong they had done to him. Joseph's reply revealed remarkable humility and a profound trust in the sovereignty of God: "'Don't be afraid. Am I in the place of God? You intended to harm me, but God intended it for good to accomplish what is now being done, the saving of many lives. So then, don't be afraid. I will provide for you and your children.' And he reassured them and spoke kindly to them" (Gen. 50:19–21).

King David likewise observed that God allowed evil men to flourish for a time. Although he could not understand why, David was convinced that God was in control and that all his ways are good. This confidence inspired David to obey God even in the midst of severe persecution. His feelings and insights are recorded in Psalm 37, which has provided great encouragement to me during times of opposition or mistreatment by others. David's deeply held confidence is reflected in the first six verses of that psalm:

> Do not fret because of evil men
>   or be envious of those who do wrong;
> for like the grass they soon wither,
>   like green plants they will soon die away.
> Trust in the LORD and do good;
>   dwell in the land and enjoy safe pasture.
> Delight yourself in the LORD
>   and he will give you the desires of your heart.
> Commit your way to the LORD;
>   trust in him and he will do this:
> He will make your righteousness shine like the dawn,
>   the justice of your cause like the noonday sun.

Like Joseph, the apostle Peter was often mistreated and wrongly imprisoned. At times he too struggled with questions and fears. Even so, he continued to trust God, draw on his grace, and do his best to obey God's revealed will. This is particularly apparent in Peter and John's prayer after they had been arrested and threatened by the Jewish authorities: "Sovereign Lord, . . . you made the heaven and the earth and the sea, and everything in them. . . . Indeed Herod and Pontius Pilate met together with the Gentiles . . . [and] did what your power and will had decided beforehand should happen. Now, Lord, consider their threats and enable your servants to speak your word with great boldness" (Acts 4:24, 27–29). When the authorities' threats later turned into floggings, Peter and the other apostles continued to trust in God, "rejoicing because they had been counted worthy of suffering disgrace for the Name" (Acts 5:41).

The apostle Paul had the same habit of trusting God regardless of his circumstances. On one occasion in Philippi, he and Silas were falsely accused, severely flogged, and thrown into prison. Incredibly, instead of wallowing in doubt or despair, they spent the night "praying and singing hymns to God" (Acts 16:25). God responded by bringing about an earthquake, the conversion of the jailer and his family, and an apology from the city officials.

Trusting God proved to be the pattern in Paul's life. Even when the Lord did not immediately relieve his sufferings, Paul continued to view everything that happened to him as God's sovereign will (2 Cor. 4:7–18). This doesn't mean that Paul never had doubts or that he never asked God to relieve his suffering (2 Cor. 12:7–8). But when the Lord's response did not match Paul's request, he was willing to believe that God had something better in mind (vv. 9–10).

This was especially evident during Paul's many imprisonments, which he always considered to be part of God's plan for advancing his kingdom (Eph. 4:1; Phil. 1:12–14; Col. 4:3). The longer Paul walked with God, the more he trusted him. Therefore, Paul did not spend his time thinking about when he would be released from prison. In fact, instead of asking his supporters to pray for his prison door to be opened, Paul urged them to pray that "God may open a *door for our message*" (Col. 4:3, emphasis added; cf. Eph. 6:19–20). Knowing that he was safely in God's hands no matter what his circumstances, Paul was always free. This knowledge saved him from crippling worry and allowed him to respond effectively to the opportunities God had set before him.

God has continued to provide us with examples of the kind of trust that honors him. One of the most profound examples in recent years was given by Jim and Elisabeth Elliot. In 1956 Jim and four other missionaries were murdered when they tried to carry the gospel to the Aucas, an isolated tribe in South America. Elisabeth was deeply grieved by the loss of her husband, and she had to wrestle through many unanswered questions. As this excerpt from her subsequent book reveals, however, she continued to trust in the sovereignty of God:

> To the world at large this was a sad waste of five young lives. But God has his plan and purpose in all things. . . . The prayers of the widows themselves are for the Aucas. We look forward to the day when these savages will join us in Christian praise. Plans were promptly formulated for continuing the work of the martyrs.[7]

The widows carried on the work their husbands had begun; three years after the killings, God answered their prayers and began to open Auca hearts to the gospel. Even some of the men who had killed the five missionaries eventually came to Christ. Although Elisabeth praised God for the conversions he brought about, she acknowledged that they were not the sole measure of God's purpose in her husband's death. In 1981 she added an epilogue to her book, which included these words:

> The Auca story . . . has pointed to one thing: God *is* God. If he is God, he is worthy of my worship, and my service. I will find rest nowhere but in his will, and that will is infinitely, immeasurably, unspeakably beyond my largest notions of what he is up to. God is the God of human history, and he is at work continuously, mysteriously, accomplishing his eternal purposes in us, through us, for us, and in spite of us. . . . Cause and effect are in God's hands. Is it not the part of faith simply to let them rest there? God is God. I dethrone him in my heart if I demand that he act in ways that satisfy my idea of justice. . . . The one who laid the earth's foundations and settled its dimensions knows where the lines are drawn. He gives all the light we need for trust and obedience.[8]

Similar trust has been displayed in the life of Joni Eareckson Tada. In 1967 Joni was paralyzed from the shoulders down as the result of a diving accident. She too struggled for a time with many questions and doubts. By God's grace, however, she did not succumb to resentment or hopelessness. Instead, as the Lord steadily increased her faith and knowledge, she learned to see her situation as an opportunity to exalt Christ and minister to disabled people. She now leads an organization that ministers to hundreds of thousands of people throughout the world. When writing about God's sovereignty, she says:

> Nothing is a surprise to God; nothing is a setback to his plans; nothing can thwart his purposes; and nothing is beyond his control. His sovereignty is absolute. Everything that happens is uniquely ordained of God. Sovereignty is a weighty thing to ascribe to the nature and character of God. Yet if he were not sovereign, he would not be God. The Bible is clear that God is in control of everything that happens. [9]

As Moses learned, when God gives a disability, he also gives us the means to deal with it (Exod. 4:11–12). God does not delight in our afflictions, but when they are in his will for us, he delights in working everything out for our good and for his glory (Rom. 8:28)—whether he removes the affliction or not!

> If examining the sovereignty of God teaches us anything, it teaches us that real satisfaction comes not in understanding God's motives, but in understanding his character, in trusting in his promises, and in leaning on him and resting in him as the Sovereign who knows what he is doing and does all things well. [10]

Each of the people mentioned in this section experienced extremely difficult problems and wrestled with the same kinds of questions and concerns we have today. What was it that allowed them to keep going in spite of these challenges? Among other things, they had the humility to recognize the limits of their own understanding and the wisdom to bow before God's eternal purposes. They rejoiced in their salvation and were grateful for the way God was working to change them. And through prayer, study, and experience, they learned to trust in the sovereignty of God. Even in the midst of incredible hardship or injustice, they believed that God was in control and that he loved them with an everlasting love. That trust released them from the burden of unanswered questions, helping them overcome the fears and doubts that naturally challenged them. That trust opened their hearts to receive God's grace and then breathe grace to others in the midst of the challenges God brought into their lives.

Trust Is a Decision

Your view of God will have a profound effect on how much you trust him. If you do not believe that he is both sovereign and good, trust will be an elusive thing, for a god who is loving but not in control is simply "a heavenly Santa Claus . . . who means well, but cannot always insulate his children from trouble and grief."[11] Such a god offers little security or hope in the face of affliction and fails to inspire either trust or obedience.

On the other hand, if you believe that God is sovereign and good, you will be able to trust him and obey him, even in the midst of difficult circumstances. A woman I counseled several years ago learned this principle when she was about to leave her husband. Her experience was so encouraging that I later asked her to write an anonymous letter for the benefit of others who were facing similar problems. Here is what she wrote:

Dear Friend,

If you are in counseling, maybe you are feeling as I did. You're saying you want to improve your marriage, but what you really want deep inside is to get out. You can't take the way you are living anymore, and you wish your husband would just disappear, leaving behind lots of cash.

The day I first called about Christian conciliation, I was ready to take thirty painkillers if I'd had them. I was full of anger, resentment, and hatred for what my life had become. I had reached the point where I couldn't even talk to my husband. I'm not talking about serious conversations—I couldn't even answer a simple question with a yes or no. When he entered a room, I left. When he touched me, I cringed. I felt trapped, and I would drive by apartment complexes with the idea of finding a place where the kids and I could run away and live.

This had gone on for so long that I didn't see how it could ever change. Talking to Ken was going to be my last effort to change things, but I really felt that the marriage was hopeless, and I told my husband that I wanted out.

After talking with Ken, I prayed and prayed about the biblical principles he had explained to me. I was deeply concerned about my future. I began to see that God is sovereign, and I realized my marriage was not an "accident." I also saw that I had no right to leave my husband. On a retreat God showed me through Scripture (Deut. 30:11–20; please read it) that really committing myself to my marriage was God's way. He set before me a choice—his way or my way. If I chose my own way, I was on my own.

I decided to trust God and go his way. I agreed to go with my husband to a Christian counselor. It was very hard at times. Sometimes I couldn't even talk, but we went for a few months, and things started to get better.

We were "getting along," yet I was deeply bothered by the fact that I felt no love for my husband. I no longer felt anger or hatred toward him, but there was no warmth either. Although our relationship had improved, I knew marriage had to be much more than just "getting along."

I didn't believe God had brought us through so much to leave us in a relationship that was so empty. I wanted to continue to trust the Lord and to depend on him for hope. When I looked up "hope" in my Bible concordance, I found this verse: "And hope does not disappoint us, because God has poured out his love into our hearts by the Holy Spirit, whom he has given us" (Rom. 5:5). To me this verse meant that by hoping in God for my future I would not be disappointed. He would give me love for my husband. I could depend on him. I was following his way, and therefore I could trust in him to meet my needs.

And do you know what? Something absolutely amazing happened. I'm in love with my husband. I enjoy being with him. I appreciate his sense of humor. I depend on him as a friend. He's my favorite lunch date, and I find myself wanting to give him a hug and a kiss while he's watching television.

The Lord has turned around my feelings. I thank him almost every day that he didn't let me go my own way. I would have thrown away so much and never realized how God can work when I let him. The change in our family is truly a miracle!

A year after she wrote this letter, I called her to ask how things were going in her marriage. She said her relationship with her husband "still went up and down at times," and they occasionally needed further counsel to deal with issues in their marriage. She told me that she and her husband were both growing in their faith. Even when she was frustrated with her husband, she seldom struggled with the hopelessness that had plagued her two years earlier. She also said she was confident that God knew what he was doing in her life, and she trusted that things would continue to improve as he kept working in both of them.

Then she said something that touched me deeply. She and her husband had just invested in an apartment, and she had been painting it that day. Remembering the times she had driven around looking for a place to run away to, she began to think about what it would be like to live there alone. She said she had shuddered at the thought of how empty and lonely she would be without her husband. "I am so glad," she said, "that I trusted God and didn't go my own way."[12]

Summary and Application

When you are involved in a conflict, you too must decide whether or not you will trust God. Trusting God does not mean believing that he will do all that you want, but rather believing that he will do everything he knows is good. If you do not trust God, you will inevitably place your trust in yourself or another person, which ultimately leads to grief. On the other hand, if you believe that God is sovereign and that he will never allow anything into your life unless it can be used for good, you will see conflicts not as *accidents* but as *opportunities*. This kind of trust glorifies God and inspires the faithfulness needed for effective peacemaking.

If you are presently involved in a conflict, these questions will help you to apply the principles presented in this chapter:

1. Have you been looking at this dispute as something that happened by chance, as something done to you by someone

else, or as something that God allowed in your life for a specific purpose?

2. What questions, doubts, or fears do you have because of this dispute?

3. Read Psalms 37 and 73. What do these psalms warn you not to do? What do they instruct you to do? List the comforting promises they provide.

4. How would your feelings, attitudes, and behavior change if you started seeing this dispute as an assignment from a perfectly loving and all-powerful God?

5. What good might God bring about if you respond to this conflict in a biblical manner?

6. Go on record with the Lord by writing a prayer based on the principles taught in this chapter.

PART 2

GET THE LOG OUT
OF YOUR EYE

*How can I show Jesus' work
in me by taking responsibility
for my contribution
to this conflict?*

You hypocrite, first take the plank out of your own eye,
and then you will see clearly to remove the speck from
your brother's eye.

Matthew 7:5

At last he had his chance. Clutching his prepared statement in his hand, Mark sat down in the front pew, ready to get even with the elders. Six months ago they had refused to support his promotion to senior pastor. They had stood silently by when Mark was slandered in a congregational meeting. Worst of all, some of them had repeatedly talked about him behind his back, voicing their doubts about his ability to fill the shoes of their retiring pastor.

After months of escalating tension, the elders finally called in a team of trained conciliators from Peacemaker Ministries. During two three-day visits, the conciliators taught peacemaking to the congregation, facilitated personal discussions, and encouraged Mark and the elders to set an example for the church by acknowledging their own contributions to the problem. But Mark could not let go of his perception that the elders' repeated sins against him far outweighed his few mistakes.

Now, with the second set of weekend meetings drawing to a close, the elders were going to make a corporate confession of their wrongs to the congregation. Their prepared statement did not go as far as Mark and his wife thought it should, however, so he and Donna planned to publicly elaborate on the elders' sins against them.

As the service began, one of the conciliators preached a brief message on reconciliation and then explained the goals and format of the meeting. He then gave the microphone to the head elder. Reading from a prepared statement, he acknowledged several ways that the elders had wronged Pastor Mark. Then he looked straight at Mark and Donna and said, "We have sinned against you both and caused you great pain. We are so very sorry." It was evident from the tears in his eyes and the emotion in his voice that he was speaking from his heart.

Then another elder stepped up, confessed his own sins, and asked for forgiveness from the associate pastor and the congregation. A third elder did the same. The conciliators had expected only two or three of them to speak, but before long seven of the nine elders had come forward to add their personal confessions to the statement that had already been read.

Mark was battling with his thoughts. He was still angry and hurt, but the elders' words had put a crack in the wall he had built around his heart. His wife sensed that he needed a few moments to collect his thoughts, so she stood up and stepped to the microphone.

Turning to the elders, Donna said, "I came here tonight planning to tell everyone how much you have hurt Mark and me. But in the last few minutes, God has shown me how wrong *I* have been. I finally understand what the Lord has been trying to tell me in

1 John 3:15. By holding on to my hatred, I have been murdering each of you in my heart for months. I am so much guiltier than you are. I do forgive you, and I ask you to forgive me." As she walked back to her seat, Donna's face showed the freedom she felt. Her bitterness had been washed away.

Mark's feet felt like they were made of lead as he rose and walked toward the microphone. The war in his heart was building to a climax. He could hold on to his anger and try to get even with the elders for the pain they had caused him, or he could find freedom and peace by forgiving them and confessing his own wrongs. With growing emotion, he realized that he could not do both.

Help me, God, he silently prayed as he reached the microphone. Suddenly his fingers opened and his notes fell to the floor. Turning to face the elders, he spoke words that he had never expected to say that night.

"Donna was wrong. *I* am actually the guiltiest person of all. As associate pastor I should have set an example of humility and submission. I should have trusted God to work through the elders and the congregation to select the next senior pastor of this church. Instead, I let my desire for this position control me, so I took matters into my own hands. I exalted myself and became defensive when people raised honest concerns about my abilities. I became angry that people were talking about me behind my back, but then I did exactly the same thing. Instead of going to talk with those who had spoken against me, I avoided them and wallowed in resentment. Even when some people asked for my forgiveness, I refused to give it. I have failed miserably as your pastor. And worst of all, I dragged Donna into my bitterness. I ask God for his forgiveness, and I hope that he will give you grace to forgive me too."

The elders rose as one to embrace Mark. Reaching out, they drew Donna into the circle. After a few moments, another voice was heard behind them. Two additional microphones had been placed before the congregation. An elderly man stood before one of them, wanting to take his share of the blame. Before he was done speaking, a woman had moved to the other microphone, compelled by the same Spirit to find peace through confession. Then another and another confessed sin, slander, divisiveness, and hardness of heart. Everyone pointed to himself or herself. Each person became his own accuser.

After forty-five minutes of confession, quietness fell over the congregation. One of the conciliators closed the meeting in prayer. When he finished, he sensed that God was not done working. So he suggested that people turn around and greet one other with the exhilarating truth, "The Lord has forgiven all your sins!" The people shared this good news with each other and hugged and talked for so long that the conciliators finally made a quiet exit. They knew that these people were in good hands—God's hands.

This incident is one of many true examples of the "Golden Result." The Golden Result is a corollary to the Golden Rule, which calls us to do to others as we would have them do to us. The Golden Result says that *people will usually treat us as we treat them.* If we blame others for a problem, they will usually blame in return. But if we say, "I was wrong," it is amazing how often the response will be, "It was my fault too."

I have seen this result in hundreds of cases over the past twenty-one years. Whether the dispute involves a personal quarrel, divorce, lawsuit, or church division, people generally treat one another as they are being treated. When one person attacks and accuses, so does the other. And when God moves one person to start getting the log out of his or her own eye, it is rare that the other side fails to do the same.

The Golden Result occurs most often with people who understand and cherish the gospel. When we admit that our own sins are so serious that Jesus had to die for us, and remember that he has forgiven us for all our wrongs, we can let go of our illusion of self-righteousness and freely admit our failures. When we do this, we experience the wonderful gift of God's forgiveness. And in many cases, he will be pleased to use our confessions to help others see the logs in their eyes.

4

IS THIS REALLY WORTH
FIGHTING OVER?

A man's wisdom gives him patience,
it is to his glory to overlook an offense.

Proverbs 19:11

Jesus had much to say about resolving conflict. One of his most familiar commands is recorded in Matthew 7:3–5:

Why do you look at the speck of sawdust in your brother's eye and pay no attention to the plank in your own eye? How can you say to your brother, "Let me take the speck out of your eye," when all the time there is a plank in your own eye? You hypocrite, first take the plank out of your own eye, and then you will see clearly to remove the speck from your brother's eye.

This passage is sometimes interpreted as a warning against talking with others about their faults. If you read it carefully, however, you will see that it does not forbid loving correction. Rather, it forbids *premature and improper* correction. Before you talk to others about their faults, Jesus wants you to face up to yours. Once you have dealt with *your* contribution to a conflict, you may approach others about theirs.

As you examine your role in a conflict, it is helpful to look for two types of fault. First, you may have an *overly sensitive attitude,* which causes you to be offended too easily by others' behavior. Second, you may have contributed to the conflict through your own *sinful behavior.* We will look at attitude issues in this chapter and at behavior issues in the following two chapters.

Define the Issues

As you evaluate your role in a conflict, it is helpful to clearly define the issues that separate you from other people. Conflicts generally involve two kinds of issues: material and personal. *Material* issues involve substantive matters such as property, money, rights, and responsibilities. These issues may be expressed by questions like these: Where will we spend our vacation? Should we build a new church? How much money does Ted owe Sue? How can we get this property sold? Was it right for Bill to fire Don? Did Alice breach the contract? These issues should usually be resolved through cooperative *negotiation,* which will be described in chapter 11.

Personal issues relate to what goes on inside or between persons. These matters involve our attitudes and feelings toward others that result from how we have treated one another. Personal issues are often expressed in thoughts and statements like these: "I am upset about your lying to me." "She is stubborn and unreasonable." "I don't like the way he always criticizes me." "I'm sure he is trying to cheat me." "You did that just to embarrass me." These kinds of issues must generally be resolved either by *overlooking* an offense or through *confession, loving correction, and forgiveness,* which will be discussed in subsequent chapters.

Some disputes involve only material issues and others only personal issues. In a large majority of conflicts, however, both kinds of issues get tangled up together. This connection is succinctly illustrated in Luke 12:13–15: "Someone in the crowd said to him, 'Teacher, tell my brother to divide the inheritance with me.' Jesus replied . . . 'Watch out! Be on your guard against all kinds of greed; a man's life does not consist in the abundance of his possessions.'"

The material issue in this conflict was, How should the family inheritance be divided? The personal issues involved the brothers' greed and estrangement, which kept them from resolving the material issue in a cooperative and generous way.

Material and personal issues often feed on and aggravate each other. This dynamic can turn minor disagreements into full-blown quarrels. For example, when I come home from a long trip, I am looking forward to my wife's wonderful cooking. She, on the other hand, is often weary of cooking and would prefer to eat out. The material issue is fairly simple, isn't it?—Should we eat at home or go out tonight? But this simple issue has at times escalated into conflict. If Corlette presses me to go out, I have sometimes grumbled that she doesn't care about how sick I am of restaurant food. And she has reacted with a comment about my insensitivity to how hard she has worked in my absence. I counter with a comment about watching our budget, and she raises a question about my new computer. Pretty soon issues of eating out, selfishness, lack of sensitivity, domestic responsibilities, and my new computer are all tangled together in a surprising mess.

Once these combinations of issues emerge, you can seldom resolve the initial material issue satisfactorily unless you also address the associated personal issues. First you must stop dragging in more issues, and then you must sort through the issues that have already surfaced. Try to agree on the primary material issue or issues. (Should we eat out or stay home tonight?) Then identify the primary personal issues. (Corlette is tired of cooking. Ken is sick of restaurants. Corlette feels taken for granted. Ken thinks Corlette is being selfish.) Then list the secondary issues. (Is Corlette neglecting our budget? Did Ken really need the new computer? Should Ken learn how to cook?)

Once you have sorted the issues out, you can begin to decide what steps to take to resolve the problem. It is often helpful to look at each issue and ask, "Is this really worth fighting over?" When significant personal or material issues are involved, the answer to this question will be yes, and you will need to follow the steps described in subsequent chapters. (It is usually helpful to address major personal issues first, which often leads to progress on material issues. At other times, you will need to alternate between personal and material issues, with progress in one area opening the way for progress in others.)

In many cases, however, if you look at a particular issue from a biblical perspective, you will realize that it is simply not worth fighting over. Such matters should be dropped or settled as quickly and quietly as possible. Below are some of the principles that will help you discern when an issue should be overlooked or pursued.

Overlook Minor Offenses

In many situations, the best way to resolve a conflict is simply to overlook the personal offenses of others. This approach is highly commended throughout Scripture:

> "A man's wisdom gives him patience; it is to his glory to overlook an offense" (Prov. 19:11; cf. 12:16; 15:18; 20:3).
>
> "Starting a quarrel is like breaching a dam; so drop the matter before a dispute breaks out" (Prov. 17:14; cf. 26:17).
>
> "Above all, love each other deeply, because love covers over a multitude of sins" (1 Peter 4:8; cf. Prov. 10:12; 17:9).
>
> "Be completely humble and gentle; be patient, bearing with one another in love" (Eph. 4:2).
>
> "Bear with each other and forgive whatever grievances you may have against one another. Forgive as the Lord forgave you" (Col. 3:13; cf. Eph. 4:32).

When we overlook the wrongs of others, we are imitating God's extraordinary forgiveness toward us: "The LORD is compassionate and gracious, slow to anger, abounding in love. He will not always accuse, nor will he harbor his anger forever; he does not treat us as our sins deserve or repay us according to our iniquities" (Ps. 103:8–10).

Since God does not deal harshly with us when we sin, we should be willing to treat others in a similar fashion. This does not mean that we must overlook all sins, but it does require that we ask God to help us discern and overlook minor wrongs.

Overlooking offenses is appropriate under two conditions. First, the offense should not have created a wall between you and the other person or caused you to feel differently toward him or her for more than a short period of time. Second, the offense should not be causing serious harm to God's reputation, to others, or to the offender. (We will discuss these criteria more fully in chapter 7.)

Overlooking is not a *passive* process in which you simply remain silent for the moment but file away the offense for later use against someone. That is actually a form of denial that can easily lead to brooding over the offense and building up internal bitterness and resentment that will eventually explode in anger. Instead, overlooking is an *active* process that is inspired by God's mercy through the gospel. To truly overlook an offense means to deliberately decide not to talk about it, dwell on it, or let it grow into pent-up bitterness. If you cannot let go of an offense in this way, if it is too serious to overlook, or if it continues as part of a pattern in the other person's life, then you will need to go and talk to the other person about it in a loving and constructive manner.

Check Your Attitude—and Change It

One of the reasons we sometimes find it difficult to overlook offenses is that we have an overly sensitive attitude or a tendency to dwell on what others have done. One way to guard against this problem is to check your attitude in the light of God's Word.

Paul's letter to the Philippians contains an excellent formula for examining our attitudes during a conflict. Apparently, Paul had heard that two followers of Jesus in Philippi were having an argument. As part of his open letter to the church in that city, Paul took time to urge these two friends to seek peace:

> I plead with Euodia and I plead with Syntyche to agree with each other in the Lord. Yes, and I ask you, loyal yokefellow, help these women who have contended at my side in the cause of the gospel, along with Clement and the rest of my fellow workers, whose names are in the book of life.
>
> Rejoice in the Lord always. I will say it again: Rejoice! Let your gentleness be evident to all. The Lord is near. Do not be anxious

about anything, but in everything, by prayer and petition, with thanksgiving, present your requests to God. And the peace of God, which transcends all understanding, will guard your hearts and your minds in Christ Jesus.

Finally, brothers, whatever is true, whatever is noble, whatever is right, whatever is pure, whatever is lovely, whatever is admirable—if anything is excellent or praiseworthy—think about such things. Whatever you have learned or received or heard from me, or seen in me—put it into practice. And the God of peace will be with you.

Philippians 4:2–9

Paul does not explain every action that Euodia and Syntyche need to take to settle their differences. Instead, he focuses on the steps they can take to develop a proper attitude toward their situation and toward each other. Paul has broken his instructions into five basic principles, which you too can use whenever you are involved in a conflict.

1. Rejoice in the Lord always. As usual, Paul urges us to be God-centered in our approach to conflict. Moreover, he wants us to be *joyfully* God-centered. Realizing we may skip over this point, Paul repeats it: "Rejoice in the Lord always. I will say it again: Rejoice!" What on earth is there to rejoice about when you are involved in a dispute? If you open your eyes and think about God's lavish goodness to you, here is the kind of joyful worship you could offer to him, even in the midst of the worst conflict:

Oh Lord, you are so amazingly good to me! You sent your only Son to die for my sins, including those I have committed in this conflict. Because of Jesus I am forgiven, and my name is written in the Book of Life! You do not treat me as I deserve, but you are patient, kind, gentle, and forgiving with me. Please help me to do the same to others.

In your great mercy, you are also kind to my opponent. Although he has wronged me repeatedly, you hold out your forgiveness to him as you do to me. Even if he and I never reconcile in this life, which I still hope we will, you have already done the work to reconcile us forever in heaven. This conflict is so insignificant compared to the wonderful hope we have in you!

This conflict is so small compared to the many other things you are watching over at this moment, yet you still want to walk beside me as I seek to resolve it. Why would you stoop down to pay such attention to me? It is too wonderful for me to understand. You are extravagant in your gifts to me. You offer me the comfort of your Spirit, the wisdom of your Word, and the support of your church. Forgive me for neglecting these powerful treasures until now, and help me to use them to please and honor you.

I rejoice that these same resources are available to my opponent. Please enable us to draw on them together so that we see our own sins, remember the gospel, find common ground in the light of your truth, come to one mind with you and each other, and restore peace and unity between us.

Finally, Lord, I rejoice that this conflict has not happened by accident. You are sovereign and good, so I know that you are working through this situation for your glory and my good. No matter what my opponent does, you are working to conform me to the likeness of your Son. Please help me to cooperate with you in every possible way and give you glory for what you have done and are doing.

Salvation through the gospel, the motivation and power to change, sound guidance through God's Word and Spirit, the resources of the body of Christ, opportunities that come through a sovereign God—all these blessings are available when you are "in the Lord." But remember, Satan does not want you to think like this; he wants to keep you worried about your conflict, wrapped up in yourself, and looking anywhere except at God. Resist him! Go to the Lord repeatedly in prayer and worship, and delight in his goodness to you. You will be surprised at the freedom and power that such rejoicing brings.

2. Let your gentleness be evident to all. The second step in developing a proper attitude toward conflict is to "let your gentleness be evident to all" (cf. Gal. 6:1–2). The Greek word translated as "gentleness" in this passage is rich in meaning. It means, "forbearing, large-hearted, gentle, courteous, considerate, generous, lenient, moderate. In summary, it is describing a quality that is the opposite of irritability, rudeness, and abrasiveness."[1]

Being gentle in the midst of conflict is a powerful way to breathe grace to others, especially when your behavior is "evident to all." Such gentleness reflects Christ's presence and power in your life, which honors him. It also guards you from speaking and acting harshly, which would only make matters worse. Finally, your gentleness may trigger the Golden Result and encourage similar behavior in your opponent.

Gentleness is especially appropriate if the person who wronged you is experiencing unusual stress. If so, the wrong done to you may be a symptom of a deeper problem. By responding in a gentle and compassionate manner, you may minister powerfully to the other person. One day my daughter, Megan, did this to me. I was having a problem at the ministry and took my anxiety out on my family by speaking irritably to them. Soon they were all walking on eggshells and trying to stay out of my way. After watching my sinful behavior for a while, Megan approached me and gently asked, "Dad, is there something bothering you? You aren't normally so grumpy." Her tone of voice conveyed such sincere concern for me that I melted. I told her what was going on in my heart and admitted I was wrong to have treated everyone so harshly. She put her hand on my arm, and said, "I forgive you, Dad. Can we pray about it?" What a wonderful way to minister to my anxieties and help me change my attitude.

3. Replace anxiety with prayer. The third step in developing a godly attitude toward conflict is to get rid of anxious thoughts. When Paul writes, "Be anxious about nothing," he is not talking about trivial concerns. The Greek word that we translate as "anxious" means laden with cares and trouble, pressured, squeezed, burdened, under stress. Such feelings tend to multiply when we are in the middle of a dispute, especially if it involves a person who is important to us or if major issues are at stake.

Paul knew that we cannot just stop being anxious. Worried thoughts have a way of creeping back into our minds, no matter how hard we try to ignore them. Therefore, he instructs us to *replace* worrying with "prayer and petition, with thanksgiving." When you are in a dispute, it is natural to dwell on your difficult circumstances or on the wrong things that the other person has done or may do to you. The best way to overcome this negative thinking is to replace it with more constructive thoughts, such as praising God for his grace through the gospel, thanking him for the many things he has already done for you in this and other situations, and praying for assistance in dealing with your current challenges (cf. Matt. 6:25–34).

When you remind yourself of God's faithfulness in the past and ally yourself with him today, you will discover that your anxiety is being steadily replaced with confidence and trust (cf. Isa. 26:3). In fact, recalling God's faithfulness and thanking him for his deliverance in the past was one of the primary ways the Israelites overcame their fears when they faced overwhelming problems (e.g., Psalms 18, 46, 68, 77, 78, 105, 106, 107, 136; Neh. 9:5–37).

When you place your focus on God through prayer, you can begin to experience something that does not seem logical: The hostility, anxiety, and inner conflict with which you have been dealing will begin to give way to a peace so unexpected that Paul says it will "transcend all understanding." Although this peace may be only internal at first ("guarding your heart and mind"), it will often grow into an external peace—or reconciliation—that will likewise surpass the comprehension of those who have been observing your conflict. When God works in his people, things begin to happen that don't make sense to the world. What a wonderful way to catch people's attention and bring praise to God!

4. See things as they really are. As you replace anxiety with prayer, you will be ready to follow Paul's fourth instruction, which is to develop a more accurate view of others. If you respond to conflict like most people, you will tend to focus on the negative characteristics of the person who is disagreeing with you, exaggerating his faults and overlooking his virtues. The more distorted your perspective becomes, the more likely you are to imagine the worst about the other person, which may lead you to misjudge his or her values, motives, and actions. A negative perspective can also lead to bitterness, which is characterized by dwelling on the hurt and thinking how little you deserve it.

The best way to overcome this tendency is to think deliberately about aspects of others that are true, noble, right, pure, lovely, admirable, excellent, or praiseworthy (see Phil. 4:8). Paul is not saying that we should think *only* about the good things in others, for he clearly understood the necessity of addressing sin and encouraging repentance (Gal. 6:1–2; Col. 3:16). Rather, Paul is teaching us to counterbalance our natural tendency to focus *only* on what is bad in those who oppose us.

This change in perspective does not come naturally for most of us. It requires a deliberate decision, followed by perseverance. If you shift your focus to positive things, you can experience the principle described in Proverbs 11:27: "He who seeks good finds goodwill, but evil comes to him who searches for it." If you look for something bad in another person, you will usually be able to find it. On the other hand, if you look for what is good, you are likely to find that too—and then more and more that is good.

As you regain a more balanced view of the other person, you will often find it easier to overlook minor offenses. I have experienced this process many times in my marriage. One day Corlette said something that really hurt me. I don't remember what she said, but I remember going out into the backyard a few minutes later to rake leaves. The more I dwelt on her words, the more deeply I slid into self-pity and resentment. I was steadily building up steam to go back into the house and let her know how wrong she was. But then God brought Philippians 4:8 to my mind.

Ha! I thought. *There's nothing noble, right, or lovely about the way she's treating me!* But the Holy Spirit wouldn't give up. The verse would not go away; it kept echoing in my mind. Finally, to get God off my back, I grudgingly conceded that Corlette is a good cook. This small concession opened the door to a stream of thoughts about my wife's good qualities. I recalled that she keeps a beautiful home and practices wonderful hospitality. She has always been kind toward my family, and she never missed an opportunity to share the gospel with my father (who eventually put his trust in Christ just two hours before he died). I realized that Corlette has always been pure and faithful, and I remembered how much she supports me through difficult times in my work. Every chance she gets, she attends the seminars I teach and sits smiling and supportive through hours of the same material (always saying she has learned something new). She is a marvelous counselor and has helped hundreds of children. And she even took up backpacking because she knew I loved it! I realized that the list of her virtues could go on and on.

Within minutes my attitude toward her was turned upside down. I saw her offensive comment for what it was—a momentary and insignificant flaw in an otherwise wonderful person. I dropped my rake and went inside, but not to unload a storm of resentment and criticism. To her surprise, I walked in, gave her a big hug, and told her how glad I was to be married to her. The conversation that followed led quickly to a warm reconciliation.

Even if a change in focus does not allow you to overlook every offense, it can often help you in two other ways. First, by recalling what is good in another person, you often will realize how much you will lose if your differences are not resolved. Many marriages, friendships, and business relationships are lost because people focus exclusively on a point of disagreement and forget about all that they have enjoyed in and with one another. Remembering the good may provide the motivation it takes to work through the painful differences that temporarily separate people.

Second, the process of focusing on the good in others can trigger the Golden Result. Your negative view of others is bound to show, and they will be inclined to respond in kind. Conversely, as you focus on what is good about another person and openly acknowledge those qualities, he or she may begin to do the same in return. As you gain a more accurate assessment of each other and as goodwill grows between you, you will both have a greater freedom to deal honestly and realistically with your differences. This will increase your ability to set aside imagined problems and offenses and give proper attention to areas of genuine disagreement. When both of you bring your attention and energy to bear on fewer, more clearly defined issues, you are more likely to find workable solutions. As mentioned earlier, making progress on the personal issues that divide you will generally open the way for progress on the material issues.

5. Practice what you've learned. Paul's final instruction to Euodia and Syntyche (and to us) is both straightforward and encouraging: "Whatever you have learned or received or heard from me, or seen in me—put it into practice. And the God of peace will be with you." Paul knew what he was talking about when it came to conflict. He had to deal with intense conflict and opposition during his stay with the Christians in Philippi (see Acts 16:16–40), so they had seen him in action. He had taught and demonstrated how to deal with disputes, but he understood our human tendency to be hearers rather than doers of the Word. Therefore, he exhorted these women and the rest of the Philippian church to put their knowledge into practice. Otherwise, all their learning was in vain.

Paul's instruction applies equally well in *your* life. When you find yourself estranged from another person, especially when that person professes to be a follower of Jesus, it is not good enough simply to study the Bible. Knowledge isn't really knowledge (in a biblical sense) unless you put it into practice. When you use God's principles to check your attitude and make needed changes, you will be surprised how often you can overlook offenses and experience the truth in Paul's marvelous promise: "The God of peace will be with you."

Count the Cost

Another way to avoid unnecessary conflict is to consider the cost of unresolved conflict. Conflict is often much more expensive than we expect it to be. Unresolved disputes can consume large amounts of time, energy, and money, leaving you emotionally and spiritually exhausted. Worst of all, as long as a disagreement is unresolved, there is the potential for further damage to a relationship. This is one of the reasons for Jesus' command to settle disputes with others as quickly as possible: "Settle matters quickly with your adversary who is taking you to court. Do it while you are still with him on the way, or he may hand you over to the judge, and the judge may hand you over to the officer, and you may be thrown into prison. I tell you the truth, you will not get out until you have paid the last penny" (Matt. 5:25–26).

Unresolved conflict can lead to many types of "prisons" and can exact penalties we never anticipate. In addition to robbing you of time, property, or money, prolonged conflict can damage your relationships and destroy your reputation. It can also imprison you in a dungeon of self-pity, resentment, or bitterness. As the verses preceding Jesus' warning indicate (vv. 21–24), ongoing hostility can destroy you from the inside and alienate you from God (cf. Ps.

73:21–22). Moreover, the anxiety and negative thinking generated by conflict can spill over and hurt people who are close to you, such as your family or coworkers.

It is all too easy to ignore these costs when we are actually embroiled in a dispute. This is why we need to make a conscious effort to count the costs of a conflict at the outset of a dispute and compare them to the benefits of quickly settling the matter. I was once asked to help four partners divide the assets of a business. One of the men wanted much more than the other three were willing to give him. He was not a Christian, and he made it clear that he would not participate in a negotiation or mediation process If he could not have what he wanted, he was fully prepared to file a lawsuit. For several weeks the other partners had firmly refused to concede to his demands. When I met with those three and asked them why they wouldn't settle, they said, "It isn't just the money; it's the principle of the matter."

In response, I asked, "How much is this principle costing you? How much time has already been taken away from your business, and how much more time will a lawsuit consume? More importantly, what effect has this conflict had on you personally and on your families?"

There was a long pause, and then one of the partners pulled out his calculator. After a few key strokes, he said, "I'd say we've already devoted five thousand dollars of our time to this, and a lawsuit could easily cost us ten times that amount." Another partner admitted that he hadn't been sleeping well because of the tensions created by the conflict. He also conceded that his critical attitude had created problems with his wife and children. The third partner agreed.

When these three men added up the real cost of their dispute and compared it to the cost of settling the matter, they saw that the wisest thing to do was to settle the matter as quickly as possible. Although it was difficult for them to do at the time, one of them later told me that within two weeks of the settlement he was completely free of the matter. "When I look back," he said, "I have a hard time understanding why we didn't settle it much earlier. It sure wasn't worth all that fighting."

What about "Rights"?

Some people resist overlooking offenses and settling disputes by arguing, "I have my rights—and it wouldn't be *just* to let him off so easily." Whenever I hear this comment from a Christian, I ask, "Where would you spend eternity if God administered justice that was not tempered with mercy?" The answer is obvious: We would all be condemned to hell. Fortunately, God does not treat us as our sins deserve: To those who have trusted in Christ, he is compassionate and merciful—and he expects us to treat one another the same way. As Jesus taught, "Be merciful, just as your Father is merciful" (Luke 6:36; cf. Micah 6:8; Matt. 5:7; James 2:12–13).

The truth of the matter is that it may actually be *unjust* in God's eyes to exercise certain rights. Much of what is legally permissible today is not right when viewed from a biblical perspective. As Supreme Court justice Antonin Scalia has noted:

> What is lawful is not always right. Confusing the two concepts is particularly easy for the English-speaking because we use the word "right" to refer both to legality and to moral appropriateness. . . . We say "I have a *right* to plead the Fifth Amendment and refuse to answer questions about possible criminal activity"—even when the consequences of exercising that "right" may cause an innocent person to be convicted. Exercising such a "right" is certainly wrong.[2]

Many conflicts arise or grow worse because people use their rights wrongly. For example, church leaders may use their authority in a heavy-handed way, or members may use church bylaws to manipulate an entire congregation. It is sometimes possible to avoid moral obligations or liabilities by pleading the statute of frauds ("I gave my word, but there's nothing in writing") or the statute of limitations ("I may have wronged him, but it's too late for him to complain"). Others reap windfalls from less powerful people by rigidly enforcing contract rights or business advantages. In addition, some of what employees and employers can do by law today is inconsistent with biblical teachings regarding the workplace.

When exercising a right allows you to avoid a moral responsibility or to take unfair advantage of others, you have not acted justly in the eyes of God, regardless of what a court might say. Therefore, always strive to exercise only those rights that would pass both a legal and a heavenly review. The basic principle to follow at all times is to "do to others what you would have them do to you" (Matt. 7:12).

God may even call you to give up a right that would be morally and legally justified. One way to imitate his mercy is to show sympathy, kindness, and compassion toward someone who is in need of help, even if he does not deserve it (see the parable of the good Samaritan, Luke 10:30–37). One way to do this is to refrain from exercising legitimate rights and thus release others from their obligations (see the parable of the unmerciful servant, Matt. 18:21–35). The Bible is filled with examples of this kind of mercy that leads to a willing relinquishment of rights.

Abraham relinquished his rights and gave his nephew Lot the first choice of land when they settled in Canaan (Gen. 13:5–12). Joseph did not exercise his right to bring his brothers to justice for kidnapping and selling him into slavery (Gen. 50:19–21). King David chose not to punish Shimei for cursing him when he was fleeing from Absalom (2 Sam. 16:5–12; 19:19–23; cf. Exod. 22:28). Paul gave up his right to financial support from the church in Corinth (1 Cor. 9:3–15). In addition, he once relinquished his right to a just trial and consequently was flogged (Acts 16:22–24). Jesus did not exercise his right to be exempt from the temple tax (Matt. 17: 24–27), and he declined to call down legions of angels to rescue him from the Jews (Matt. 26:53–54). Most importantly, he willingly laid down his right to justice by allowing himself to be crucified as a substitute for sinful men (1 Peter 2:22–25).

On the other hand, the Bible teaches that it is sometimes appropriate to exercise our rights, to talk with others about their wrongs, and to hold them fully accountable for their responsibilities. For example, after Paul was flogged in Philippi, he asserted his rights and insisted that the civil authorities apologize for their unjust conduct (Acts 16:35–39). On other occasions Paul quickly asserted his rights as a Roman citizen to avoid a flogging and also to secure an appeal of his case (Acts 22:25–29; 25:11).

As these examples indicate, there are times when it is proper to assert rights, as well as times when we should willingly lay them aside. How can you know when to do which? Paul's first letter to the Corinthians provides a guiding principle. In it Paul discusses various rights the Corinthians were concerned about, including legal rights (6:1–8), marital rights (7:1–40), dietary rights (8:1–13; 10:23–33), and the rights of apostles (9:1–18). He concludes his discussion of rights with words that we looked at earlier:

> So whether you eat or drink or whatever you do, do it all for the glory of God. Do not cause anyone to stumble, whether Jews, Greeks or the church of God—even as I try to please everybody in every way. For I am not seeking my own good but the good of many, so that they may be saved. Follow my example, as I follow the example of Christ.
>
> 1 Corinthians 10:31–11:1

Here again the concept of stewardship serves as a helpful guiding principle. Rights are not something you deserve and possess for your own benefit. Rather, they are *privileges* given to you by God, and he wants you to use them for his glory and to benefit others, especially by helping them know Christ. As a steward, it is also appropriate to consider your needs and personal responsibilities (Phil. 2:3–4). Thus, whenever there is a question about your rights, you should ask yourself questions like these:

"Will exercising my rights honor God by showing the power of the gospel in my life?"

"Will exercising my rights advance God's kingdom—or will it advance only my interests at the expense of his kingdom?"

"Will exercising my rights benefit others?"

"Is exercising my rights essential for my own well-being?"

A review of the examples mentioned above shows how the stewardship principle was lived out by many people in the Bible. Paul gave up his right to financial support "rather than hinder the gospel of Christ" (1 Cor. 9:12). When he allowed himself to be flogged by the Philippian authorities and then insisted that they apologize to him, he alarmed them and vividly reminded them of their responsibility to administer justice properly (Acts 16:36–38). This probably caused them to act more carefully in the future, which would be to the benefit of the fledgling church in Philippi (Acts 19:35–41; 22:22–29). Likewise, when Paul asserted his rights as a Roman citizen to avoid being flogged, to defend himself in court, and to appeal his case to Caesar, he was securing the opportunity to carry the gospel to the Gentiles and to testify about Christ in Rome (Acts 9:15–16; 22:25; 23:11; 25:11).

Similarly, Abraham's deference to Lot prevented conflict that would have dishonored God in the eyes of those around them (Gen. 13:5–10). Joseph's mercy to his brothers reunited the house of Israel and allowed it to grow to great numbers (Gen. 50:19–21; Exod. 1:6–7). When David had mercy on Shimei, he demonstrated forgiveness and reconciliation to war-torn Israel and discouraged his followers from taking revenge against others (2 Sam. 19:22–23). Jesus relinquished his right to be exempt from the temple tax so that he would not offend the Jews and generate unnecessary distractions to his ministry (Matt. 17:27). Transcending all these examples, Jesus' decision to lay down this rights at Calvary allowed him to carry out his salvation mission and save all of those who put their faith in him (1 Peter 2:22–25; cf. Isa. 53:1–7; Phil. 2:5–11).[3]

By exercising or laying down their rights with God's kingdom in mind, all of these people drew attention to the goodness and power of God, brought him praise, expanded the ultimate outreach of the gospel, and sought the good of others. This should be our goal as well. In many cases it will be preferable for us to give up rights in order to prevent unnecessary conflicts that would detract from our daily purpose to serve Christ and to spread the gospel. But in other cases the best way to advance God's kingdom will be to assert our rights. For example, asserting rights may sometimes be the best way to help others learn that they are accountable for their decisions and must "pay the penalty" for their wrongs (Prov. 19:19). Such accountability may help them realize that one day they will be answerable to God. You may also need to exercise certain rights to provide for your family or others who depend on you.

When you are weighing your personal interests and responsibilities, be careful not to twist the concept of stewarding to your advantage. I have seen many people who believe that stewardship means *preserving* everything they have. Thus, they refuse to lay down any rights or sacrifice any property in the interest of peace. Jesus condemns this notion—he does not want us to either stockpile or spend anything for our own pleasure or convenience. Instead, he wants us to invest our resources wisely and gain the maximum return for his kingdom (Matt. 25:24–27). This certainly means protecting our rights and assets from *wasteful* sacrifices, but it also means expending them willingly on spiritually profitable ventures. Just as seed must be sacrificed to produce a crop, our personal rights and material assets must sometimes be surrendered to sow the gospel and produce a spiritual harvest (John 12:24–26).

The principle of relinquishing rights to advance God's kingdom was illustrated in one of my first conciliation cases. Ted worked for a government agency. As a new believer, he was excited about his salvation and wanted to have a positive witness for Christ among his coworkers. Ted and his supervisor, Joan, had never gotten along well, partly because Ted continually tried to tell her how to run her department. His enthusiasm for Christ provoked her further. As her frustration toward Ted increased, Joan gave him particularly difficult work assignments, even though she knew he had a back problem. Eventually he injured his back and had to leave work for several months. Although he received some disability benefits, Ted lost several thousand dollars due to missed wages and additional medical expenses. As a result, he filed a lawsuit against Joan and the agency.

By the time Ted came to see me, he had returned to work and the lawsuit was moving slowly through the court system. During our first conversation, Ted and I identified several ways he had contributed to the conflict with Joan. Seeing his own fault more clearly, Ted began to consider settling the lawsuit by accepting the five thousand dollars the agency had offered him a few days earlier. Although his damages exceeded that amount, his attorney advised him to accept the settlement. On the other hand, several of Ted's friends were encouraging him to demand more money or continue the litigation.

A few days later Ted surprised me by saying that he was going to drop his lawsuit without accepting the settlement offer. The more he had reflected on his own fault in the matter, the less comfortable he felt about accepting money from the agency. At the same time, he had concluded that laying down his right to restitution would be an effective way to demonstrate the mercy and forgiveness that he himself had received from God.

The next morning, Ted went to talk with Joan. He admitted that he had been disrespectful, arrogant, and rude, and he asked for her forgiveness. Joan seemed suspicious of his motives and said little in response. Ted went on to explain that he had forgiven her for ordering him to move the heavy boxes and that he was dropping his lawsuit. Finally, he said he hoped they could start over in their relationship and learn to work together in the future.

More suspicious than ever, Joan asked why he was doing this. He replied, "I became a Christian a year ago, and God is slowly helping me to face up to a lot of my faults, including those that contributed to the problems between you and me. God has also shown me that his love and forgiveness for me is absolutely free and that I can do nothing to earn or deserve it. Since he has done that for me, I decided I want to act the same way toward you."

Amazed by his answer, Joan mumbled something like, "Oh, I see. Well, let's let bygones be bygones. Thanks for coming in."

Although Joan's response wasn't quite what Ted had hoped for, he walked out of her office knowing that God had forgiven him and that he had at least given Joan a glimpse of that forgiveness. Ted soon discovered that Joan was telling others about their meeting. The next day a union representative who had heartily supported the lawsuit against Joan confronted Ted and asked whether he had really dropped his lawsuit. When Ted said yes, the man asked, "Is it true that you did it because you're a Christian?" Ted again said yes, and the man's scowl turned to a look of puzzlement. As the man walked away, Ted heard him say to a bystander, "Well, that's the first time I've ever seen a Christian's faith cost him anything."

Like ripples in a pond, word of Ted's actions spread throughout the department. A few days later, two coworkers asked to meet with him over lunch once a week to discuss the Bible. Later, other coworkers asked him questions about his faith. For the first time since Ted's conversion, he felt he was really helping people to learn about God's love.

Although Joan continued to treat Ted rudely at times, he learned to submit to her authority and use her provocations as further opportunities to show God's work in his life. When she was replaced a few months later, there was no doubt in Ted's mind who had arranged for him to have a more pleasant and supportive boss.

Three years later I asked Ted whether he regretted his decision to give up the settlement. "No," he replied, "that was the best five thousand dollars I ever spent. God used those events to bring several people to Christ. He also helped me to overcome some major sins in my life. I only wish I had settled it more quickly."

Summary and Application

There are many conflicts that require a lot of time and effort to resolve. But there are far more that can be resolved simply by overlooking minor offenses or relinquishing rights for the sake of God's kingdom. Therefore, before focusing on your rights, take a careful look at your responsibilities. Before you go to remove the speck from your brother's eye, ask yourself, "Is this really worth fighting over?"

If you are presently involved in a conflict, these questions will help you to apply the principles presented in this chapter.

1. Define the material issues in this conflict.
2. Define the personal issues in this conflict.
3. Which personal issues are having the greatest influence on you? On your opponent?
4. What has the other person done that has offended you?
5. Check your attitude:
    a. What can you rejoice in the Lord about in this situation?
    b. Have you been gentle or irritable and rude toward others? From this point on, how could you make the gentleness of Christ more evident to others?
    c. What have you been worried or anxious about? How has God shown himself to be loving, powerful, and faithful to you in previous conflicts or difficulties? What would you like him to do for you or accomplish through this conflict?

    d. What is good about the person with whom you
       are in conflict? What is right about his or her concerns?
       Do you have any good memories of your relationship?
       How has God helped you through that person?
    e. What principles taught in Scripture are most difficult
       for you to put into practice in this situation? Will you
       apply those principles? How?

6. What effect is this dispute having or likely to have on
    a. Your witness for Christ
    b. Your family life
    c. Your occupation
    d. Your finances or property
    e. Your friendships
    f. Your relationship with God
    g. Your service to your church and community

7. Consider your rights:
    a. What legal rights could you exercise in this situation?
       Would it be morally right to do so?
    b. What other rights could you exercise? How might
       exercising these rights glorify God, advance his
       kingdom, benefit others, and benefit you? How might
       laying down these rights glorify God, advance his
       kingdom, benefit others, and benefit you?

8. Which of the offenses described in answer to question 4
   can you simply overlook? How might overlooking them please
   and honor God?

9. Which of the material issues described in answer to question 1 can you simply give in on?

10. Go on record with the Lord by writing a prayer based on the
   principles taught in this chapter.

5

CONFLICT STARTS
IN THE HEART

What causes fights and quarrels among you? Don't
they come from your desires that battle within you?

James 4:1

All I wanted was a little peace and quiet when I came home
from a long day at the office. But I was not getting it. My
children, Megan and Jeff, had been trying to control each other
all week, and their constant friction had exhausted their mother's
patience. Instead of resolving their quarrels with her usual calm,
Corlette found herself resorting to sharp words and threats of, "Wait
until your father comes home!" So instead of walking through the
door and finding smiling children and a serene, affectionate wife,
I found nothing but sullen faces, irritable voices, and the general
sense that I had walked into a war zone. Each evening Corlette
and I worked to break the cycle of conflict, but it would start again
in a day or two. By Sunday morning I was feeling frustrated and
resentful toward my children.

Corlette had gone to church early that morning to meet with some other women, and I followed thirty minutes later with the kids. As we approached the car, a new contest began.

"It's my turn to sit in the front seat!"

"No, you got to yesterday!"

"Well, you shouldn't sit there anyway. You're so small the airbag could kill you."

"I don't care. I'm not sitting in the backseat!"

Then a new voice entered the exchange. "Be quiet!" I shouted. Then, pointing to each child in turn, "You get in the backseat right now, and you get in the front seat. I don't want to hear another word out of either of you!"

Climbing into the car myself, I gave vent to the anger that had been building in me all week. I even adjusted the rearview mirror so I could glare at Megan as I lectured her in the backseat. Among other things, I told them I was very angry at the way they had behaved all week and that I was now going to make things miserable for them. When I finally paused to take a breath, Jeffrey saw his opening.

"Daddy," he said meekly, "do you think you should pray to Jesus and ask him if it's rightful anger?"

His words must have been guided by the Holy Spirit, because they instantly cut me to the core. I saw an empty parking lot and pulled in. Before I had even turned off the ignition, I knew what I needed to say. Turning to my children, I went to the heart of our conflict.

My behavior that morning, as well as my family's behavior that week, is described with painful accuracy in James 4:1–3:

> What causes fights and quarrels among you? Don't they come from your desires that battle within you? You want something but don't get it. You kill and covet, but you cannot have what you want. You quarrel and fight. You do not have, because you do not ask God. When you ask, you do not receive, because you ask with wrong motives, that you may spend what you get on your pleasures.

James is making a specific application of the fundamental principle Jesus taught in Matthew 15:19: "Out of the heart come evil thoughts, murder, adultery, sexual immorality, theft, false testimony, slander." Our hearts are the wellsprings of all our thoughts, desires, words, and actions. Therefore, it is also the source of our conflicts (Luke 12:13–15).

These passages describe the root cause of conflict: *unmet desires in our hearts*. When we want something and feel that we will not be satisfied unless we get it, that desire starts to control us. If others fail to meet our desires, we sometimes condemn them in our hearts and fight harder to get our own way. Let us look at this progression one step at a time.

The Progression of an Idol[1]

I Desire

Conflict always begins with some kind of desire. Some desires are inherently wrong, such as vengeance, lust, or greed, but many desires are not. For example, there is nothing innately wrong about desiring things like peace and quiet, respectful children, a loving spouse, more time with your grandchildren, a new computer, professional success, or a growing church. These are good things, and it is fine to want them and seek them in reasonable ways.

If someone is standing in the way of a good desire, it is appropriate to talk together about it. As you talk, you may discover ways that both of you can grow and benefit each other. If you cannot make progress privately, it is reasonable to seek help from a pastor, trusted adviser, or mediator.

But what if the other person persistently fails to satisfy your desire? If he is an employee, it may be appropriate to fire him, and if he is an employer, you may need to look for a new job. But what if the other person is your spouse, a child, a longtime friend, or a member of your church? These relationships should not be easily forsaken, so when one of these people disappoints you, you will need to choose between two courses of action. On the one hand, you can trust God and seek your fulfillment in him (Ps. 73:25). You can ask him to help you to continue to grow and mature no matter what the other person does (James 1:2–4). And you can continue to love the person who is blocking your desire, pray for God's sanctifying work in his or her life, and wait for the Lord to open the door for progress at a later time (1 John 4:19–21; Luke 6:27). If you choose this course, God promises to bless you and, no matter what the other person does, to use your difficult situation to conform you to the likeness of Christ (Rom. 8:28–29).

But there is another course we often follow. We keep fighting to achieve our desire, dwelling on our disappointment, and allowing our desire and disappointment to control our lives. At the very least, this course results in self-pity and bitterness toward those who stand in our way. At worst, it utterly destroys important relationships and draws us away from God. Let us look at how this downward spiral continues.

I Demand

Unmet desires have the potential of working themselves deeper and deeper into our hearts. This is especially true when we come to see a desire as something we need or deserve and therefore must have in order to be happy or fulfilled. There are many ways to justify or legitimize a desire.

"I work hard all week. Don't I deserve a little peace and quiet when I come home?"

"I just want the children to get along and work hard in school."

"I spend hours managing our budget! A new computer could save me hours of work."

"God calls me to provide for our family. I deserve to have more appreciation and support for the long hours I put in."

"I just want to have the kind of intimacy God intended for marriage."

"She's my granddaughter. If I don't see her more, she'll think I don't love her."

"God has made me the pastor of this church, so people should respect me."

"He's my pastor, so he should visit me faithfully in the hospital."

"I've worked harder than anyone else on this project. I deserve the promotion."

"I fulfilled my part of the contract and deserve to be paid."

There is an element of validity in each of these statements. The trouble is that if these seemingly legitimate desires are not met, we can find ourselves in a vicious cycle. The more we want something, the more we think we need and deserve it. And the more we think we are entitled to something, the more convinced we are that we cannot be happy and secure without it.

When we see something as being essential to our fulfillment and well-being, it moves from being a desire to a demand. "I wish I could have this" evolves into "I must have this!" This is where trouble sets in. Even if the initial desire was not inherently wrong, it has grown so strong that it begins to control our thoughts and behavior. In biblical terms, it has become an idol.

Most of us think of an idol as a statue of wood, stone, or metal worshiped by pagan people. But the concept of idolatry is much broader and far more personal than that. An idol is anything apart from God that we depend on to be happy, fulfilled, or secure. In biblical terms, it is something other than God that we *set our heart on* (Luke 12:29; 1 Cor. 10:19), that motivates us (1 Cor. 4:5), that masters and rules us (Ps. 119:133; Eph. 5:5), or that we trust, fear, or serve (Isa. 42:17; Matt. 6:24; Luke 12:4–5). In short, it is something we love and pursue more than God (see Phil. 3:19).

Given its controlling effect on our lives, an idol can also be referred to as a "false god" or a "functional god." As Martin Luther wrote, "To whatever we look for any good thing and for refuge in every need, that is what is meant by 'god.' To have a god is nothing else than to trust and believe in him from the heart. . . . To whatever you give your heart and entrust your being, that, I say, is really your god."[2]

Even sincere Christians struggle with idolatry. We may believe in God and say we want to serve him only, but at times we allow other influences to rule us. In this sense we are no different from the ancient Israelites: "Even while these people were worshiping the LORD, they were serving their idols. To this day their children and grandchildren continue to do as their fathers did" (2 Kings 17:41).

It is important to emphasize the fact that idols can arise from good desires as well as wicked desires. It is often not what we want that is the problem, but that we want it too much. For example, it is not unreasonable for a man to want a passionate sexual relationship with his wife or for a mother to want to stay at home with a newborn baby. Nor is it wrong for an employer to want diligent workers or for a pastor to desire respect from his deacons. These are good desires, but if they turn into demands that must be met in order for us to be satisfied and fulfilled, they can lead to bitterness, resentment, or self-pity that can destroy a family, business, or church.

How can you discern when a good desire might be turning into a sinful demand? You can begin by prayerfully asking yourself "X-ray" questions that reveal the true condition of your heart.

What am I preoccupied with? What is the first thing on my mind in the morning and the last thing on my mind at night?

How would I answer the question: "If only _____, then I would be happy, fulfilled, and secure"?

What do I want to preserve or to avoid at all costs?

Where do I put my trust?

What do I fear?

When a certain desire is not met, do I feel frustration, anxiety, resentment, bitterness, anger, or depression?

Is there something I desire so much that I am willing to disappoint or hurt others in order to have it?

As you search your heart for idols, you will often encounter multiple layers of concealment, disguise, and justification. One of the subtlest cloaking devices is to argue that we want only what we legitimately deserve or what God himself commands. That is what I was doing the Sunday I was so angry with my children. Throughout the week I had been trying to convince myself that all I wanted was for them to obey God's commandments to honor their mother and to love one another. (I even quoted the specific verses to them repeatedly through the week!) But as my anger intensified, it became apparent that there was another desire lurking in my heart. I wanted to come home to peace and quiet, to smiling children and a loving and undistracted wife—not for God's glory, but for my own comfort and convenience.

Of course, we all struggle at times with these kinds of mixed motives; in a fallen world we will never have entirely pure hearts. But this is never an excuse to let selfish desires rule us, as I did that morning.

How could I tell which motives were actually ruling my heart? All I had to do was look at how I felt and reacted when my desires were not being met. If God-centered desires had been dominating my heart that week, my attitude toward my disobedient children would have been characterized by God's discipline toward me. "The LORD is compassionate and gracious, slow to anger, abounding in love" (Ps. 103:8). As I drew on God's grace, my actions would have been in line with the corrective guidelines found in Galatians 6:1: "If someone is caught in a sin, you who are spiritual should restore him gently." My discipline could still have been direct and firm, but it would have also been wrapped in gentleness and love, and it would have left no residue of unforgiveness.

But this was not how I was feeling or acting. My behavior throughout the week was marred by an increasing coolness and smoldering resentment toward my children, even after we had supposedly worked through the process of confession, discipline, and forgiveness. On Sunday morning my frustration finally overflowed in harsh and angry words. These sinful attitudes and actions clearly showed that I was not concerned primarily about my children acting well in order to obey and honor God. Instead, I was being ruled by my desire for peace and quiet for the sake of my own comfort and convenience. I had let a good desire grow into a consuming demand, and I was serving this idol instead of my God. To paraphrase 2 Kings 17:41, even though I claimed I was worshiping the Lord, I was actually serving my idol.

I Judge

As my example shows, idolatrous demands usually lead us to judge other people. When they fail to satisfy our desires and live up to our expectations, we criticize and condemn them in our hearts if not with our words. As David Powlison writes:

> We judge others—criticize, nit-pick, nag, attack, condemn—because we literally play God. This is heinous. [The Bible says,] "There is

only one Lawgiver and Judge, the one who is able to save and to destroy; but who are you to judge your neighbor?" Who *are* you when you judge? None other than a God wannabe. In this we become like the Devil himself (no surprise that the Devil is mentioned in James 3:15 and 4:7). We act exactly like the adversary who seeks to usurp God's throne and who acts as the accuser of the brethren. When you and I fight, our minds become filled with accusations: your wrongs and my rights preoccupy me. We play the self-righteous judge in the mini-kingdoms we establish.[3]

This insight should leave us shaking in our boots! When we judge others and condemn them in our hearts for not meeting our desires, we are imitating the devil (see James 3:15; 4:7). In doing so, we have doubled our idolatry problem: Not only have we let an idolatrous desire rule our hearts, but we have also set ourselves up as judging minigods. This is a formula for excruciating conflict.

I am not saying that it is inherently wrong to evaluate or even judge others within certain limits. As we will see in chapter 7, Scripture teaches that we should observe and evaluate others' behavior so that we can respond and minister to them in appropriate ways, which may even involve loving correction (see Matt. 7:1–5; 18:15; Gal. 6:1).

We cross the line, however, when we begin to sinfully judge others, which is characterized by a feeling of superiority, indignation, condemnation, bitterness, or resentment. Sinful judging often involves speculating on others' motives. Most of all, it reveals the absence of a genuine love and concern toward them. When these attitudes are present, our judging has crossed the line and we are playing God.

The closer we are to others, the more we expect of them, and the more likely we are to judge them when they fail to meet our expectations. For example, we may look at our spouse and think, *If you really love me, you above all people will help meet my need.* We think of our children and say, "After all I've done for you, you owe this to me."

We can place similar expectations on relatives, close friends, or members of our church. Expectations are not inherently bad. It is good to hope for the best in others, and it is reasonable to anticipate receiving understanding and support from those who are closest to us.

But if we are not careful, these expectations can become conditions and standards that we use to judge others. Instead of giving people room for independence, disagreement, or failure, we rigidly impose our expectations on them. In effect, we expect them to give allegiance to our idols. When they refuse to do so, we condemn them in our hearts and with our words, and our conflicts with them take on a heightened intensity.

I Punish

Idols always demand sacrifices. When someone fails to satisfy our demands and expectations, our idol demands that he should suffer. Whether deliberately or unconsciously, we will find ways to hurt or punish people so that they will give in to our desires.

This punishment can take many forms. Sometimes we react in overt anger, lashing out with hurtful words to inflict pain on those who fail to meet our expectations. When we do so, we are essentially placing others on the altar of our idol and sacrificing them, not with pagan knives, but with the sharp edge of our tongues. Only when they give in to our desire and give us what we want will we stop inflicting pain upon them.

We punish those who don't "bow" to our idols in numerous other ways as well. Our children may use pouting, stomping, or shooting dirty looks to hurt us for not meeting their desires. Adults and children alike may impose guilt or shame on others by walking around with a pained or crushed look on their faces. And some people resort to physical violence or sexual abuse to punish and control others.

As we grow in faith and awareness of our sin, most of us recognize and reject overt and obviously sinful means of punishing others. But our idols do not give up their influence easily, and they often develop more subtle means of punishing those who do not serve them.

Withdrawal from a relationship is a common way to hurt others. This may include acting cool toward the other person, withholding affection or physical contact, acting sad or gloomy, refusing to look him or her in the eye, or even abandoning the relationship altogether.

Sending subtle, unpleasant cues over a long period of time is an age-old method of inflicting punishment. For example, a friend of mine mentioned to me that his wife was not pleased with the fact that he was giving so much time to a particular ministry. He closed by saying, "And as we all know, when Momma ain't happy, ain't nobody happy!" He laughed as he said it, but his comment made me think of the proverb, "A quarrelsome wife is like a constant dripping on a rainy day" (Prov. 27:15). A woman has a unique ability to set the tone in a home. If she is not careful, she can pervert that gift and use it to create an irritable, unpleasant, uncomfortable atmosphere that tells her family, "Either get in line with what I want, or you will suffer." Such behavior is an act of unbelief. Instead of relying on God's means of grace to sanctify her family, she depends on her own tools of punishment to manipulate them into change. Of course, a man can do the same thing. By being perpetually critical and unhappy, he too can make everyone in the family miserable until they give in to his idols. The usual result of such behavior is a superficial, splintered family.

As James 4:1–3 teaches, inflicting pain on others is one of the surest signs that an idol is ruling our hearts. When we catch ourselves punishing others in any way, whether deliberately and overtly or unconsciously and subtly, it is a warning that something other than God is ruling our hearts.

The Cure for an Idolatrous Heart

As we have seen, an idol is any desire that has grown into a consuming demand that rules our hearts; it is something we think we must have to be happy, fulfilled, or secure. To put it another way, it is something we love, fear, or trust.

Love, fear, trust—these are words of worship. Jesus commands us to love God, fear God, and trust God only (Matt. 22:37; Luke 12:4–5; John 14:1). Anytime we long for something apart from God, fear something more than God, or trust in something other than God to make us happy, fulfilled, or secure, we worship a false god. As a result, we deserve the judgment and wrath of the true God.

Deliverance from Judgment

There is only one way out of this bondage and judgment: It is to look to God himself, who loves to deliver people from their idols. "I am the LORD your God, who brought you out of Egypt, out of the land of slavery. You shall have no other gods before me" (Exod. 20:2–3).

God has provided the cure for our idolatry by sending his Son to experience the punishment that we deserve because of our sin. Through Jesus Christ we can become righteous in God's sight and find freedom from sin and idolatry. "Therefore, there is now no condemnation for those who are in Christ Jesus, because through Christ Jesus the law of the Spirit of life set me free from the law of sin and death" (Rom. 8:1–2).

To receive this forgiveness and freedom, we must acknowledge our sin, repent of it, and put our trust in Jesus Christ (see Acts 3:19; Ps. 32:5). When we do, we are no longer under God's judgment. Instead, he brings us into his family, makes us his children and heirs, and enables us to live a godly life (Gal. 4:4–7). This is the good news of the gospel—forgiveness and eternal life through our Lord Jesus Christ.

Deliverance from Specific Idols

Yet there is more good news. God wants to deliver us not only from our general problem with sin and idolatry, but also from the specific, day-to-day idols that consume us, control us, and cause conflict with those around us.

This deliverance is not done in blanket fashion, sweeping away all our idols in one great spiritual experience. Instead, God calls us to identify and confess our idols one by one and then cooperate with him as he steadily removes them bit by bit from our hearts.

God uses three vehicles to convey his grace to help us in this identification and deliverance process: his Bible, his Spirit, and his church. The Bible is "living and active. Sharper than any double-edged sword, it penetrates even to dividing soul and spirit, joints and marrow; it judges the thoughts and attitudes of the heart" (Heb. 4:12). As you diligently study and meditate on the Bible and sit under regular, sound preaching, God will use his Word like a spotlight and a scalpel in your heart. It will reveal your idolatrous desires and show you how to love and worship God with all your heart, mind, strength, and soul.

The Holy Spirit aids our deliverance from idols by helping us understand the Bible, identify our sin, and pursue a godly life (1 Cor. 2:10–15; Phil. 2:13). Therefore, we should pray on a daily basis for the Spirit to guide, convict, and strengthen us in our walk with Christ.

Finally, God has established the church to channel his grace to you. Through the church we can receive the sacraments of baptism and the Lord's Supper, which unite us with Christ and strengthen us in our faith. Through the church we are also surrounded by brothers and sisters in Christ who can teach us, lovingly point out our idols, and provide encouragement and guidance in our spiritual growth (Gal. 6:1; Rom. 15:14). This requires that we commit ourselves to consistent involvement in a solid, biblical church and seek regular fellowship and accountability from spiritually mature believers.

Through these three vehicles of grace, God will help you examine your life and progressively expose the idols that rule your heart and deliver you from them. This miraculous process involves several key steps.

> When you find yourself in conflict, work backwards through the progression of an idol to identify the desires that are controlling your heart. Ask yourself these questions: How am I punishing others? How am I judging others? What am I demanding to have? What is the root desire of that demand?
>
> Prayerfully ask yourself the X-ray questions provided earlier in this chapter. They will help you discern any excessive desires that have become ruling idols in your heart.
>
> Keep track of your discoveries in a journal so that you can identify patterns and steadily go after specific idols.
>
> Pray daily that God would rob your idols of their influence in your life by making you miserable whenever you give in to them.
>
> Describe your idols to your spouse or an accountability partner and ask him or her to pray for you and to lovingly approach you when there are signs that the idol is still controlling you.

Realize that idols are masters of change and disguise. As soon as you gain a victory over a particular demand or form of punishment, your idol can reappear in a related form, with a new justification and more subtle means of judging and punishment.

If you are dealing with an idol that is difficult to identify or conquer, go to your pastor or some other spiritually mature advisor and seek his or her counsel and support.

Most of all, ask God to *replace* your idols with a growing love for him and a consuming desire to worship him and him alone (more on this below).

If someone told you that you had a deadly cancer that would take your life if you did not get treatment, you would probably spare no effort or expense in pursuing the most rigorous treatment available. Well, you do have cancer—a cancer of the soul. It is called sin and idolatry. But there is a priceless cure that is freely available. It is called the gospel of Jesus Christ, and it is administered through the Word, the Spirit, and the church. The more rigorously you avail yourself of these means of grace, the greater effect they will have in delivering you from the idols that plague your soul and disrupt your relationships.

Replace Idol Worship with Worship of the True God

In his excellent book *Future Grace,* John Piper teaches that "sin is what you do when you are not fully satisfied in God."[4] The same may be said about idolatry. In other words, if we are not fulfilled and secure in God, we will inevitably seek other sources of happiness and security.

Therefore, if you want to squeeze the idols out of your heart and leave no room for them to return, make it your top priority to aggressively pursue an all-consuming worship of the living God. Ask him to teach you how to love, fear, and trust him more than anything in this world. Replacing idol worship with worship of the true God involves several steps.

Repent before God. When we repent and confess our sins and idols, believing in our forgiveness through Christ, we also confess our faith in Christ. Repentance and confession of our faith in the one God is true worship (1 John 1:8–10). "The sacrifices of God are a broken spirit; a broken and contrite heart, O God, you will not despise" (Ps. 51:17; see Isa. 66:2b).

Fear God. Stand in awe of the true God when you are tempted to fear others or are afraid of losing something precious. "The fear of the LORD is the beginning of [all wisdom]" (Prov. 1:7). "Do not be afraid of those who kill the body but cannot kill the soul. Rather, be afraid of the One who can destroy both soul and body in hell" (Matt. 10:28). "If you, O LORD, kept a record of sins, O Lord, who could stand? But with you there is forgiveness; therefore you are feared" (Ps. 130:3–4).

Love God. Desire the one who forgives us and provides everything we need, instead of looking to other things that cannot save you. "Jesus replied: 'Love the Lord your God with all your heart and with all your soul and with all your mind'" (Matt. 22:37). "Those who seek the LORD lack no good thing" (Ps. 34:10). "Seek first his kingdom and his righteousness, and all these things will be given to you as well" (Matt. 6:33). "Whom have I in heaven but you? And earth has nothing I desire besides you. My flesh and my heart may fail, but God is the strength of my heart and my portion forever" (Ps. 73:25–26).

Trust God. Rely on the one who sacrificed his Son for you and has proven himself to be absolutely dependable in every situation. "It is better to take refuge in the LORD than to trust in man" (Ps. 118:8). "Commit your way to the Lord; trust in him and he will do this: He will make your righteousness shine like the dawn, the justice of your cause like the noonday sun" (Ps. 37:5–6). "His divine power has given us everything we need for life and godliness through our knowledge of him who called us by his own glory and goodness. Through these he has given us his very great and precious promises, so that through them you may participate in the divine nature and escape the corruption in the world caused by evil desires" (2 Peter 1:3–4).

Delight in God. Learn to find your greatest joy in thinking about God, meditating on his works, talking to others about him, praising him, and giving him thanks. "Delight yourself in the LORD and he will give you the desires of your heart" (Ps. 37:4). "My mouth is filled with your praise, declaring your splendor all day long" (Ps. 71:8). "Rejoice in the Lord always. I will say it again: Rejoice!" (Phil. 4:4). "Be joyful always; pray continually; give thanks in all circumstances, for this is God's will for you in Christ Jesus" (1 Thess. 5:16–18).[5]

As these passages indicate, God has designed a wonderful cycle for those who want to worship him above all things. As you love, praise, give thanks, and delight yourself in God, he will fulfill your desires with the best gift: more of himself. And as you learn to delight more and more in him, you will feel less need to find happiness, fulfillment, and security in things of this world. By God's grace, the influence of idolatry and its resulting conflict in your life can be steadily diminished, and you can enjoy the intimacy and security that comes from worshiping the one true God.

This is what happened the morning I blew up at my children. The Holy Spirit graciously exposed my idolatry through my son's insightful question, "Daddy, do you think you should pray to Jesus and ask him if it's rightful anger?" Even as I pulled into the empty parking lot, God revealed the answer in my heart: My anger was anything but rightful. It sprang from my worshiping an idol of comfort and convenience. I confessed this to my children and asked them to forgive me for my anger and harsh words. They responded with hugs of forgiveness and confessions that they too had been serving idols that week. The Lord lovingly enabled us to cast down the gods of conflict and remind one another that the true God is so much better than the idols we had been serving. We were a few minutes late to church that morning, but our worship was more sincere, joyful, and exhilarating than it had been for a long time.

Summary and Application

James 4:1–3 provides a key principle for understanding and resolving conflict. Whenever we have a serious dispute with others, we should always look carefully at our own hearts to see whether we are being controlled by unmet desires that we have turned into idols. These desires love to disguise themselves as things we need or deserve, or even as things that would advance God's kingdom.

But no matter how good or legitimate a desire may look on the surface, if we have gotten to the point where we cannot be content, fulfilled, or secure unless we have it, that desire has evolved into an idol that has diverted our love and trust from God. Fortunately, God delights to deliver us from our slavery to idols and enable us to find true freedom, fulfillment, and security in his love and provision. And as we break free from the desires that have fueled our conflicts, we can resolve seemingly hopeless disputes and become more effective peacemakers.

If you are presently involved in a conflict, these questions will help you apply the principles presented in this chapter to your situation:

1. Work backwards through the progression of an idol to identify the desires that are controlling your heart. Ask yourself these questions:
    a. How am I punishing others?
    b. How am I judging others?
    c. What am I demanding to have?
    d. What is the root desire of that demand?
2. What makes you think that you need or deserve to have any of these desires satisfied?
3. In order to more clearly identify your idols (desires turned into demands), ask yourself these questions:
    a. What am I preoccupied with? (What is the first thing on my mind in the morning and/or the last thing at night?)
    b. How would I fill in this blank?: "If only _____, then I would be happy, fulfilled, and secure."
    c. What do I want to preserve or avoid at any cost?
    d. Where do I put my trust?
    e. What do I fear?
    f. When a certain desire is not met, do I feel frustration, anxiety, resentment, bitterness, anger, or depression?
    g. Is there something I desire so much that I am willing to disappoint or hurt others in order to have it?

4. How are your expectations of others magnifying your demands on them and your disappointment in their failure to meet your desires?
5. How are you judging those who do not meet your desires? Are you feeling indignation, condemnation, bitterness, resentment, or anger?
6. How are you punishing those who do not meet your desires?
7. What has God done to deliver you from your idols? What can you do to receive this deliverance?
8. How can you cultivate a more passionate love for and worship of God?
9. Go on record with the Lord by writing a prayer based on the principles taught in this chapter.

6

CONFESSION BRINGS FREEDOM

He who conceals his sins does not prosper,
  but whoever confesses and renounces them finds mercy.

Proverbs 28:13

God's grace, as revealed in the gospel of Christ, is the driving force behind peacemaking. "For God so loved the world that he gave his one and only Son, that whoever believes in him shall not perish but have eternal life" (John 3:16). This incredible news reveals our radical sinfulness—nothing could save us except the death of God's only Son. But it also reveals the depths of God's radical mercy—he gave his Son to die for us! As we reflect on and rejoice in the gospel of Christ, two things happen. Our pride and defensiveness are stripped away, and we can let go of our illusion of self-righteousness, honestly examine ourselves, and find freedom from guilt and sin by admitting our wrongs. At the same time, the gospel shows us how important reconciliation is to God, which inspires us to do everything we can to repair any harm we have caused to others and to be reconciled to those we have offended.

This restoration process involves four activities: repentance, self-examination, confession, and personal change.

Repentance Is More Than a Feeling

Repentance is the first step in gaining freedom from sin and conflict. Repentance is not something we can do on our own; it is a gift of God for which we should continually pray, whereby he convicts us of our sin and shows us the road to freedom (2 Tim. 2:24–26). Repentance does not mean we simply feel sad and uncomfortable. Nor does it involve a mere apology. To repent literally means to change the way we think. Thus, repentance is sometimes described as "coming to our senses" (see Luke 15:17; 2 Tim. 2:25–26). It involves a waking up to the fact that we have been deceiving ourselves and that our ideas, attitudes, values, or goals have been wrong. If this change in thinking is genuine, it will lead to a renouncing of sin and a turning to God (Ezek. 14:6; Acts 3:19). This process is described in Isaiah 55:7: "Let the wicked forsake his way and the evil man his thoughts. Let him turn to the LORD, and he will have mercy on him, and to our God, for he will freely pardon."

Although repentance is often accompanied by sorrow, simply feeling bad does not prove that one is repentant. In fact, there is a world of difference between mere remorse and genuine repentance. As Paul explained to the Corinthians, "I am happy, not because you were made sorry, but because your sorrow led you to repentance. . . . Godly sorrow brings repentance that leads to salvation and leaves no regret, but worldly sorrow brings death" (2 Cor. 7:9–10).

Worldly sorrow means feeling sad because you got caught doing something wrong or because you must suffer the unpleasant consequences of your actions, such as financial loss, a broken marriage, a damaged reputation, or nagging guilt. Any normal person will feel regretful when faced with these unpleasant circumstances. Before long, however, worldly sorrow dies away, and most people begin to behave just as they did before. Instead of changing their thinking and conduct, they simply try harder not to get caught again. This kind of limited remorse leads only to further grief.

In contrast, godly sorrow means feeling bad because you have offended God. It means sincerely regretting the fact that what you did was morally wrong, regardless of whether or not you must suffer unpleasant consequences. It involves a change of heart—which is possible only when you understand that sin is a personal offense against God himself (2 Chron. 6:37–39; cf. Jer. 31:19). Godly sorrow will not always be accompanied by intense feelings, but it implies a change in thinking, which should lead to changes in behavior.

When Paul said that repentance leads to salvation, he was referring not only to eternal salvation, but also to the fact that the penitent would be delivered from sinful habit patterns (2 Cor. 7:10). The fact that genuine repentance should lead to changed behavior is confirmed elsewhere in Scripture. For example, John the Baptist warned people to "produce fruit in keeping with repentance" (Matt. 3:8). Similarly, Paul continually preached that people should "turn to God and prove their repentance by their deeds" (Acts 26:20).

Examine Yourself

One evidence of sincere repentance is a willingness to thoroughly examine ourselves so that we can uncover both our mistakes and our sins. Mistakes are the result of errors in judgment rather than sin. Although it is right to acknowledge and repair mistakes that have hurt others, we do not need to go through the same in-depth process that is needed to confess and correct our sins.

Literally speaking, to sin means "to miss the mark." It may also be described as failing to be and do what God commands and doing what God forbids (1 John 3:4). Sin is not an action against an impersonal set of rules. Rather, it is a rebellion against God's personal desires and requirements. This is true even when our thoughts, words, or actions are not consciously directed against God himself. Even seemingly small wrongs against other people are serious in God's eyes, because every wrong is a violation of his will (Gen. 39:9; Num. 5:6–7; Ps. 51:3–4; James 2:10–11).

In fact, we can sin against God by omission—by doing nothing. As James 4:17 tells us, "Anyone, then, who knows the good he ought to do and doesn't do it, sins." Therefore, if we are involved in a conflict and neglect opportunities to serve others (by failing to bear their burdens, gently restore them, etc.), we are guilty of sin in God's eyes.

Because most of us do not like to admit that we have sinned, we tend to conceal, deny, or rationalize our wrongs. If we cannot completely cover up what we have done, we try to minimize our wrongdoing by saying that we simply made a "mistake" or an "error in judgment." Another way to avoid responsibility for our sins is to shift the blame to others or to say that they made us act the way we did. When our wrongs are too obvious to ignore, we practice what I call the 40/60 Rule. It goes something like this: "Well, I know I'm not perfect, and I admit I am partially to blame for this problem. I'd say that about 40 percent of the fault is mine. That means 60 percent of the fault is hers. Since she is 20 percent more to blame than I am, she should be the one to ask for forgiveness." I never actually say or think these exact words, but I often catch myself resorting to this tactic in subtle ways. By believing that my sins have been more than canceled by another's sins, I can divert attention from myself and avoid repentance and confession.

Of course, we are only kidding ourselves when we try to cover up our sins. As 1 John 1:8 indicates, "If we claim to be without sin, we deceive ourselves and the truth is not in us" (cf. Ps. 36:2). Whenever we refuse to face up to our sins, we will eventually pay an unpleasant price. This is what King David discovered when he did not immediately repent of his sins. Psalm 32:3–5 describes the guilty conscience, emotional turmoil, and even physical side effects he experienced until he confessed his sins to God.

If it is difficult for you to identify and confess your wrongs, there are two things you can do. First, ask God to help you see your sin clearly and repent of it, regardless of what others may do (Ps. 139:23–24). Then prayerfully study his Word and ask him to show you where your ways have not lined up with his ways (Heb. 4:12). Second, ask a spiritually mature friend to counsel and correct you (Prov. 12:15; 19:20). The older I get, the less I trust myself to be objective when I am involved in a conflict. Time after time I have been blessed by asking a friend to candidly critique my role in a conflict. I have not always liked what my friends have said, but as I have humbled myself and submitted to their correction, I have always seen things more clearly.

As you examine your role in a conflict, there are many areas you could consider. Here are a few of the areas where you are most likely to sin when you are at odds with others.

Using Your Tongue as a Weapon

Scripture warns us that the tongue is often a chief cause of conflict. "Consider what a great forest is set on fire by a small spark. The tongue also is a fire, a world of evil among the parts of the body. It corrupts the whole person. . . . It is a restless evil, full of deadly poison" (James 3:5–6, 8b). Sinful speech can take many forms.

Reckless words, spoken hastily and without thinking, inflame many conflicts. "Reckless words pierce like a sword, but the tongue of the wise brings healing" (Prov. 12:18; cf. Prov. 13:3; 17:28; 21:23; 29:20). Although we may seldom set out deliberately to hurt others with our words, sometimes we do not make much of an effort *not* to hurt others. We simply say whatever comes to mind without thinking about the consequences. In the process, we may hurt and offend others, which only aggravates conflict.

Grumbling and complaining irritates and discourages other people. It also takes our eyes off of the good things God and others do for us. When others feel we are critical of them or ungrateful for what they do, it is only a matter of time before conflict breaks out (Phil. 2:14; James 5:9).

Falsehood includes any form of misrepresentation or deceit (Prov. 24:28; 2 Cor. 4:2), including lying, exaggeration, telling only part of the truth, or distorting the truth by emphasizing favorable facts while minimizing those that are against us. Anytime we use words that give a false impression of reality, we are guilty of practicing deceit. In doing so, we are following the example of Satan himself, who is known as the "father of lies" (John 8:44; cf. Gen. 3:13; Rev. 12:9).

Gossip is often both the spark and the fuel for conflict. "A perverse man stirs up dissension, and a gossip separates close friends" (Prov. 16:28). "Without wood a fire goes out; without gossip a quarrel dies down" (Prov. 26:20). To gossip means to betray a confidence or to discuss unfavorable personal facts about another person with someone who is not part of the problem or its solution. Even if the information you discuss is true, gossip is always sinful and a sign of spiritual immaturity (2 Cor. 12:20; cf. Prov. 11:13; 20:19; 1 Tim. 5:13).

Slander involves speaking false and malicious words about another person. The Bible repeatedly warns against such talk (e.g., Lev. 19:16; Titus 2:3) and commands us to "have nothing to do" with slanderers who refuse to repent (2 Tim. 3:3–5). We should be especially sobered by the fact that the Greek word *diabolos,* translated as "slanderer" or "accuser," is used thirty-four times in the Bible as a title for the devil, the world's chief slanderer.

Worthless talk can also contribute to conflict, even if you intend no harm. It violates God's high standard for talking to or about others: "Do not let any unwholesome talk come out of your mouths, but only what is helpful for building others up according to their needs, that it may benefit those who listen" (Eph. 4:29). Worthless talk also shows a disregard for Jesus' warning, "But I tell you that men will have to give account on the day of judgment for every careless word they have spoken" (Matt. 12:36). If you memorize these passages and use them consciously as a filter for your words, it can help you to avoid many kinds of careless, critical, worthless words and to speak only those things that will benefit others, build them up, and promote spiritual growth.[1]

Sinful words contribute greatly to conflict. Furthermore, they can destroy us from the inside out. As 2 Timothy 2:16 warns, "Avoid godless chatter, because those who indulge in it will become more and more ungodly." If you indulge in reckless talk, falsehood, gossip, slander, or worthless talk, you will not only stir up conflict, but also erode your own character and relationship with God. Therefore, for the sake of peace and spiritual growth, renounce all such talk and seek God's help in overcoming it.

Controlling Others

Few things cause as much conflict as trying to control other people. Some attempts to control others are blatantly self-serving, such as maximizing our own profit or influence at another person's expense (Gen. 29:15–30). But the more common type of control involves trying to persuade, manipulate, or force people to do things that simply make our lives more comfortable and convenient. Sometimes we justify our control by saying we are trying to help others make decisions that are in their own best interests. Although it is appropriate to share genuine concerns about others' decisions and offer them sincere advice, we cross the line and invite conflict when we refuse to respect their decisions and persist in trying to change their minds, especially if it is really for our own comfort, convenience, or peace of mind (see 2 Tim. 2:24–26).

Breaking Your Word

A great deal of conflict is the direct result of someone's failure to keep a commitment, whether it was expressed in a contract, a marriage vow, an oath to God, or by a simple yes or no (Matt. 5:33–37; cf. Num. 30:2; Deut. 23:23; Prov. 2:17). God expects us to keep our word, even if we made an unwise commitment, things did not turn out as we expected, or it will be difficult to fulfill a commitment (Ps. 15:4; Josh. 9:1–19; Eccles. 5:1–7). If you have made an impulsive commitment or if unforeseen circumstances make it difficult to keep your word, you may appeal to the other person for mercy and ask (not demand) to be released from your obligation (Prov. 6:1–5; cf. Matt. 18:22–33). In some cases, you may also be freed from your commitment if the other party fails in a substantial way to keep his or her word (e.g., Matt. 19:9; 1 Cor. 7:15). If you cannot be released in a biblical way, ask God to help you keep your word and learn from your mistake.

Failing to Respect Authority

Another common source of conflict is the abuse of or rebellion against the authority God has established in the church, the government, the family, and the workplace. All legitimate authority has been established by God, primarily for the purpose of maintaining peace and order (Rom. 13:1–7). He has given those in authority strict commands not to take advantage of their positions, but rather to diligently serve and look out for the well-being of those whom they are called to lead (Mark 10:42–45; cf. Eph. 5:25–33; 6:4, 9; 1 Peter 3:7; 5:1–3). When leaders misuse their authority and use it for their own ends, God himself will eventually hold them accountable for that sin (Deut. 24:15; Job 31:13–14; Jer. 22:13; Mal. 3:5; Col. 4:1; James 5:4).

At the same time, God commands those under authority to submit to those over them, both for his sake and for their own good (Eph. 5:21–24; 1 Thess. 5:12–13; 1 Tim. 6:1–2; Titus 2:9–10; Heb.

13:17). Because submission to authority is not a popular concept these days, a variety of excuses are offered to justify overthrowing God's authority structure. But those who rebel against biblically established authority are rebelling against God himself (Rom. 13:2). R. C. Sproul writes, "All authority is under Christ. When we disobey lesser authorities, we are guilty of disobeying Christ. You cannot serve the King and honor his authority by rebelling against his appointed governors. To say you honor the kingdom of Christ while you disobey his authority structure is to be guilty not only of hypocrisy but of cosmic treason."[2]

Respect for authority is so important that Jesus commands us to submit to those over us, even when they behave hypocritically or harshly (Matt. 23:1–3; 1 Peter 2:13–3:6). In other words, God calls us to respect the *positions* of those in authority even when their *personalities* leave much to be desired.

Authority does have its limits, however. Since God has not given anyone the authority to command you to sin, it is right to disobey any instructions that contradict the clear teaching of Scripture (Acts 4:18–19; 5:29; cf. Dan. 3:9–18; 6:6–10). When a person in authority instructs you to do something that you believe is unwise, unfair, or sinful, it is appropriate to make an appeal and respectfully try to persuade that person to do what is right and wise (Esther 7:1–6; Prov. 25:15; Acts 4:5–17; 24:1–26:32). When doing so, it is helpful to try to discern the purpose or goal of the person in authority and seek to offer creative alternatives that will accomplish the same end (assuming it is a proper one) but do it in a biblical and efficient manner (e.g., 1 Sam. 25:1–35; Dan. 1:6–16; 2:14–16; Eccles. 8:2–5).[3] If this does not lead the person in authority to change course, you should obey any instructions that do not violate Scripture and trust God to take care of the results (1 Peter 2:19–23).[4]

Forgetting the Golden Rule

Perhaps the most common cause of conflict is our failure to follow the Golden Rule, which Jesus taught in Matthew 7:12: "So in everything, do to others what you would have them do to you, for this sums up the Law and the Prophets." To see whether you have violated this teaching, ask yourself questions like these:

Would I want someone else to treat me the way I have been treating him?

How would I feel if I found out people were saying about me what I've said about her?

If our positions were reversed, how would I feel if he did what I have done?

If someone broke a contract for the same reasons I am using, would I feel that was right?

If I was an employee, how would I feel if I was treated the way I have treated her?

If I owned this business, would I want my employees to behave the way I am behaving?

Anytime you see that you would not want someone else to treat you the way you are presently treating others, you have fallen short of the standard Jesus established to govern all human relations. If you admit your failure to God and the person you have wronged, you can start moving down the road to forgiveness, agreement, and reconciliation.

Serving Sinful Desires

As we saw in chapter 5, destructive conflict is usually caused by unmet desires that have gained control over our hearts. These consuming desires, which may also be referred to as idols of the heart, may include the following:

Improper desires for physical pleasure, also known as lusts of the flesh, may lead to sexual immorality, overeating, gambling, laziness, or other forms of self-indulgence (1 John 2:15–17; cf. Gal. 5:16–21; Eph. 4:19).

Pride and the desire to always be right can make us defensive, reluctant to admit our wrongs, slow to accept advice, and quick to find fault with others (Prov. 8:13; 2 Cor. 5:12; James 3:14; 1 John 2:15–17).

Love of money or other material possessions, which can also appear as envy, can lead to a preoccupation with financial security; tempt us to lie, break contracts, mistreat employees, or compulsively pursue unnecessary things; or make it difficult for us to forgive debts or show mercy to others (1 Tim. 6:10; Eph. 5:5; Matt. 6:24; Luke 12:16–21; 27–31; Acts 5:1–3).

Fear of man may involve an actual fear of what others can do to us (Prov. 29:25; Luke 12:4–5) or an excessive concern about what others think about us, which can lead to a preoccupation with acceptance, approval, popularity, personal comparisons, or pleasing others (John 9:22; 12:42–43; Gal. 1:10; 1 Thess. 2:4). This idol can make us reluctant to address serious sin, tempt us to gossip or do other things we know are not right, and make us reluctant to admit our wrongs or ask for help, which often prolongs conflict.

Good things that we want too much. As discussed in the previous chapter, some of the most difficult idols to deal with are good desires that we elevate to demands, such as a longing for love, respect, comfort, convenience, or success. These things, while beneficial in themselves, can become the source of terrible conflict if we let them take control of our hearts.

The Seven A's of Confession

As God opens your eyes to see how you have sinned against others, he simultaneously offers you a way to find freedom from your past wrongs. It is called confession. Many people have never experienced this freedom because they have never learned how to confess their wrongs honestly and unconditionally. Instead, they use words like these: "I'm sorry if I hurt you." "Let's just forget the past." "I suppose I could have done a better job." "I guess it's not all your fault." These token statements rarely trigger genuine forgiveness and reconciliation. If you really want to make peace, ask God to help you breathe grace by humbly and thoroughly admitting your wrongs. One way to do this is to use the Seven A's.

1. Address Everyone Involved

As a general rule, you should confess your sins to every person who has been directly affected by your wrongdoing. Since all sins offend God by violating his will, all sins should be first confessed to him (see Ps. 32:5; 41:4).

Whether a sin should be confessed to other people as well as to God depends on whether it was a "heart sin" or a "social sin." A heart sin takes place only in your thoughts and does not directly affect others. Therefore, it needs to be confessed only to God.

A social sin involves words or actions that actually affect other people. (This may include acts of commission, such as slandering, stealing, or lying, or acts of omission, such as failing to help someone in need or ignoring someone.) Social sins should be confessed to those who have been affected by them, whether it is a single individual or a group of people who were affected by, or even witnessed, your actions (e.g., Luke 19:8; Acts 19:18). Whatever the case, your confession should reach as far as your offense.

2. Avoid **If,** **But,** *and* **Maybe**

The best way to ruin a confession is to use words that shift the blame to others or that appear to minimize or excuse your guilt. The most common way to do this is to say, "I'm sorry if I've done something to upset you." The word *if* ruins this confession, because it implies that you do not know whether or not you did wrong. The message you are communicating is this: "Obviously you're upset about something. I don't know that I have done anything wrong, but just to get you off my back I'll give you a token apology. By the way, since I don't know whether I have done anything wrong, I certainly don't know what I should do differently in the future. Therefore, don't expect me to change. It's only a matter of time before I do the same thing again."

Clearly, that is no confession at all. It is a superficial statement designed to get someone to stop bothering you or to transfer fault for breaking a relationship. Small wonder that genuine forgiveness rarely follows such words. Notice how the following so-called confessions are similarly diluted by the words in italics.

"*Perhaps* I was wrong."

"*Maybe* I could have tried harder."

"*Possibly* I should have waited to hear your side of the story."

"*I guess* I was wrong when I said those critical things about you."

"I shouldn't have lost my temper, *but I was tired.*"

Each of these statements would have value if the italicized words were left out. These words neutralize the rest of the confession and destroy its ability to convey sincere repentance and soften the heart of someone who has been offended.

The word *but* is especially harmful, because it has the strange ability to cancel all the words that precede it:

"I'm sorry I hurt your feelings, *but* you really upset me."

"I should have kept my mouth closed, *but* she asked for it."

"I know I was wrong, *but* so were you!"

Whenever statements like these are made, most people sense that the speaker believes the words following *but* more than those that precede it. Thus, a confession containing *but* rarely leads to reconciliation. The same is true when you use *however, if, maybe,* or any other word indicating reluctance to accept full responsibility for what you have done. As Tony Evans once preached, "If it contains an 'if' it ain't a confession." Therefore, make it a point to strike such words from your vocabulary anytime you need to make a confession.

3. Admit Specifically

The more *detailed* and specific you are when making a confession, the more likely you are to receive a positive response. Specific admissions help convince others that you are honestly facing up to what you have done, which makes it easier for them to forgive you. In addition, being specific will help you identify the behavior you need to change. For example, instead of saying, "I know I'm not much of an employee," you might say, "I know I've had a very negative attitude the last few months, which has led me to be critical of others and to disrupt the operation of this office. It was especially wrong of me to criticize your work in front of others yesterday."

As you strive to be specific in your confessions, make it a point to deal with your attitudes as well as actions. As we have seen, conflict starts in the heart with unmet desires that give rise to sinful attitudes like selfishness, ingratitude, envy, jealousy, bitterness, resentment, self-righteousness, disloyalty, insensitivity, and stubbornness. If you explicitly identify your sinful desires and attitudes, as well as your words and actions, others are far more likely to believe that you are genuinely repentant.

It is often wise to admit specifically that what you did violated God's will. As the prodigal son said, "Father, I have sinned against heaven and against you" (Luke 15:21). Such words show that you realize that what you did was not a minor error in judgment, but rather a serious violation of God's will. One of the most convincing ways to show that you realize you have been morally wrong is to identify the biblical principles you violated. Here are a few examples of how this can be done:

> "My critical comments have not only hurt you, but they have offended God as well. I have disobeyed his command to not slander others."
>
> "I've finally realized that I have completely failed to be the kind of husband God wants me to be. In Ephesians he says I should love you as Christ loved his church, but I haven't even come close to living up to that standard."
>
> "Last night I spent quite a while studying what the Bible says about employment relationships, and I realize that I have not treated you the way God wants me to. In particular, I violated Ephesians 6:9 when I threatened you."

Such statements demonstrate to the other person that you know your behavior was wrong. They also help you focus on the biblical principles you need to ask God to help you obey in the future, which will help you make the changes needed to avoid similar wrongdoing.

4. Acknowledge the Hurt

If you want someone to respond positively to a confession, make it a point to acknowledge and express sorrow for how you have hurt or affected them. Your goal is to show that you understand how the other person felt as a result of your words or actions. Here are two examples of how this can be done:

> "You must have been terribly embarrassed when I said those things in front of everyone. I'm very sorry I did that to you."
>
> "I can see why you were frustrated when I didn't deliver the parts on time. I'm sorry I failed to keep my commitment to you."

Sometimes it is helpful to ask the other person how he or she felt as a result of your behavior. This is especially wise when you suspect that the other person was deeply hurt by your conduct but is reluctant to tell you so. Another way to show that you are trying to understand how you affected others is to describe a similar experience from your own life. For example:

> "I can imagine how you feel. I was falsely accused by an employer too, and it was one of the worst experiences of my life. I'm sorry I have put you through the same thing."
>
> "I'm sure you were hurt by what I did. I remember when a close friend of mine failed to keep a promise to help me with a business I was just starting. I worked for months, but without his help it just wouldn't work. I was really hurt by what he did. I'm sorry I failed you in a similar way."

Although you should not dwell excessively on feelings, it is important to show that you understand how other people feel and to express genuine sorrow for hurting them. Once their feelings have been acknowledged and they see that you regret what you have done, most people will be more willing to move ahead with forgiveness.

5. Accept the Consequences

Explicitly accepting the consequences of your actions is another way to demonstrate genuine repentance. The prodigal son demonstrated this principle. After acknowledging that he had sinned against God and his father, he decided to say, "I am no longer worthy to be called your son; make me like one of your hired men" (Luke 15:19).

Similarly, if you have repeatedly violated an employer's trust, you may need to say, "You have every right to fire me because of what I have done, and I wouldn't blame you if you did." Or, if you damaged someone's property, you may need to say, "It will take me some time to earn the extra money, but I will see that your property is repaired or replaced as quickly as possible." (It was a statement like this that made Zacchaeus's confession so credible; see Luke 19:8.) Or, if you helped spread false information about someone, you could say, "Beginning this evening, I will call every person I talked to and admit that my statements were not true." The harder you work to make restitution and repair any damage you have caused, the easier it will be for others to believe your confession and be reconciled to you. (See appendix C for more specific guidance on when and how to make restitution.)

6. Alter Your Behavior

Another sign of sincere repentance is to explain to the person you offended how you plan to alter your behavior in the future. On a personal level, this could involve describing some of the attitude, character, and behavior changes you hope to make with God's help. You could mention that you plan to meet with a friend, church leader, or counselor who can offer you advice and hold you accountable for the changes you hope to make.

If you are an employer, you could write out a new policy on how you will train and supervise employees to prevent future misunderstandings and conflicts. If you are a pastor, you could describe how you will guide future changes in the church to prevent miscommunication and make sure that everyone has a chance to participate properly in decisions. To acknowledge that you cannot change on your own and are depending on God, it is often helpful to begin describing your plan for change with the words, "With God's help, I plan to . . ."

A written plan for change has several benefits. It shows you take the matter seriously and are willing to spend substantial time planning how to change. Listing specific goals and objectives helps remind you what you have committed yourself to, and it provides a standard by which your progress can be measured. It is often helpful to ask the person you have wronged to suggest how you can change. Write those suggestions down and check back with that person periodically to see whether he or she believes you are following through on your commitments. By doing so, you will be able to chart your progress more objectively, and your actions will continue to demonstrate that your confession was genuine.

7. *Ask for Forgiveness (and Allow Time)*

If you follow the six steps described above, many people will readily say they forgive you. If the person to whom you have confessed does not express forgiveness, however, you may ask, "Will you please forgive me?" This question is a signal that you have done all that you can by way of confession and that the responsibility for the next move has shifted to the other person. This will often help the offended person make and express the decision to forgive you. (The details of forgiveness will be discussed in chapter 10.)

Be careful, however, not to use this question as a means to pressure someone into forgiving you. Some people can forgive quickly, while others need some time to work through their feelings. My wife is like this. Sometimes, when I have deeply hurt her and later confessed, she needs a while to think and pray. If I press her to say "I forgive you" too quickly, I add to her burdens by introducing feelings of guilt, which can give rise to resentment and bitterness. On the other hand, if I respect her need for some time, she usually comes back to me fairly soon and willingly expresses her forgiveness.

If you sense that the person to whom you confessed is simply not ready to forgive you, it may be helpful to say something like this: "I know I have deeply hurt you, and I can understand why you would have a hard time forgiving me. I hope that you will soon be able to forgive me, because I want very much to be reconciled.

In the meantime, I will pray for you. I will do my best to repair the damage I caused as quickly as possible, and with God's help, I will work to overcome my temper. If there is anything else I can do, please let me know."

Time alone will not always bring forgiveness. Sometimes forgiveness is inhibited because a confession was inadequate. Therefore, when forgiveness is delayed, you may need to go back to the person you wronged and cover some of the elements of confession more thoroughly. For example, you may not have explained adequately how you intend to repair the damage you have done. Or you may have failed to understand and express regret for the way you hurt the other person. If you probe sensitively, you can often discover what is blocking forgiveness and then take care of it.

If forgiveness is still delayed, you have a few options. If the person is a Christian who apparently doesn't understand what forgiveness means, you may offer a pamphlet or book dealing with forgiveness (see chapter 10). Another possibility would be to encourage the person to talk over the problem with a pastor or a mature Christian friend. If none of these efforts works after a reasonable period of time, you may need to enlist a pastor to help bring about reconciliation. If these avenues are unavailable or ineffective, prayer and the steps outlined in chapter 12 will be your last resort.

Not every confession will require all seven steps. Minor offenses can often be handled with a fairly simple statement. The more serious the offense, however, the wiser it is to make a thorough confession using all of the Seven A's.

Before I leave the topic of confession, I must offer an important warning. Any time we use a process like the Seven A's, we can turn it into a meaningless ritual and completely miss what God wants us to do (see Mark 7:5–13; Luke 11:42). This usually happens when we use the process for our own benefit instead of seeing it as a means to glorify God and serve other people. I have caught myself going through the Seven A's simply to get a burden off my shoulders and minimize the consequences of my sin. In the process, I heaped greater burdens on the person I had already wronged. (Since I had "fulfilled my duty," the other person felt coerced to forgive me, even though he sensed that my confession was mechanical and insincere.)

Ask God to keep you from this sin. When you go to confess a wrong, remember that you are there to serve the other person and not to gain comfort for yourself. Focus on showing God's loving work in your life and on ministering to the person you have harmed. And regardless of his or her response, strive earnestly to fulfill your commitment to repair any damage you have caused and to alter your choices in the future. This is the fastest road to genuine peace and reconciliation.

You *Can* Change

The final step in finding freedom from a particular sin is to work with God to change your attitudes and behavior in the future. This process fulfills the third opportunity of peacemaking, namely, growing to be more like Christ.

God is eager to help us to grow and change (see Phil. 1:6, 2:13; Rom. 8:28–29; 1 Cor. 6:9–11; 2 Peter 1:4). There is no sin or habit in your life that cannot be overcome by his grace. If you have trusted in Jesus, God has already given you a new mind and a new nature (Eph. 4:22–24). And he promises to work in you so that you can learn to replace your old sinful behavior with godly attitudes and habits (Eph. 4:22–32). There are four ways that you can cooperate with God in this process.

Pray. Thank God for the saving work he has already done in your life and ask him to give you faith to believe that you really can change. Pray that he will open your eyes to see where he wants you to grow, and ask him to give you strength on a daily basis to put off your old ways of thinking and behaving and to put on new ways that imitate Christ (Ps. 139:23–24; Phil. 1:9–11; Col. 1:9–12).

Delight yourself in the Lord. As we saw in chapter 5, the best way to squeeze idolatrous desires out of our hearts is to learn to love and worship God with all our heart, mind, strength, and soul. As you focus on the Lord, you will discover that he can provide what idols promise but can never deliver. He alone can give lasting joy, peace, happiness, and security (Eph. 1:18–19). As you delight yourself more and more in him, he will purify your heart and fill it with desires he is eager to satisfy (Ezek. 36:25–26; Ps. 37:4; Matt. 5:3–13). And out of that new heart he will bring forth the character of Christ (James 3:17–18).

Study. The Bible frequently emphasizes the close connection between transformed thinking and growth in character (Rom. 8:6–8; 12:1–2; 1 Cor. 2:9–16; Eph. 1:17–19; 4:22–24; Phil. 1:9–11; Col. 1:9–12). Wisdom, knowledge, and understanding—all involving our minds—are important prerequisites to spiritual fruitfulness. God does not mysteriously infuse our minds with these qualities; rather, as we regularly and carefully study his Word, he helps us understand his principles and his ways so that our minds are truly "made new" and we learn how to walk in his ways.

Practice. As Paul warned the Philippians, we cannot change unless we put what we are learning into practice (Phil. 4:9). In other letters he used athletic metaphors to teach that godly character qualities must be developed through disciplined practice in which we seek to overcome our weaknesses, master the proper techniques, and make a desired behavior natural and automatic (1 Cor. 9:24–27; Phil. 3:14; 2 Peter 1:4–8). As we have seen, conflict provides excellent opportunities for such practice. When an argument develops, give close attention to controlling your tongue. When your desires clash with another's, recall Jesus' example and willingly submit. Or, if you have been offended, ask God to help you resist resentment and forgive as he has forgiven you. With God's help and faithful practice, you can develop a Christ-like character, which will demonstrate your repentance and enable you to enjoy the benefits of peace.

Summary and Application

To be a peacemaker, you need to deal honestly with your contribution to a conflict. As Paul told Timothy, "If a man cleanses himself from [sin], he will be an instrument for noble purposes, made holy, useful to the Master and prepared to do any good work" (2 Tim. 2:21). This cleansing process is inspired by Jesus' promise that he has forgiven our sins and wants to purify us from the idols and habits that cause conflict (1 John 1:9). He calls us to cooperate in this process of repentance, self-examination, confession, and personal change. The more faithfully you draw on his grace and pursue these steps, the more useful you will be to him in making peace. At the same time, after you get the log out of your own eye, you will be better prepared to gently restore others.

If you are presently involved in a conflict, these questions will help you apply the principles presented in this chapter.

1. As you look back at the way you have handled this conflict, do you see a need for repentance and confession? Why?
2. As you have talked to and about others in this situation, have you used your tongue as a weapon in any of the following kinds of speech? If so, describe what you said.
   Reckless words
   Grumbling and complaining
   Falsehood
   Gossip
   Slander
   Worthless talk that does not benefit or build others up
3. Have you tried to control others in this situation? Why and how?
4. Are you guilty of any of the following sins in this situation? If so, describe what you did or failed to do.
   Uncontrolled anger
   Bitterness
   Vengeance
   Evil or malicious thoughts
   Sexual immorality
   Substance abuse
   Laziness
   Defensiveness
   Self-justification
   Stubbornness
   Resistance to godly advice
   Greed
   Deficient work
   Withholding mercy and forgiveness
   Improper concessions
   Compulsive behavior

Breaking your word

Misusing authority

Rebelling against authority

Failing to treat others as you want to be treated

5. Have any of the following idols influenced your behavior in this situation? How?

Lusts of the flesh

Pride

Love of money

Fear of others (or excessive concern about what others think of you)

Good things you want too much (desires elevated to demands)

6. How have your sins contributed to this conflict?

7. Write an outline for your confession.

a. Address everyone involved. To whom do you need to confess?

b. Avoid *if, but,* and *maybe.* What excuses or blaming do you need to avoid?

c. Admit specifically. What desires have you allowed to rule you, and what sins have you committed? What biblical principles have you violated?

d. Acknowledge the hurt. How might others feel as a result of your sin?

e. Accept the consequences. What consequences do you need to accept? How can you reverse the damage you have caused?

f. Alter your behavior. What changes do you intend to make, with God's help, in the way you think, speak, and behave in the future?

g. Ask for forgiveness. What might make the person you have wronged reluctant to forgive you? What can you do to make it easier for him or her to forgive you?

8. How do you want to change as a result of this conflict? Pick one character quality you wish to change. Specifically, what steps can you take to practice that quality?

9. Go on record with the Lord by writing a prayer based on the principles taught in this chapter.

PART 3

GENTLY RESTORE

*How can I lovingly serve others
by helping them take
responsibility for their contribution
to this conflict?*

Brothers, if someone is caught in a sin, you who are
spiritual should restore him gently.

Galatians 6:1

Janet waited patiently for all of Larry's students to file through
the door. When she saw that he was finished with his work
and placing papers into his briefcase, she walked casually into his
classroom.

Giving him a friendly smile, she asked, "Larry, do you have a
few minutes to talk?"

Larry looked up, his eyes filled with suspicion. "I'm pretty busy
right now. What do you want to talk about?"

"I'd like to ask your forgiveness for the way I spoke to you last week and talk about how we are relating to each other, but if this isn't a convenient time, I could come back later."

His surprised look showed that this was not what he was expecting to hear from Janet. "No, that's OK. I've got a few minutes."

"Thanks. Well, like I said, I need to ask your forgiveness for what I said in the teachers' lounge last Wednesday. When you joked about me in front of Steve and Joyce, I lost my temper and lashed back at you. I was wrong, and I'm sure I embarrassed you. Would you please forgive me?"

Taken off guard by her transparency, all he could think to say was, "That's OK. I know I can be sort of abrasive at times. Just forget about it."

"Forgetting can take a long time. I'd appreciate it if you would say you forgive me."

"Sure, whatever. I forgive you. Let's just drop it."

Janet had been planning this conversation for days with the help of a trained reconciler in her church. They had anticipated that Larry might try to brush their differences aside, so they had role-played how to keep the conversation going. Janet now put that planning into practice.

"Since I blew up at you in front of Steve and Joyce, I want you to know that I plan to go to them and admit I was wrong. Is there anything else I can do to make this right with you? Anything else I've done to offend you?"

"No," he responded, "not that I can think of."

"Maybe you can help me understand something. If I haven't done anything else to offend you, why do you say sarcastic things about me in front of others?"

"Hey, I'm just kidding around. Can't you take a joke?"

"Maybe you don't mean to hurt me, but it doesn't feel like a joke, Larry. It's embarrassing to be made fun of in front of the people I work with every day. I don't think they find it funny either. And I don't think I'm the only person who's staying clear of the teachers' lounge just to avoid your jokes."

"Oh, so now I'm the big bad wolf," he responded sarcastically. "And all the little pigs need to run home to hide!"

"That's just what I mean, Larry. You seem to have a habit of calling people names and tearing them down. It's not a good example for our students. And I'm sorry to say that I've overheard some of the staff mocking your faith behind your back. Do you know what they're saying?"

Larry didn't actually want to know, but he felt compelled to say, "What?"

"They're calling you a hypocrite, Larry. They can't understand how you can claim to be a Christian and yet speak so critically all the time."

Larry cringed at Janet's words, and he began looking for a way to end the conversation. Before he could speak, however, Janet spoke gently.

"I don't think you mean to do it. I believe you want to have a positive witness, but it seems like you're stuck in the habit of saying hurtful things to people. I've struggled with the same problem, Larry. I've hurt so many people with my words. Just ask my family! But God is so forgiving. He doesn't treat us as our sins deserve. And he wants to free us from our hurtful habits. He doesn't want you and me fighting with each other. He would be so pleased if we forgave each other and worked together to improve our relationship and our witness around here."

Larry had never been approached like this in his life. The truth in Janet's words stung, but her tone of voice and her reminder of God's forgiveness held out a glimmer of hope. He slumped in his chair and sighed with weariness and regret.

"I don't deserve your forgiveness," he said. "I've torn you apart all year, just like everyone else. I've always used sarcasm when I don't know how to relate to people. I go home night after night knowing I blew it, but I just can't seem to change. Is there really hope for a jerk like me?"

"Of course there is!" Janet replied as she pulled up a chair across from Larry's desk. "If God can help me get control of my tongue, he can help anyone. Let's pray right now and ask him to show us how we can turn our past differences into an opportunity to demonstrate his power in our lives."

Talking to other people about a conflict is usually an unpleasant experience. We often let tensions build to the exploding point and then confront people with a list of their wrongs. They become defensive and react with a list of our wrongs, which leads to a painful battle of words. Those who are more verbally skilled may win a few arguments this way, but in the process they lose many important relationships.

The gospel opens the door for an entirely different approach to talking to others about their role in a conflict. Remembering God's mercy toward us, we can approach others in a spirit of love rather than condemnation. And instead of using guilt and shame to force others to change themselves, we can breathe grace by holding out to them the wonderful news that God wants to free them from sin and help them grow to be like his Son.

There are many helpful communication skills we can learn as well; these enable us to listen more carefully and speak more clearly and graciously. Godly communication usually leads to better understanding and agreement. As your words are seasoned with wisdom and grace, talking to others about their wrongs can become an avenue for strengthening relationships, serving other people, and bringing praise to God.

7

JUST BETWEEN THE TWO OF YOU

If your brother sins against you, go and show him his
fault, just between the two of you. If he listens to you,
you have won your brother over.

Matthew 18:15

Conflict presents unique opportunities to serve other people.
When others are weighed down with problems and stress,
God will sometimes use us to encourage them and help carry
their burdens. In other situations, we may be able to give helpful
advice, provide a positive example, or suggest creative solutions
to problems. Best of all, conflict can provide the opportunity to
demonstrate the love of Christ and give witness to the gospel, even
to people who are attacking us.

One of the most challenging ways to serve others in the midst of
conflict is to help them see where they have been wrong and need
to change. Although many offenses can and should be overlooked,
some problems are so harmful that they must be discussed. In this
chapter we will explore some basic guidelines on when and how

you should go and talk privately to another person about his or her contribution to a conflict.

Restoring Means More than Confronting

When Christians think about talking to someone else about a conflict, one of the first verses that comes to mind is Matthew 18:15: "If your brother sins against you, go and show him his fault, just between the two of you." If this verse is read in isolation, it seems to teach that we must always use direct confrontation to force others to admit they have sinned. If the verse is read in context, however, we see that Jesus had something much more flexible and beneficial in mind than simply standing toe to toe with others and describing their sins.

Just before this passage, we find Jesus' wonderful metaphor of a loving shepherd who goes to look for a wandering sheep and then rejoices when it is found (Matt. 18:12–14). Thus, Matthew 18:15 is introduced with a theme of restoration, not condemnation. Jesus repeats this theme just after telling us to "go and show him his fault" by adding, "If he listens to you, you have won your brother over." And then he hits the restoration theme a third time in verses 21–35, where he uses the parable of the unmerciful servant to remind us to be as merciful and forgiving to others as God is to us (Matt. 18:21–35).

Jesus is clearly calling for something much more loving and redemptive than simply confronting others with a list of their wrongs. He wants us to remember and imitate his shepherd love for us—to seek after others to help them turn from sin and be restored to God and those they have offended. This restoration theme is echoed throughout Scripture, as we are urged to "help," "restore," "save," and "forgive" those who are caught in sin (see 1 Thess. 5:14; Gal. 6:1; James 5:20).

Although this restoration process may sometimes require direct confrontation, the Bible teaches that there are often better ways to approach people regarding their wrongs. In fact, Scripture rarely uses words we would translate as "confront" to describe the process of talking to others about their faults. Instead, it calls us to use a wide spectrum of activities to minister to others, including confessing, teaching, instructing, reasoning with, showing, encouraging, correcting, warning, admonishing, or rebuking (Matt. 5:23–24; Luke 17:3; Acts 17:17; 1 Thess. 5:14; 2 Tim. 2:24; 4:2). God wants us to adjust the intensity of our communication to fit the other person's position and the urgency of the situation (1 Tim. 5:1; Titus 1:13). We are also warned not to let disagreements with others degenerate into quarreling, arguing, or foolish controversies (Phil. 2:14; 2 Tim. 2:23–24; Titus 3:9). Clearly, there is more to restoring others than simply confronting them with their wrongs. Therefore, if we want to be effective as peacemakers, we need to ask God to help us be discerning and flexible so that we can use whatever approach will be most effective in a given situation.

We should also note that Scripture provides numerous favorable examples of approaching others indirectly instead of bluntly describing their wrongs. Jesus did not directly confront the Samaritan woman at the well about living in adultery. Instead, he approached the issue indirectly by using questions and discussion that engaged her in the process of thinking about and assessing her own life (John 4:1–18). Jesus frequently used parables and stories as roundabout ways to help people see their sins (see, e.g., Matt. 21:33–45; Luke 15). The apostle Paul could be similarly indirect. Instead of hitting the Athenians head-on with their idolatry, he first engaged them on a point of common interest and moved gradually into the good news of the one true God (Acts 17:22–31). Esther may have the record for the indirect approach, taking two days and two banquets to get to the point of telling the king about the injustice of his decree to kill all of the Jews (Esther 5–7).

As these and many similar passages indicate, we need to let go of the idea that showing someone his fault always requires direct confrontation. Although that approach will be appropriate in some situations, we should never do it automatically. Instead, we should ask God to help us discern the most winsome and effective way to approach a particular person at a particular time and to open the way for genuine reconciliation. (In the next chapter we will look more closely at how to approach people indirectly using stories and metaphors.)

Sooner or Later, Face-to-Face

Matthew 18:15–20 is understood by some people to require that we must always talk personally and privately with someone who has offended us before we can ask others to get involved in the situation. The Bible clearly commends face-to-face meetings as an important step in reconciling people, but it does not teach that this is the only way to begin a reconciliation process. In fact, it is sometimes better to involve other people in resolving a conflict *before* trying to meet personally with someone who has wronged you. These people may act as neutral intermediaries who shuttle between you and the other person or as representatives who initially speak for you in joint meetings.

For example, before Jacob met his brother Esau in person he sent servants and gifts on ahead to set the stage for a friendly encounter (Genesis 32–33). When Joseph's brothers feared that he would finally take revenge on them for their sins against him, they sent someone to speak on their behalf to appeal to Joseph for mercy (Gen. 50:15–16). Abigail intervened between her husband and an enraged David and was highly commended for her initiative and wisdom (1 Sam. 25:18–35). When David was estranged from his son Absalom, Joab enlisted a Jewish woman to approach the king to soften his heart toward his son (2 Sam. 14:1–23). Similarly, when the apostles would not meet with Paul after his conversion, Barnabas intervened to speak on Paul's behalf and appeal for reconciliation (Acts 9:26–27).

As these stories indicate, there are many biblically legitimate ways to approach someone with whom we have a conflict. Personal conversations are often best, but in some cases involving other people right away will be even better. There are several situations in which this may be true today:

When you are dealing with a person who comes from a culture or tradition in which it is customary to resolve problems through intermediaries such as family representatives or trusted leaders

When going to someone personally and privately is likely to make them lose face in the sight of others

When either of the parties might feel intimidated by the other
person, perhaps because of a difference in verbal skills or differing positions of authority or influence

When one person was abused by the other and there is a possibility that the abuser will use a private conversation to manipulate
or silence the person who has been abused

When there is a third party who has a much closer relationship
than you do with the person who may be caught in sin, and
that third party is willing to raise the issue with the offender

Whatever the situation might be, we should always show respect
for the concerns, traditions, limitations, and special needs of others
and ask God to show us how to communicate with them in the way
that is most appropriate and helpful to them (Phil. 2:3–4).

However, whether we begin with a private meeting or work
through intermediaries, we must not let personal preferences or
cultural traditions divert us from seeking genuine reconciliation,
which requires a sincere expression and confirmation of confession and forgiveness. Although in unusual situations this might
conceivably take place without a personal meeting between the
parties (e.g., cases of child abuse), the Bible teaches that a face-
to-face meeting is usually essential to genuine reconciliation. This
principle is presented in three ways in the Bible.

First, many of the passages related to restoring relationships
clearly contemplate a direct conversation between the conflicting
parties (see Matt. 5:23–24; 18:15; Luke 17:3). Second, Scripture
provides many examples of marvelous reconciliation that came
about after personal meetings between people who had wronged
each other, including Jacob and Esau (Gen. 33:6–12), Joseph and
his brothers (45:1–5; 50:15–21), and Paul and the apostles (Acts
9:27–28). Third, the Bible also gives examples of disastrous results when the involvement of intermediaries allowed the parties
to delay or avoid personal meetings involving genuine confession
and forgiveness.

Perhaps the most tragic illustration of a failed reconciliation is
that of David and Absalom. After Absalom killed his own brother,
Joab was able to negotiate a pardon from the king that allowed Absalom to return to Jerusalem. But then Joab made a fatal mistake.

When David said, "[Absalom] must go to his own house; he must
not see my face" (2 Sam. 14:24), Joab failed to urge the king to
see his son and be reconciled to him immediately. This prolonged
estrangement embittered Absalom toward his father (14:28–32)
and eventually led to a rebellion that resulted in thousands of
deaths (2 Samuel 15–18). A similar tragedy unfolds in Genesis
34 when Shechem's father mediates a superficial agreement but
fails to urge Shechem to confess his wrongs personally to Dinah,
Jacob, and Jacob's sons. Jacob's sons fail to forgive Shechem and
later slaughter his entire city.

These stories illustrate a key element of God's design for human
relationships. God does not intend for people to relate to one another at a distance or through other people. Genuine relationship
involves *personal* communication. As Exodus 33:11 says, "The LORD
would speak to Moses face to face, as a man speaks with his friend"
(see also 2 John 12). If this is the ideal for a true friendship, it is
also the ideal for a relationship that has been broken by conflict
and needs to be restored. Although other people can sometimes
help get the restoration process started, its ultimate goal should
usually be a personal, face-to-face meeting between those who
have been estranged, so they can express and confirm repentance,
confession, and forgiveness and experience together the grace and
reconciliation of God.

If Someone Has Something against You

If you learn that someone has something against you, God wants
you to take the initiative in seeking peace—even if you do not believe
you have done anything wrong. If you believe that another person's
complaints against you are unfounded or that the misunderstanding
is entirely the other person's fault, you may naturally conclude that
you have no responsibility to take the initiative in restoring peace.
This is a common conclusion, but it is false, for it is contrary to
Jesus' specific teaching in Matthew 5:23–24: "Therefore, if you
are offering your gift at the altar and there remember that your
brother has something against you, leave your gift there in front
of the altar. First go and be reconciled to your brother; then come
and offer your gift." Note that this command is not limited to situ-

ations where the other person has something *justifiable* against you. Jesus said to be reconciled if your brother has *something* against you, implying that the obligation exists whether or not you believe his complaint is legitimate.

There are several reasons why you should initiate reconciliation even if you do not believe you are at fault. Most importantly, Jesus commands you to go. Also, as I explained previously, peace and unity among believers significantly affects how others will receive the gospel. Seeking peace with an alienated brother enhances your Christian witness, *especially* if he is the one who has done the wrong (Luke 6:32–36).

In addition, you can have greater peace of mind if you have honestly faced any complaints someone might have against you. Only by carefully listening to others can you discover sins of which you were not aware or help others realize that their complaints are unfounded. Either way, you will gain a clear conscience, which is an essential ingredient of internal peace and a close relationship with God.

Finally, you should initiate reconciliation out of love for your brother and concern for *his* well-being. Just before Jesus' command to seek reconciliation, he warned of the danger of unresolved anger: "You have heard that it was said to the people long ago, 'Do not murder, and anyone who murders will be subject to judgment.' But I tell you that anyone who is angry with his brother will be subject to judgment. . . . anyone who says, 'You fool!' will be in danger of the fire of hell" (Matt. 5:21–22).

Bitterness, anger, and unforgiveness are serious sins in God's eyes. If your brother indulges in these feelings, they will separate him from God and expose him to judgment (Eph. 4:30–31; cf. Isa. 59:1–2). In addition, these sinful feelings can eat away at your brother's heart like an acid and leave him spiritually, emotionally, and physically scarred (Ps. 32:1–5; 73:21–22; Prov. 14:30). This damage can occur even if someone is mistaken in believing you have done something wrong. Therefore, you should go to the person out of love and do everything within your power to resolve the matter. This may require either confessing your own wrongs or helping the other person realize there is no basis for the complaint. Although you cannot force someone to change his or her mind about you, you can make every effort to "live at peace" by clearing up misunderstandings and removing obstacles to reconciliation (Rom. 12:18; cf. 14:13–19). This may require repeated attempts and great patience, but the benefit to both of you makes it well worth the effort.

I recall one Sunday when I visited a small ranching community and preached a message on Matthew 5:21–24. After church a friend took me out to lunch. Part way through our meal, a man I had seen in church that morning walked into the restaurant. Seeing me, he came over to our table, smiling with delight.

"I have to tell you what just happened!" he said. "Your sermon really shook me up, because I've got a neighbor who hasn't talked to me for two years. We had an argument about where to run a fence. When I wouldn't move it to where he thought it should be, he just turned his back on me and stomped away. Since I thought I was in the right, I've always figured it was up to him to make the first move at being friends again. This morning I saw that the Lord wants *me* to be the one to seek reconciliation, so right after church I drove over to his house to talk with him. I told him I was sorry for being so stubborn two years ago and that I wanted to be friends again. He just about fell over. He said he felt bad all along for stomping away that day, but he didn't know how to come talk with me. Man, was he glad I came to talk with him!"

When Someone's Sins Are Too Serious to Overlook

God also calls you to go and talk to someone about a conflict if that person's sins are too serious to overlook. This is why Jesus said, "If your brother sins, rebuke him, and if he repents, forgive him" (Luke 17:3). It is sometimes difficult to decide whether another person's sin is so serious that you need to go and talk about it. Below are a few of the situations that may warrant this kind of attention.

As discussed earlier, there may be some situations in which it is best to work initially through intermediaries who have a closer relationship with the other person. It is generally best to keep these kinds of discussions as private as possible, however, so the other person is spared embarrassment. Therefore, in the following discussion, I will focus primarily on the situation where you are in a position to approach the other individual personally and privately.

Is It Dishonoring God?

Sin is too serious to overlook if it is likely to bring significant dishonor to God (see, e.g., Matt. 21:12–13; Rom. 2:23–24). If someone who professes to be a Christian is behaving in such a way that others are likely to think less of God, of his church, or of his Word, it may be necessary to talk with that person and urge him to change his behavior. This doesn't mean that we should call attention to every minor offense, for God himself is patient and forbearing with much of what we do wrong. But when someone's sin becomes visible enough to obviously and significantly affect a Christian's witness, it needs to be addressed.

Is It Damaging Your Relationship?

You should also go and talk about offenses that are damaging your relationship with another person. If you are unable to forgive an offense—that is, if your feelings, thoughts, words, or actions toward another person have been altered for more than a short period of time—the offense is probably too serious to overlook. Even minor wrongdoing can damage a relationship if it is repeated. Although something minor may be easily forgiven the first few times, frustration and resentment can eventually build up. When this happens, it may be necessary to bring the matter to the other person's attention so that the offensive pattern can be changed.

Is It Hurting Others?

An offense or disagreement is also too serious to overlook when it results in significant harm to you or others. This can happen in various ways. The offender may be hurting or imperiling others in a direct way (e.g., child abuse or drunk driving). The person may also be setting an example that will encourage other Christians to behave in a similar manner. Knowing that "a little yeast works through the whole batch of dough," Paul commands Christians to address serious and open sin quickly and firmly to save other believers from being led astray (1 Cor. 5:1–13; cf. 2 Tim. 4:2–4; Prov. 10:17). An offense can also adversely affect others if it is made public and other Christians take sides. When the peace and unity of the church are threatened in this way, the underlying problem needs to be addressed before it causes serious division (Titus 3:10).

Is It Hurting the Offender?

Finally, sin needs to be addressed when it is seriously harming the offender, either by direct damage (e.g., alcohol abuse) or by impairing his or her relationship with God or other people. Looking out for the well-being of other Christians, especially those in your own family or congregation, is a serious responsibility. Unfortunately, because many Christians have adopted the world's view that everyone should be allowed to "do his own thing," some believers will do nothing, even when they see a brother or sister ensnared in serious sin. This is not the kind of love Jesus demonstrated, nor is it consistent with the clear teaching of Scripture:

"Do not hate your brother in your heart. Rebuke your neighbor frankly so you will not share in his guilt" (Lev. 19:17).

"Rescue those being led away to death; hold back those staggering toward slaughter. If you say, 'But we knew nothing about this,' does not he who weighs the heart perceive it? Does not he who guards your life know it? Will he not repay each person according to what he has done?" (Prov. 24:11–12).

"Better is open rebuke than hidden love. Wounds from a friend can be trusted, but an enemy multiplies kisses" (Prov. 27:5–6; cf. 9:8; 19:25; 28:23).

"If your brother sins against you, go and show him his fault, just between the two of you. If he listens to you, you have won your brother over" (Matt. 18:15).

"Brothers, if someone is caught in a sin, you who are spiritual should restore him gently. But watch yourself, or you also may be tempted" (Gal. 6:1).

"My brothers, if one of you should wander from the truth and someone should bring him back, remember this: Whoever turns a sinner from the error of his way will save him from death and cover over a multitude of sins" (James 5:19–20).

Although these verses endorse constructive confrontation, they are not a license to be a busybody. The Bible repeatedly warns us not to be eagerly looking for opportunities to point out the faults of others (e.g., 2 Thess. 3:11; 1 Tim. 5:13; 2 Tim. 2:23; 1 Peter 4:15). In fact, anyone who is *eager* to go and show a brother his sin is probably disqualified from doing so. Such eagerness is often a sign of pride and spiritual immaturity, which cripple our ability to minister effectively to others (Gal. 5:22–6:2). The best confronters are usually people who would prefer not to have to talk to others about their sin but will do so out of obedience to God and love for others.

At the other extreme are those who are reluctant to talk about sin under any circumstances. They often point to Matthew 7:1—"Do not judge, or you too will be judged"—and say that the Bible forbids us to pass judgment on how others live. However, when studied in the light of the verses quoted above, which specifically tell us to evaluate and talk to others about their behavior, Matthew 7:1–5 cannot be interpreted as forbidding personal correction. Instead, the passage explains when and how correction should occur. Jesus is saying that if you follow his instructions properly, "you will see clearly to remove the speck from your brother's eye" (Matt. 7:5). This unquestionably implies his approval of appropriate correction.

Some people refuse to talk to others about sin or conflict because of another passage: "Do not resist an evil person. If someone strikes you on the right cheek, turn to him the other also" (Matt. 5:39). This passage does not forbid personal correction. Rather, it forbids people to take the law into their own hands and to seek *vengeance* against those who wrong them.[1] This verse teaches that Christians should be willing to endure personal injury without retaliation when that injury comes as a direct result of their Christian witness (cf. 1 Peter 1:6–7; 2:12–3:18; 4:12–19). In the normal disagreements of daily living, however, Christians have the responsibility to address serious sin, especially when it is found in a fellow believer.

Others avoid correcting others by saying, "Who am I to tell someone else what to do?" While it is true that we have no right to force our personal opinions on other people, we do have a responsibility to encourage fellow believers to be faithful to God's truths, which are presented in Scripture. Thus, if you believe that the Bible contains authoritative instruction from God, and if you have a genuine love for God and for your brother, you will not shirk your responsibility to talk with that brother in appropriate ways to help him live in line with God's standards (e.g., Rom. 15:14; Col. 3:16; 2 Tim. 2:24–26).

Another way to avoid going to others is to say, "Isn't it *God's* job to show people where they are wrong?" It is true that God is the only one who can convict people of sin and change their hearts, which he does through the power of the Holy Spirit. But God often uses another person to speak the words that a sinner needs to hear to see the need to repent (e.g., 2 Sam. 12:1–13; 2 Tim. 2:24–26). We cannot change people on our own, but through loving correction we can be used by God to help people see where they have a problem with sin.

A Christian's responsibility to help others deal with serious sins can be understood more clearly by studying two particular words used in Galatians 6:1. In this passage Paul told the Galatians to restore a brother who is "caught in a sin." The Greek word that is translated as "caught" *(prolambano)* means to be overtaken or surprised. Thus, the brother who needs our help is one who has been ensnared when he was off guard. He is like a fisherman who wasn't paying attention and got entangled in his net as it was going overboard, and now he is hanging desperately to the side of the boat, in danger of being drowned. Both the fisherman and the man caught in sin have the same need—their problems have become so serious that they may not be able to save themselves. They need someone else to step in and sever the cords that entangle them. Just as you would not stand by and watch a fisherman drown while tangled in his net, neither should you stand by and watch another Christian be destroyed by his sin.

It also helps to understand what Paul told the Galatians to do with a brother caught in sin. Instead of ignoring him or throwing him out, the Galatians were instructed to "restore him gently." The word translated as "restore" *(katartizo)* means to mend, repair, equip, complete, or prepare. This word is used several times in the New Testament—to describe fishermen *mending* and *preparing* their nets (Matt. 4:21), to describe Paul's *supplying* what is lacking in the Thessalonians' faith (1 Thess. 3:10), to describe Jesus' *equipping* believers with everything good for doing his will (Heb. 13:21) and God's *restoring* those who have suffered and making them "strong, firm and steadfast" (1 Peter 5:10). Each of these activities has the goal of making something or someone useful for its intended purpose. For example, just as nets are designed to serve people in a specific way, we are designed to serve God in a specific way. Thus, we can see that the goal of *katartizo,* as used in Galatians 6:1, is to mend broken people and restore them to usefulness in God's kingdom.

Understanding these two words will help you decide whether an offense is too serious to be overlooked. First, keep the picture of being "caught" in mind. If a sin does not appear to be doing serious harm to a brother or damaging his relationships, it may be best simply to pray that God will show him his need for change. On the other hand, if the sin appears to be dragging your friend under, do not delay in going to him. Second, remember the *katartizo* principle. Has that person's sin significantly hurt his spiritual health and reduced his usefulness to God (as a large hole would decrease the usefulness of a fishing net)? If so, there may be a need for "mending," which might be accomplished through a gracious conversation. For a look at how this can happen, read once more the story that preceded this chapter.[2]

Special Considerations

Having laid down some basic guidelines on when it is appropriate to go and show others their faults, it may be helpful to look at a few situations or concerns that require special consideration.

Going to Non-Christians

The Bible teaches we should be concerned about the well-being of others regardless of whether they are Christians or non-

Christians (Luke 10:25–37; Gal. 6:10). We are also commanded to "live at peace with everyone" (Rom. 12:18). Therefore, most of the principles given above apply to conflicts with non-Christians. Of course, you should modify your approach somewhat, being sensitive to their perspectives and needs. Instead of referring to specific Bible verses, you may appeal to commonly held interests or values, such as preserving a marriage or maintaining a good reputation. (There will be more on this in chapter 11.) Even so, most of the principles described throughout this book will be applicable to resolving a conflict with a non-Christian. And in some cases, God will use your faithful efforts at peacemaking to help the other person come to faith in Christ.

Going to a Person in Authority

Your responsibility to go to someone who is caught in sin does not vanish just because that person is in a position of authority over you (e.g., an employer or a church elder). Since these people are as human as you are, they will also sin and need correction (see 1 Tim. 5:19–20). Of course, you may need to exercise special care in choosing your words when you talk with such a person. Speak in a respectful manner, and do all you can to affirm your regard for that person's authority (see, e.g., Dan. 1:11–14). In doing so, you may not only encourage needed changes, but also increase that person's respect for you (cf. 1 Sam. 25:23–35).

Dealing with Abuse

One of the most difficult offenses to address is one that involves an abuse of power or authority, such as physical or sexual abuse. In rare situations, a victim of abuse may have gained sufficient strength to go and talk directly to his or her abuser. In most situations, however, it is not wise or constructive for a victim to talk privately with the abuser. Many abusers are very adept at manipulation and intimidation, and they will use the conversation as an opportunity for further abuse. Therefore, it is usually best to involve others in the confrontation process.

If the abuser is a Christian, his church has a responsibility to confront his sin, promote genuine repentance and confession, support counseling, and require him to submit to necessary legal consequences. This involvement can and should be carried out in cooperation with actions that civil authorities must take to deal with the abuse.

At the same time, the church should be ministering lovingly and diligently to the victim of abuse. This calls for compassion and understanding, acknowledging any role the church may have played in failing to properly protect the victim, providing needed counseling, and changing policies and practices to prevent similar abuse in the future.[3]

Go Tentatively and Repeatedly

It is wise to remember that many differences and offenses are the result of misunderstandings rather than actual wrongs. Therefore, when you approach another person, do so in a tentative manner. Unless you have clear, firsthand knowledge that a wrong has been done, give the other person the benefit of the doubt and be open to the possibility that you have not assessed the situation correctly. A cautious, fair-minded manner will usually promote a more relaxed atmosphere and encourage honest dialogue rather than defensive rebuttals.

Be prepared for the fact that your first meeting may not be successful. Since the other person may doubt your sincerity or may not be accustomed to dealing with differences in such a direct and honest way, your initial attempt at reconciliation may do nothing more than plant seeds that you will need to cultivate in following days. The Greek verb used for "go" in Matthew 18:15 implies a *continual* action. If you don't succeed at first, try to discern what went wrong (perhaps by reviewing portions of this book), seek appropriate counsel, and correct your mistakes. Give the other person time to think (and give God time to work), and then go again. You should continue seeking to resolve the matter privately until it becomes apparent that further personal conversations are truly pointless or are likely to do harm. At that point you should consider whether it would be wiser to overlook the matter entirely.

If doing so is inappropriate, you will need to seek help from others, which will be discussed in chapter 9.

After the Log Is Out of Your Eye

As Jesus teaches in Matthew 7:3–5, you should not try to talk to others about their wrongs until you have dealt with your contribution to a problem. When you follow Jesus' teaching, your confession will sometimes encourage the other person to admit sins. But not everyone will respond so cooperatively. In some cases the other person will acknowledge little or no responsibility for the problem, which will put you in an awkward position. If you proceed to bring up that person's wrongs, he may become defensive and believe that your earlier confession was a sham. On the other hand, if you just walk away without discussing the other person's wrongs, he may not come to grips with the need for change. So what do you do? Generally speaking, there are four possible courses to follow:

1. You may simply overlook the offense. Confess your contribution to the problem, let go of what the other person did, and get on with your life. This route will be appropriate if the other person's sin is relatively minor and has not permanently affected your relationship. It will also be appropriate if your fault in the matter far outweighs the other person's, in which case you should devote your attention to the changes you need to make instead of saying anything about the other's faults.

2. You may build on the other's superficial confession. Your confession may encourage the other person to make some form of admission, even if it is incomplete or halfhearted. (For example: "I guess I sort of lost my temper too." "Well, it wasn't all your fault." "I can see why you were frustrated.") Sometimes it is appropriate to pick up on another's words and reflect them back in more detail. Below are some examples of what you might say.

> "I appreciate your admitting that you lost your temper, Bob. May I explain how that made me feel?"
> "I appreciate your saying that. What do you think you did wrong?"
> "Why do you think I was frustrated?"

3. You may need to talk about the other person's sin now. This will be appropriate when the conflict is so serious or the other person's attitude and behavior is so harmful that the situation must be dealt with immediately or further problems are likely to occur. If you do proceed to address the other person's behaviors, plan your words carefully in advance to reduce the likelihood that he or she will question your motives. For example:

> "Bill, I appreciate your forgiveness, and I will really work at controlling what I say in the future. In fact, I'd appreciate it if you would let me know if you ever hear me talking like that again. In the same way, I believe there are some things you could do differently in the future that might help to avoid similar problems. May I explain what I mean?"

> "Linda, there's no question that my careless words contributed to this problem, and I really am sorry for aggravating you. At the same time, I'm not sure you realize how you contributed to this problem. As much as I would like to drop the matter, I'm afraid we'll have similar problems again unless we get all of our concerns on the table. May I explain how I see your conduct in this matter?"

4. You may postpone confrontation until another time. This will be appropriate if the matter is not urgent and if immediate confrontation is not likely to be productive. If you genuinely repent of your wrongs and sincerely work at changing your attitude and behavior, a variety of results may take place. First, you may eventually decide that the other person's wrongs were actually insignificant, in which case you may not need to bring them up. Second, the effort you make to change and to restore your relationship may convict the other person and eventually motivate him to come to you and admit past wrongs. Third, if the offense is repeated later, you will be in a better position to approach the offender if you have made an obvious effort to deal with your faults. Since your repentance and changed conduct will make it more difficult for the other person to shift the blame, he or she may finally start to face up to the misbehavior.

If you know you need to confess your wrongs to another person, pray and think carefully beforehand about whether or not it will be wise to talk about the other person's wrongs during the same conversation. Although you will often not be able to make a final decision on the matter until you see how that person responds to your confession, it is wise to have a tentative plan in mind even before you meet. This will help you avoid careless words and respond constructively to what the other person says.

Summary and Application

Although it is often best simply to overlook the sins of others, there will be times when doing so only prolongs alienation and encourages them to continue acting in a hurtful manner. If you know that someone has something against you, go to that person and talk about it as soon as possible. Similarly, if someone's sins are dishonoring God, damaging your relationship, hurting others, or hurting that person, one of the most loving and helpful things you can do is go and help him or her see the need for change. With God's grace and the right words (including your own confession), such a conversation will often lead to restored peace and stronger relationships.

If you are presently involved in a conflict, these questions will help you apply the principles presented in this chapter.

1. Do you have any reason to believe that someone else has something against you? If so, why?
2. How has the other person sinned in this situation?
3. Would it be better to overlook the offense against you or to go and talk with the other person about it? What would be the probable benefits and drawbacks of each course of action?
4. Is the other person's sin too serious to overlook? More specifically:
    Is it dishonoring God? If so, how?
    Is it damaging your relationship? If so, how?
    Is it hurting others? If so, how?
    Is it hurting that person? If so, how?
    Is it making that person less useful to the Lord?
5. Which of the other person's sins need to be discussed?

6. Would it be better to go in person or to involve others right away? Why?
7. Would it be best to raise the issue directly, or might this person respond better to an indirect approach? How could you use a story, an analogy, or a point of common interest to open your discussion?
8. Do you need to confess any of your sins before you talk about what the other person has done wrong? If so, what will you do if the other person does not confess his or her sins?
9. Go on record with the Lord by writing a prayer based on the principles taught in this chapter.

8

SPEAK THE TRUTH
IN LOVE

Speaking the truth in love, we will in all things grow
up into him who is the Head, that is, Christ.

Ephesians 4:15

Words play a key role in almost every conflict. When used properly, words promote understanding and encourage agreement. When misused, they usually aggravate conflicts and drive people further apart. If your words seem to do more harm than good when you try to resolve a disagreement, don't give up. With God's help you can improve your ability to communicate constructively. In this chapter we will look at some foundational communication principles and skills and explore practical ways to use them in the midst of conflict.

Bring Hope through the Gospel

When someone has disappointed or offended me, my natural tendency is to come at them with "the law," lecturing them about what they have done wrong and what they should now do to make things right. This approach generally makes people defensive and reluctant to admit their wrongs, which makes a conflict worse.

The Lord is graciously working to teach me a better way to approach others about their failures. Instead of coming at them with the law, I am learning to bring them the gospel. In other words, rather than dwelling on what people should do or have failed to do, I am learning to focus primarily on what God has done and is doing for them through Christ. This approach is demonstrated and commended throughout Scripture.

Consider again Jesus' conversation with the Samaritan woman. Instead of hammering away at her sinful lifestyle, Jesus spent most of his time engaging her in a conversation about salvation, eternal life, true worship, and the coming of the Messiah (John 4:7–26). She responded eagerly to this gospel-focused approach, let down her defenses, and put her trust in Christ. Although Jesus changed this focus when rebuking hard-hearted Pharisees, his typical approach to bringing people to repentance was to bring them the good news of God's forgiveness (see, e.g., Luke 19:1–10; John 8:10–11).

The apostle Paul had a similar approach, even when he had to deal with serious sin. In his first letter to the Corinthians, he had to address divisions, immorality, lawsuits, food sacrificed to idols, and the misuse of the Lord's Supper and spiritual gifts. But before addressing these terrible sins, Paul's gracious greeting held out hope for forgiveness and change by reminding the Corinthians of what God had already done for them through Christ:

> To the church of God in Corinth, to those sanctified in Christ Jesus and called to be holy. . . . I always thank God for you because of his grace given you in Christ Jesus. For in him you have been enriched in every way—in all your speaking and in all your knowledge—because our testimony about Christ was confirmed in you. Therefore you do not lack any spiritual gift as you eagerly wait for our Lord Jesus Christ to be revealed. He will keep you strong to the end, so that you will be blameless on the day of our Lord Jesus Christ. God, who has called you into fellowship with his Son Jesus Christ our Lord, is faithful.
>
> 1 Corinthians 1:2–9

What a marvelous way to set the stage for repentance and change! Paul did the same thing in his letters to other churches and individuals. He always kept Jesus in the center of his instruction and correction. For example, when writing the Ephesians, Paul devoted the first half of his letter to a detailed description of God's redemptive plan. When he finally got around to addressing errors in the congregation, his readers were already standing on a foundation of hope and encouragement.

Paul did the same thing with the Philippians and Colossians, who also needed correction and instruction. He begins both letters by drawing attention to what God has done in each of these churches (Phil. 1:3–11; Col. 1:3–23). Then he continues to refer to the gospel as he moves from issue to issue. For example, in the midst of admonishing the Colossians, Paul injects this marvelous clause: "*Therefore, as God's chosen people, holy and dearly loved,* clothe yourselves with compassion, kindness, humility, gentleness and patience" (Col. 3:12; emphasis added). Before telling them something more that they should do, Paul reminds them of who they are in Christ.

As these passages show, when we need to talk with others about their faults, we should ask for God's help to resist our tendency to hammer people into submission by dwelling on their failures. Of course, we sometimes need to show them where they have sinned and fallen short of God's ways. But that should not be the primary focus of our words, because judgment inevitably discourages. With God's help we can instead offer hope by drawing attention to the wonderful news that God has forgiven our sins through Christ and is eager to help us change our ways.

When talking with someone about gossip you might say:

> "I don't think you deliberately set out to hurt Bill, but your words may have damaged his reputation. The good news is that Jesus died to deliver you, me, and Bill—all of us—from our sins. God has given us a warning and a wonderful promise: If we conceal our wrongs, he will continue to discipline us until we repent, but if we confess our sins, he will forgive us and restore our relationships. There is such hope because of what Jesus has done for us! If you ask for his help and deal with this the way he teaches, the whole incident can be completely wiped away."

Whether I'm doing peacemaking at home, in my church, or in a formal conciliation case, I've seen this approach open the door for repentance and peace. The more hope you give by focusing on what God has done and is doing for us, the more likely others will be to listen to your concerns, acknowledge their wrongs, and move toward reconciliation.

The year before I began making the latest changes to this book, I realized that I could not consistently weave the gospel into my conversations with others until the gospel was woven deeply into my own heart. God showed me that I am a natural "law speaker;" I bring judgment much more easily than I bring grace. When I saw this, I began praying for God to give me a major heart change, to make the gospel central to everything I think, say, and do. Perhaps you see the same inclination and need for change in yourself. If so, pray that God will open your eyes more fully to the glory of what Christ has done for you. Learn to delight in reading about, meditating on, and rejoicing in Jesus' completed work on the cross. When your soul, your thoughts, and your conversation are saturated with the gospel, it will overflow into other areas of your life, bringing hope and encouragement to others, even if you are talking to them about their need for repentance and change.[1]

Be Quick to Listen

Another element of effective communication is to listen carefully to what others are saying. Knowing this is not our nature, James gave this warning to the early church: "My dear brothers, take note of this: Everyone should be quick to listen, slow to speak and slow to become angry" (James 1:19).

Good listening is particularly important for a peacemaker. It improves your ability to understand others, it shows that you realize you do not have all the answers, and it tells the other person that you value his or her thoughts and opinions. Even if you cannot agree with everything others say or do, your willingness to listen demonstrates respect and shows that you are trying to understand their perspective. This can help create an atmosphere of mutual respect that will improve communication. With God's help you can develop several listening skills.

Waiting

Waiting patiently while others talk is a key listening skill. Without this skill, you will often fail to understand the root cause of a conflict, and you may complicate matters with inappropriate reactions. As Proverbs 18:13 teaches, "He who answers before listening—that is his folly and his shame" (see also Prov. 15:28). There are several basic ways to improve your waiting ability. Try not to jump to premature conclusions about what others are thinking; give them time and hear them out. Discipline yourself not to interrupt others while they are speaking. Learn to be comfortable with silence and do not respond the moment there is a pause. And do not offer immediate solutions to every problem others bring to you. Sometimes they already know what they should do, but they need to have someone allow them to talk it through.

Attending

The human mind can think at least four times faster than a person can talk. Therefore, when you are listening to someone, your mind may be searching for something more to do. If you allow your mind to wander, or if you start rehearsing your responses, you may miss much of what others are saying. Moreover, others can usually tell when you are distracted, which discourages them in their efforts to communicate.

There are several ways you can show that you are paying attention to what others are saying. Maintain regular eye contact. Avoid negative body language, such as folding your arms, tapping your foot, or looking around. Eliminate distractions as much as possible—turn off the television, close a door to reduce noise, and sit where you will not be tempted to glance away frequently. Leaning forward slightly usually shows interest, as do warm and responsive facial expressions. Nod your head occasionally to show that you understand what the other person is saying or feeling. Occasional responses like "hmmm," "uh-huh," "I see," and "oh" tell others that their words are getting through to you. This will encourage them to continue talking, which will allow you to get as much information as possible before you respond.

Clarifying

Clarifying is the process of making sure you understand what the other person is saying. It usually involves questions and statements like these:

"Are you saying . . . ?"
"Tell me more about . . ."
"Can you give me an example?"
"I'm confused about . . ."
"Let me see if I understand . . ."

Words like these show that you are hearing and thinking about what is being said. Because these responses also show your interest in getting further information, they encourage the other person to share emotions and perceptions more fully. If he or she responds to that invitation, you can often get beyond the surface issues and discern more clearly underlying concerns, motives, and feelings.

Reflecting

Reflecting or "paraphrasing" is the process of summarizing the other person's main points in your own words and sending them back in a constructive way. Reflecting may deal with both the *content* of what the other person has said and the associated *feelings*. For example:

"You believe I didn't take time to hear you out."
"From your perspective, I was wrong when I said that about you."
"The way you see it, then, is that there isn't much hope . . ."
"This situation has created a lot of problems for you and your family."
"You seem to believe I was being dishonest about . . ."
"You must really care about this project."
"I get the impression I've really disappointed you."

"You were really hurt by my comment about you in front of the class."

"It sounds like you are upset because I gave John the job instead of you."

Reflecting does not require that you agree with what the other person says; it simply reveals whether you comprehend another person's thoughts and feelings. Reflecting shows that you are paying attention and you are trying to understand the other person. When others sense this, they are less likely to repeat themselves or use a loud voice to get their point across. Reflecting also helps to clarify what the other person is saying and allows you to focus the discussion on a specific topic rather than having to deal with several concerns simultaneously. In addition, it can slow down the pace of a conversation, which is especially beneficial when emotions are high and words may be spoken in haste. Finally, reflecting what others are saying can make them more willing to listen to what you want to say.

Agreeing

Agreeing with what another person says is an especially powerful listening response. This doesn't mean you abandon your beliefs, but rather that you acknowledge what you know is true before addressing points of disagreement. Agreeing with the person who is speaking will often encourage him or her to talk more openly and avoid unnecessary repetition.

Agreeing is especially important when you have been in the wrong. For example, responses like these can make the difference between an argument and a meaningful dialogue:

"You're right. I was wrong when I said . . ."

"You know, a lot of what you just said is true. I do need to deal with my attitude."

"I can understand why you would be upset with my being late again."

Agreeing with others, especially when they are pointing out your faults, is not easy, but it can play a crucial role in peacemaking.

When you are talking with another person, first listen for the truth, resisting the temptation to defend yourself, blame others, or focus on points of disagreement. Ask yourself, "Is there *any* truth in what he or she is saying?" If your answer is "yes," acknowledge what is true and identify your common ground before moving to your differences. Doing so is a sign of wisdom and spiritual maturity. "Let a righteous man strike me—it is a kindness; let him rebuke me—it is oil on my head. My head will not refuse it" (Ps. 141:5). "He who listens to a life-giving rebuke will be at home among the wise" (Prov. 15:31; cf. 15:5; 17:10; 25:12). By agreeing with the other person whenever possible, you can resolve certain issues easily and then focus profitably on matters that deserve further discussion.

One reason we are sometimes reluctant to admit being wrong on one issue is that we fear it will seem like we are accepting responsibility for the entire problem. The best way to overcome this hurdle is to agree with others in *specific* terms. For example:

"Now that I've heard you, I can see that part of this problem really is my fault. I was wrong not to fulfill my part of the agreement, and then I made things even worse when I complained about you to others. What else do you believe I did wrong?"

"I agree that I was wrong not to follow through on my commitment, and I need to be more faithful in the future. I believe there is more to this problem than just that, but before we talk about what you've done, I want to hear you out. Would you please be more specific about how my actions hurt you?"

These kinds of responses require genuine humility and also call for keeping a tight rein on your emotions. But they are worth the effort, for a controlled *response* will usually do more for peace than will an emotional *reaction*. The more quickly you agree with what is true and accept responsibility for your own actions, the more open the other person may be if you later say, "Okay, we've agreed on some things I did wrong. How do you think *you* contributed to this problem?" If you were humble enough to acknowledge where you were wrong, others are much more likely to do the same.

The Tongue of the Wise Brings Healing

A third element of effective communication is the ability to speak to others in a clear, constructive, and persuasive manner. Proverbs 12:18 is particularly relevant to this task: "Reckless words pierce like a sword, but the tongue of the wise brings healing." There are several habits and skills that will help you to communicate with others with wisdom.

Breathe Grace

As we have seen throughout this book, peacemakers are people who breathe grace to others in the midst of conflict. Since we cannot breathe out what we have not breathed in, this process hinges on our moment-to-moment relationship with God. We must continually "breathe in" God's grace by studying and meditating on his Word, praying to him, thanking him for his mercy and rejoicing in our salvation, worshiping him, partaking of the Lord's Supper, and enjoying the fellowship of other believers. As we are filled with his grace, we can then breathe it out to others by confessing our wrongs, bringing them hope through the gospel, lovingly showing others their faults, forgiving them as God has forgiven us, and manifesting in our words and actions the fruit of the Holy Spirit: "love, joy, peace, patience, kindness, goodness, faithfulness, gentleness and self-control" (Gal. 5:22–23; see also James 3:17–18). When even one person in a conflict is faithfully breathing out this kind of grace, others will often receive God's grace through us. As they do, they are less likely to be defensive and more inclined to listen to our concerns.[2]

Make Charitable Judgments

When you are trying to show others where they may need to change, your attitude will usually carry more weight than your actual words. If people sense that you have jumped to conclusions about them and enjoy finding fault in them, they are likely to resist correction. If, on the other hand, they sense that you are trying to believe the best about them, they will be more inclined to listen to your concerns. Therefore, ask God to help you make *charitable judgments* about others. (*Charitable* simply means "loving.")

Making a charitable judgment means that out of love for God you strive to believe the best about others until you have facts to prove otherwise. In other words, if you can reasonably interpret what someone has said or done in two possible ways, God calls you to embrace the positive interpretation over the negative, or at least to postpone making any judgment at all until you can acquire conclusive facts (see 1 Cor. 13:6; Matt. 7:12; 22:39; James 4:11–12).

If you fail to heed this principle, people will often sense that you have already made up your mind about them and that it is pointless to talk with you. This stifles communication. On the other hand, communication will usually improve if you give someone the benefit of the doubt, put things in the best possible light, avoid backing the person into a corner, and indicate that you really are open to hearing his or her side of the story.[3]

Speak the Truth in Love

God commands us not only to speak the truth to each other, but to "[speak] the truth *in love*" (Eph. 4:15; emphasis added), even to people who have wronged or mistreated us (1 Peter 3:9; cf. Luke 6:27–28; Acts 7:59–60; Rom. 12:14; 1 Cor. 4:12–13). This process starts when you ask God to put a love into your heart that is not naturally there (1 Cor. 13:1–7). Next, ask him to give you the ability to communicate this love by speaking to others with gentleness and patience and by showing genuine concern for their well-being and interests (Phil. 2:3–4).

Of course, there are times when you must speak to others in a firm or even blunt manner, especially if they have refused to pay attention to a gentle approach and are persisting in sinful behavior. Even so, it is wise to take a gentle approach first and get firmer only as necessary (1 Thess. 5:14–15). Strong words are more likely to evoke defensiveness and antagonism, and once a conversation takes on this tone, it is difficult to move to a friendlier plane.

Talk from Beside, Not from Above

When you need to show others their faults, do not talk down to them as though you are faultless and they are inferior to you. Instead, talk with them as though you are standing side by side at the foot of the cross. Acknowledge your present, ongoing need for the Savior. Admit ways that you have wrestled with the same or other sins or weaknesses, and give hope by describing how God has forgiven you and is currently working in you to help you change. (For an example of this approach, see the story on pages 139–141. When people sense this kind of humility and common bond, they will be less inclined to react to correction with pride and defensiveness.

Help Others Examine the Desires of Their Hearts

As we saw in chapter 5, the root cause of most conflict is desires in our hearts that have become so strong that they begin to consume and control us. These desires can become little gods or idols that dominate our thoughts, goals, and actions. Since these idols are often good things we have come to want too much, we are usually blind to how wrong and destructive they are. Until they are exposed and cast down, genuine peace and reconciliation will be elusive.

It is hard enough to talk to others about their sinful words and behavior; it is far more difficult to know and talk about what is going on in their hearts. In fact, unless someone specifically admits to a desire that is patently sinful, you can never know for sure what is going on in their hearts. So how can you help others recognize and repent of sinful desires that are fomenting conflict? The best starting point is to humbly describe the idols you have found in your own heart and confess how they have caused you to sin in this conflict or other similar situations. Refer specifically to passages like James 4:1–3 and Matthew 15:19, and explain how God is helping you recognize and fight against idolatrous desires in your own heart.

If the other person seems generally receptive to this concept, graciously suggest that perhaps he too is being influenced by good desires that have taken too strong of a grip on his heart. Recommend that he ask himself the X-ray questions provided in chapter 5. If he seems to trust your intentions, you could refer to specific behavior on his part that seems to reveal an underlying desire that has grown too strong. Although you cannot conclusively tell people what is going on in their own hearts, you can raise the issue and encourage them by example and by gracious teaching to examine their own hearts and break free from the idols that often fuel conflict. [4]

Choose the Right Time and Place

Timing is an essential ingredient of effective communication. If possible, do not discuss sensitive matters with someone who is tired, worried about other things, or in a bad mood. Nor should you approach someone about an important concern unless you will have enough time to discuss the matter thoroughly.

Likewise, give careful thought to where you will talk. Unless it is necessary, do not talk about sensitive matters in front of others. Try to find a place that is free of such distractions as television, other people, and loud noises. If the person with whom you need to talk is likely to be nervous or suspicious, it may be wise to select a place where he or she will feel relatively secure, perhaps at home.

Talk in Person Whenever Possible

As we discussed in chapter 7, communication is most effective when it is done as personally as possible. Therefore, face-to-face conversation is usually better than talking by telephone, because both people can see facial expressions and communicate with body language as well as with words. In contrast to a letter, oral communication allows you to see how the other person is taking your words, to clarify places where there may be some misunderstanding, and to get feedback before moving to other issues. These advantages can prevent you from making incorrect assumptions that would motivate you to write unnecessarily offensive things.

On the other hand, there are times when other forms of communication are helpful. For example, people in our society are not accustomed to having someone drop by their home for an important conversation without giving advance notice. Therefore, it may be wise to telephone to arrange for a personal conversation.

If delicate issues are involved, do not go into extended explanations over the phone. Instead, express your desire to meet as soon as it is convenient for the other person.

Letters can sometimes serve a useful purpose. If the other person has refused to respond positively to telephone calls or personal conversations, a brief letter may be the only way to invite further communication. If you must resort to communicating by letter, write as personally and graciously as possible. Avoid quoting numerous Bible references, or you will seem to be preaching. Also, at least during initial letters, do not try to explain or justify your conduct in writing, because it will probably be misunderstood. Use your letter to invite communication, and try to leave detailed explanations for a personal conversation. If time allows, set aside the first draft of a letter for a day or two. When you reread it, you may catch words that will do more harm than good. It may also be wise to ask a close friend to read the letter as well, because an objective reader may be able to identify needed changes. (If the letter contains personal or confidential information about someone else, however, you may need to delete that information before allowing anyone else to see your letter.)

The advantage of a letter is that it can be read and reread. Even if the other person doesn't like your words at first, they may seem more reasonable as the letter is read again later. The disadvantage of a letter is that it cannot change in response to the other person's reaction. Therefore, although letters are often useful, personal conversations are usually superior when it comes to reconciling people and resolving problems.

Engage Rather than Declare

One of the fastest ways to make people defensive is to abruptly announce what they have done wrong. If you launch into a direct and detailed description of their faults, they are likely to close their ears and launch a counterattack. Therefore, it is wise to think carefully about how to open a conversation in a way that shows genuine concern for the other person and engages him in listening to your words without being defensive.

If you are talking to a friend who trusts you and is not likely to react strongly to the issue you want to raise, you may be able to speak fairly candidly. You could affirm your respect and friendship and then describe your concern in direct terms.

If strong trust has not been built between you, however, or if the issue is likely to trigger defensiveness, you would be wise to broach your concern in an indirect way that engages the other person's heart and mind without putting him instantly on guard. One of the best ways to do this is to use a story that touches the other person's heart. Jesus was a master of this approach, using a wide variety of parables to engage people's hearts (Luke 10:25–37; 15:11–32). Nathan used this approach when he needed to show King David his sin (2 Sam. 12:1–13), as did Joab when he wanted to convince David to pardon Absalom (2 Sam. 14:1–22).

A similar technique is to use an analogy or metaphor that uses a familiar concept in the other person's life as an illustration of the way they themselves are behaving (Matt. 13:24–33, 44–52; Matt. 18:5, 23; 20:1). This could involve references to any topic that is important to the other person, which could include family, church, business, sports, or history. For example, when I need to talk to my son about failing to do his chores, I will often use a military metaphor. He admires soldiers, so when I appeal to his ideals of military discipline and respect, he listens more carefully. When I need to talk to my daughter about a relational issue, I will refer to a character she admires from one of the many books she reads. She aspires to noble character and close relationships, so she pays close attention when I compare her to one of her heroines. Similarly, if I need to talk with a pastor about a failure in his ministry, I will often use a shepherd metaphor, much as Nathan did when he approached David.

Whatever approach you use, your goal should be to describe your concern in a way that captures others' attention, appeals to their values, and gives hope that the issue can be resolved constructively. The more you engage another's heart and the less you declare his or her wrongs, the more likely he or she is to listen to you.

Communicate So Clearly That You Cannot Be Misunderstood

Many conflicts are caused or aggravated by misunderstandings. People may say things that are actually true or appropriate, but because they did not choose their words carefully, they leave room for others to misconstrue what they mean and take offense. One way to reduce misunderstandings is to remember a rule I was taught as an engineer: It is not good enough to communicate so that you can be understood. You should communicate so clearly that you cannot be misunderstood. (This principle is especially important for people who are in positions of leadership. Their words affect many people, and when they communicate in a way that leaves the door open for varying interpretations, they are setting the stage for misunderstanding and conflict.) Therefore, whenever you need to communicate important information, think carefully about your words and look for ways that they might be vague, imprecise, or potentially misleading. As you tighten up what you say, you can prevent many of the misunderstandings that fuel conflict.

Plan Your Words

I cannot overemphasize the importance of planning your words when you need to talk with others about their faults. In delicate situations, careful planning can make the difference between restored peace and increased hostility. The discipline of planning is highly commended in Scripture: "Those who plan what is good find love and faithfulness" (Prov. 14:22b). When you are dealing with important issues or sensitive people, you should think in advance about what you will say. In many cases, it will be wise to actually write out several things, such as:

The issues that you believe need to be addressed. (Define the problem as narrowly as possible so you can focus on the central issues and not get distracted by minor details.)

Words and topics that do not need to be included in your discussion and should be avoided because they are likely to offend the other person.

Analogies or metaphors that the other person will understand and value.

Words that describe your feelings (e.g., concerned, frustrated, confused, disappointed).

A description of the effect the problem is having on you and others.

Your suggestions and preferences for a solution to the problem.

The benefits that will be produced by cooperating to find a solution.

As you plan what to say, make every effort to use words that are gracious, clear, and constructive. It is helpful to write down some of the words you will use when discussing issues that are especially sensitive or likely to arouse strong differences of opinion. Although you cannot write a script for your entire conversation, planning some of your opening comments can help a conversation begin positively. Here are two examples of how to begin a conversation:

Telephone call: "Jim, this is Dave. I'm really sorry for what I said last Friday, and I know I was wrong to cut you off. If you have some time in the next day or two, I'd like to stop by so I can apologize in person and see how you would like to finish this project. Would that be all right with you?"

Face-to-face: "Thank you for taking time to talk with me. Lately I've had the feeling that you are disappointed with my work. If I have done something wrong or if there are specific ways I could improve my work, I would really like to hear about them. Could we sit down together and talk sometime soon?"

These kinds of opening statements clearly indicate that you do not want to continue an argument, but rather are seeking positive dialogue. Remember that *asking* for a meeting is less threatening than *telling* someone there will be a meeting. This approach will normally encourage the other person to at least give you an opportunity to talk.

In addition to planning your opening remarks, it is often wise to think of two or three ways the other person may respond to your words and then plan how you will handle each scenario. Even if the other person says something you didn't anticipate, your preparation will generally make it easier to respond. For example, you may anticipate that the person to whom you are going to talk could lose his or her temper. Here is a possible response:

"Ted, I can understand how frustrating it must be to have so much financial pressure. I can also see why you are upset about having to make a repair on the car so soon after I sold it to you. I'm trying to figure out what I should do about it, and it would help if I knew a little more about what went wrong with the engine. However, I think we could understand each other better if we talked in person, so could I stop by some evening this week?"

In responding to an angry reaction, remember that "a gentle answer turns away wrath, but a harsh word stirs up anger" (Prov. 15:1). Respond to anger with a gentle voice, relaxed posture, and calm gestures. Communicate in every way that you take the other's expression of anger seriously and want to help resolve the problems that prompt it. Plan ahead how to respond to possible objections and deal with them specifically and reasonably.

If you believe that the other person may refuse to meet with you, you may plan this kind of response:

"Ted, I need to tell you that according to our contract I do have the legal right to take the car back, keep your deposit, and let you worry about paying the repair bill. I'd rather not do that. I would still like to work this out in a way that is satisfactory to both of us. Would you at least be willing to think about what I'm suggesting, and I'll call you back in a couple of days?"

Again, don't depend on the other person to follow your script. You will need to be flexible in responding to new developments. Generally speaking, however, if you are prepared when you begin a conversation, you will feel more confident and will be able to deal with developments more constructively. In fact, if you are concerned about your ability to make yourself understood, ask a close friend to role-play with you so you can practice what you plan to say. This may be awkward at first, but it often pays great dividends, especially for people who have difficulty thinking clearly in tense situations.

Use "I" Statements

One of the most helpful skills Corlette has taught me is how to use "I" statements. The statements give information about yourself rather than attack the other person—as is the case when you make statements like "You are so insensitive" or "You are just irresponsible." A typical formula for an "I" statement is "I feel ___ when you ___, because ___. As a result ___."

The following examples fill in the blanks:

> "I feel hurt when you make fun of me in front of other people, because it makes me feel stupid and foolish. As a result, I am getting reluctant to go places with you when others may be around."

> "I feel frustrated when you fail to keep your commitments, because you play a key role in this department. As a result, I'm finding it difficult to depend on you or work with you."

> "I feel confused when you say that I never listen, because two days ago I sat here for over an hour while you shared several deep concerns with me. I really don't know what to do differently."

"I" statements can accomplish three things. First, they tell the other person how his or her conduct is affecting you. By bringing yourself into the picture, you can reduce defensiveness and encourage concern in the person you are addressing. Second, this kind of statement identifies what the other person has done that you are concerned about. By defining the problem specifically and not bringing in unrelated issues, you further reduce the chance of threatening the other person. Third, an "I" statement can explain why this issue is important to you and why you would like to discuss it. The more the other person understands your concerns and the effect the behavior is having on you (and possibly others), the more motivated and willing he or she may be to discuss and deal with the problem.

Be Objective

When you are trying to show someone his fault, keep your remarks as objective as possible. While an expression of personal perceptions and feelings may help someone understand your feelings, if you emphasize subjective opinions and judgments too much, you are likely to convey condescension or condemnation. Therefore, use objective facts whenever you can.

Along the same line, make an effort not to exaggerate. Phrases like "you always," "you never," and "every time" reduce the likelihood that others will take the rest of what you say seriously. Here are some illustrations of these principles:

Say, "You were late for work five times in the last two weeks," rather than, "You are *always* late for work."

Say, "John's grades have dropped in three classes," rather than, "Don't you see that your son's performance in school is a *mess?*"

Say, "The fact is, I have gotten to the point that I prefer not to work on committees with you," rather than, "*Nobody* likes to work with you."

Use the Bible Carefully

It is often helpful to refer to the Bible as a source of objective truth when you have a disagreement with another Christian. If this is not done with great care, however, it will alienate people rather than persuade them. Here are a few basic principles to keep in mind when you use the Scriptures as part of a discussion:

Keep Ephesians 4:29 in mind. Don't quote the Bible to tear others down, but only to build them up in the Lord.

Make sure you are using a passage for its intended purpose. Don't pull a verse out of context and try to make it say something other than its clear meaning.

If possible, encourage others to read the passage from their own Bibles; then ask, "What do you think that means?" This often achieves better results than imposing your interpretation on them.

Know when to stop. If the other person appears to be getting irritated by your references to Scripture, it may be wise to back off and give him or her time to think about it. (Backing off would not be appropriate if formal church discipline is under way and the person is clearly trying to avoid clear biblical warnings and admonishments.)[5]

Ask for Feedback

When talking to another person, one of your primary goals should be to match impact with intent. In other words, you want to make sure that what you meant to say has actually gotten across to the other person completely and accurately. If the other person responds by clarifying, reflecting, or agreeing with what you say, you will have a fairly good idea whether or not he or she is getting your message.

In many cases, however, it will be difficult to tell what impact your words are having on the other person. Therefore, you will sometimes need to ask the other person to give you some feedback. Here are some ways you can do so:

> "I'm not sure I've said this clearly. Would you mind telling me what you think I've said?"
>
> "Have I confused you?"
>
> "Have I explained myself clearly enough?"
>
> "What are you thinking about the meeting?"
>
> "What have I said that you would agree with? What would you disagree with?"

Asking questions will promote dialogue and give you an opportunity to measure how well you are communicating as well as how the other person is responding to you. As you take that information into account, you can clarify as needed and adjust what you say to suit developments. As a result, your subsequent words will normally be more relevant and productive.

Offer Solutions and Preferences

When you speak to others about issues in their lives, be prepared to offer solutions to the specific problems you have identified. If you can show a person a reasonable way out of a predicament, he or she may be more inclined to listen to you. Hope is a key ingredient in promoting repentance and change.

At the same time, try not to give the impression that you have *all* the answers. Make it clear that your suggestions are just a starting point and offer to discuss any ideas the other person has. It may be helpful to tell him or her about your preferences and encourage an exchange of preferences. Here are some examples:

> "I would prefer to renegotiate the contract rather than abandon it, but I'm open to suggestions. What would you prefer?"
> "My first choice would be to get the whole family together to discuss Dad's will in person. What do you think?"

Again, the more you can promote dialogue and reasonable thinking, the less likely people will be to remain entrenched in one position. If you give them creative ways to deal with a situation and set an example of openly weighing various options, the discussion can result in real progress.

Recognize Your Limits

Finally, whenever you are trying to show someone his fault, remember that there are limits to what you can accomplish. You can raise concerns, suggest solutions, and encourage reasonable thinking, but you cannot force change. God may use you as a spokesperson to bring certain issues to the attention of another person, but only God can actually penetrate the other person's heart and bring about repentance. Paul clearly describes this division of labor in 2 Timothy 2:24–26: "And the Lord's servant must not quarrel; instead, he must be kind to everyone, able to teach, not resentful. Those who oppose him he must gently instruct, *in the hope that God will grant them repentance leading them to a knowledge of the truth,* and that they will come to their senses and escape the trap of the devil, who has taken them captive to do his will" (emphasis added).

As we have seen throughout this book, God calls us to be concerned with faithfulness, not with results. If you prayerfully prepare, speak the truth in love, and do all you can to effectively communicate your concerns to the other person, you will have succeeded in God's eyes regardless of how others respond (see Acts 20:26–27). God will take it from there—in his time your words will produce exactly the results he wants.

Summary and Application

Ron Kraybill, a respected Christian mediator, has noted that "effective confrontation is like a graceful dance from supportiveness to assertiveness and back again."[6] This dance may feel awkward at first for those who are just learning it, but perseverance pays off. With God's help you can learn to speak the truth in love by saying only what will build others up, by listening responsibly to what others say, and by using principles of wisdom. As you practice these skills and make them a normal part of your everyday conversations, you will be well prepared to use them when conflict breaks out. In developing the skills of loving confrontation, you can see for yourself that "the tongue of the wise brings healing."

If you are presently involved in a conflict, these questions will help you apply the principles presented in this chapter.

1. When you talk to or about your opponent, what might you be tempted to say that would be harmful or worthless?
2. How can you offer hope to the other person by focusing on what God has done and is doing?
3. Which listening skills do you have a hard time with: waiting, attending, clarifying, reflecting, or agreeing? Write down some things you will do or say to overcome these weaknesses.
4. Are you trying to believe the best about the other person (i.e., making charitable judgments)? How could you demonstrate that you are doing this?
5. What can you say that would clearly communicate your love and concern for your opponent?
6. What is the best time and place to talk with your opponent?
7. Would it be wiser to communicate in person, on the phone, or by means of a letter? Why?
8. Write a brief summary of what you need to say and avoid saying, including

   The issues you believe should be addressed

   Words and topics to avoid

   Stories or comparisons that the other person will understand and value

Words that describe your feelings

A description of the effect the dispute is having on you
and others

Your suggestions and preferences for a solution

The benefits that will be produced by cooperating to
find a solution

9. How could you improve what you intend to communicate
so that you cannot be misunderstood?

10. Plan your opening statement. What are three ways that your
opponent may react to this statement? How could you respond
constructively to each of these reactions?

11. Write some of the "I" statements you could use.

12. How can you show that you are trying to be objective?

13. How can you refer to Scripture in a helpful manner?

14. How will you ask for feedback?

15. Go on record with the Lord by writing a prayer based on the
principles taught in this chapter.

9

TAKE ONE OR TWO
OTHERS ALONG

But if he will not listen, take one or two others along,
so that "every matter may be established by the testimony of two or three witnesses."

Matthew 18:16

As we have seen in the preceding chapters, the Bible encourages Christians to make every effort to resolve their
differences as personally as possible. If we draw on God's grace
and follow the principles he has given to us in Scripture, we can
resolve most conflicts on our own. But sometimes we need help.
As we saw in chapter 7, there are situations where it is best to have
someone else act as an intermediary before we even try to talk with
another person. In other cases, if we are not able to resolve our
differences in private, we may need to ask one or more respected
friends, church leaders, or other godly and unbiased individuals to
help us be reconciled. Jesus himself sets forth the framework for
seeking help from others to resolve a conflict:

If your brother sins against you,[1] go and show him his fault, just between the two of you. If he listens to you, you have won your brother over. But if he will not listen, take one or two others along, so that "every matter may be established by the testimony of two or three witnesses." If he refuses to listen to them, tell it to the church; and if he refuses to listen even to the church, treat him as you would a pagan or a tax collector.

I tell you the truth, whatever you bind on earth will be bound in heaven, and whatever you loose on earth will be loosed in heaven. Again, I tell you that if two of you on earth agree about anything you ask for, it will be done for you by my Father in heaven. For where two or three come together in my name, there am I with them.

Matthew 18:15–20

In this passage, Jesus teaches us how to minister to a fellow Christian who is caught in sin. Since prolonged conflict usually involves sin (James 4:1), this passage is directly applicable to peacemaking. (The apostle Paul probably had this teaching in mind when he instructed Christians to resolve their legal disputes with the help of fellow Christians rather than in secular courts; see 1 Cor. 6:1–8.) In this chapter we will walk through this process step-by-step and see how you can apply it as you seek to restore someone to a right relationship with God and other people.

The Matthew 18 Process

A general principle taught in Matthew 18 is that we should try to keep the circle of people involved in a conflict *as small as possible for as long as possible*. If we can resolve a dispute personally and privately, we should do so. But if we cannot settle matters on our own, we should seek help from other people, expanding the circle only as much as necessary to bring about repentance and reconciliation. This is one of the great blessings of belonging to the church: Whenever you cannot handle a problem or conflict on your own, you can turn to the body of Christ for guidance and assistance. This process of involving others may involve five steps.

Step One: Overlook Minor Offenses

Before you consider involving others in a conflict, it is wise to review the steps that you can take to resolve a dispute in private. To begin with, evaluate how you can use the situation as an opportunity to glorify God, serve others, and grow to be like Christ (see chapters 1–3). Then seriously consider resolving the dispute unilaterally by overlooking minor offenses and giving up certain personal rights (see chapter 4).

Step Two: Talk in Private

If you have wronged someone else, God calls you to go to the other person to seek forgiveness (see chapters 5 and 6). If another person has committed a wrong that is too serious to overlook, it is your responsibility to go the other person and show him his fault, making every effort to resolve personal issues and promote genuine reconciliation (see chapters 7 and 8). Or, if you are dealing with material issues that are too important to walk away from, you can try to reach an agreement through negotiation (see chapter 11). Throughout this effort, it is appropriate to seek counsel and encouragement from godly advisors who can help you see your own faults more clearly and respond to the other person wisely. If repeated efforts to resolve the matter in these private ways fail, and if the matter is too serious to overlook, you may proceed to the next step in the Matthew 18 process.

Step Three: Take One or Two Others Along

If a dispute cannot be resolved in private, Jesus tells us to ask other people to get involved. "But if he will not listen, take one or two others along, so that 'every matter may be established by the testimony of two or three witnesses'" (Matt. 18:16). Paul gives the same instruction in Philippians 4:2–3. In some cases, the others may serve as intermediaries, shuttling between both sides to promote understanding (see chapter 7). In most cases, however, they will act initially as mediators, meeting with both parties simultaneously to improve communication and offer biblical counsel. If necessary, they may eventually serve as arbitrators and provide a binding decision about how to resolve the matter (see 1 Cor. 6:1–8). There are two ways that outside people can become involved in a dispute.

By mutual agreement. If you and your opponent cannot resolve a dispute in private, you can suggest that the two of you ask one or more unbiased individuals to meet with you in an effort to facilitate more productive dialogue. These individuals may be mutual friends, church leaders, godly and respected individuals in your community, or trained Christian mediators or arbitrators. For the purposes of this discussion, I will refer to all of these persons as "reconcilers."

Although reconciler training can be very beneficial (see appendix E), reconcilers do not have to be professionally trained to serve in personal disputes. Rather, they should be wise and spiritually mature Christians who are worthy of your respect and trust (1 Cor. 6:5; Gal. 6:1). If your dispute involves technical issues, it is helpful if one or more of the reconcilers has experience in that area. For example, if your dispute involves alleged defects in the construction of a building, an experienced architect or builder might serve as a reconciler. Likewise, when legal issues are at stake, it is wise to include an attorney.

Some of the best reconcilers are people who are personally acquainted with you or your opponent, or better yet, who know both of you quite well. Such familiarity is not recommended in secular mediation, out of fear that it will allow partiality. But if you are dealing with spiritually mature reconcilers, this potential for bias should be more than offset by their commitment before God to do what is just and right. In fact, my experience has shown that someone who knows you well will have greater freedom to be honest and frank, and that is exactly what you need in a reconciler.

If your opponent balks at your suggestion to involve others, carefully explain why doing so would be beneficial. If the person is a Christian, you can refer to Matthew 18 and 1 Corinthians 6 as the biblical basis for your suggestion. Whether or not you are dealing with a fellow Christian, you can describe the practical benefits of involving others: saving time, money, and energy (when compared to more formal legal processes); avoiding publicity; receiving the benefit of others' experience and creativity. (Appendix B describes some of these benefits in detail.) You may also share materials produced by Peacemaker Ministries or encourage your opponent to talk personally with an experienced reconciler. If you give sufficient information and enough time to think about it, the other person is more likely to agree to involve a reconciler.[2]

On your initiative. While mutual agreement is always preferable, it is not actually required if your opponent professes to be a Christian. Matthew 18:16 indicates that you may seek help from reconcilers even if your opponent doesn't want it. Before you take this step, however, it is wise and often beneficial to warn your opponent what you are about to do. For example, you might say, "Bob, I would prefer to resolve this matter just between the two of us. Since that has not happened and because this involves issues that are too important to walk away from, my only other option is to obey what the Bible commands, which means asking some people from our churches to help us out. I would prefer that we go together to get that help, but if you will not cooperate, I'll ask for it by myself."

I have seen many cases where a statement like that has helped "Bob" to change his mind. If he is aware of the fact that he is partly at fault in the matter, he may not want someone from his church to get involved; therefore, he may suddenly become more willing to work with you in private. On the other hand, he may at least decide to participate in selecting the reconcilers, if for no other reason than to keep you from gaining some sort of advantage.

If your Christian opponent does not agree to cooperate, you may enlist the help of reconcilers in several ways. If you can get the help of someone your opponent is likely to respect and trust, you and that reconciler may personally visit your opponent and ask to talk. If you have good reason to believe that your opponent would be seriously offended by this approach, you may ask the reconciler to talk to your opponent individually in an effort to set up a meeting with you and the reconciler later. You may contact your opponent's church and ask for help from one of its leaders. Depending on the circumstances, a pastor or elder may either go with you or talk to your opponent privately in an effort to facilitate a joint meeting.

Regardless of how you enlist the help of reconcilers in achieving your opponent's participation, make every effort not to give them unnecessary details about the conflict. Simply explain that you and the other person are at odds and need their help. If you go into detail with the reconcilers, the other party might naturally conclude that they have already been biased in your favor. Even worse, doing so may encourage you to slander or gossip. Only when you and the other person are both present should you give a detailed explanation of your perceptions. Writing a letter to request assistance may be wiser in some situations. In this case, send a copy to your opponent so he or she will know what you have said—and not said. Here is an example of such a letter:

> Dear Pastor Smith,
>
> I am involved in a dispute with John Jones, who I believe is a member of your church. John and I have not been able to resolve this matter in private. Because I want to follow God's instructions in 1 Corinthians 6:1–8 and Matthew 18:15–20, I would deeply appreciate it if you or another leader in your church would be willing to meet with us and help us come to an agreement. In fairness to John, I will not go into any detail about the dispute in this letter other than to say that it involves John's purchase of a business from me. I will wait until he and I are with you so you can hear both of our perspectives at the same time.
>
> If you or one of the leaders in your church would be willing to help us resolve this matter, I would be able to meet with you and John any evening during the next few weeks. One of the elders from my church would be willing to meet with us as well.
>
> I know you have many other things to do, and I regret having to burden you with this request. But in the interest of peace and unity among Christians, I don't feel I can leave matters unresolved between John and me. I would deeply appreciate your assistance. (By the way, I have sent a copy of this letter to John so he knows what I have communicated to you.)

If initial attempts to arrange a meeting are unsuccessful, the reconcilers may make repeated attempts to talk with or write to your opponent. They should not give up until the opponent adamantly refuses to listen. If that happens, the church may have to move to a more formal process, which we will discuss later in this chapter.

What do reconcilers do?

Reconcilers can play a variety of roles in a conflict. Their primary role is to help you and your opponent make the decisions needed to restore peace. In doing so, they may apply many of the listening and communication skills described in chapter 8. At first they may simply facilitate communication by encouraging both sides to listen more carefully to each other. They may also help determine the facts by listening carefully themselves, by asking appropriate questions, and by helping you and the other person obtain additional facts.

As implied by Matthew 18:17 and 1 Corinthians 6:1–8, the reconcilers may also give advice on how to deal with the problem. They may encourage repentance and confession on either or both sides by pointing out any behavior that has been inconsistent with what is taught in the Bible. They may also facilitate biblical solutions to material issues by directing you to relevant principles and examples in Scripture. Finally, they may draw on their own knowledge and experience to propose practical solutions to specific problems.

If you and your opponent want them to, the reconcilers may also help resolve a deadlock. You may jointly ask the reconcilers to suggest an appropriate solution to the problem. (Wise reconcilers, however, make sure that every effort has been made to reach a voluntary solution before they give an advisory opinion.) In fact, even before you begin to discuss any issues with the reconcilers, you and your opponent may agree that if you are not able to reach a voluntary solution, you will abide by the reconcilers' counsel, provided it does not require you to violate principles taught in Scripture. If you want to, you may make this agreement legally binding, which means that the reconcilers will serve as arbitrators and render a decision that is enforceable by a civil court. Although decisions imposed by others are often less satisfactory than voluntary agreements, they are normally preferable to litigation, which can drag on for months or years at great financial, emotional, and spiritual expense.[3]

Finally, if either you or the other person refuses to resolve material issues or to be reconciled, the reconcilers may serve as "witnesses" to report to your respective churches what they have observed during reconciliation efforts (Matt. 18:16). This information may help your church or churches discern the reason for the deadlock and assist them in deciding how to resolve the matter.

Step three may be followed even when your opponent claims to be a Christian but is not acting like one. In fact, this step is specifically designed to help professed believers get their actions back in line with their words.

What if my opponent is not a Christian?

The basic principles of step three can also be applied when the other person does not profess to be a Christian. Some modifications may be needed, of course. Formal church involvement will not be possible, and you will not be able to hold the other person to the biblical standards you must follow. Furthermore, your opponent must voluntarily consent to mediation or arbitration and may need to be persuaded that the reconcilers can offer objective and helpful advice. In spite of these limitations, the process can still be beneficial and productive, especially if you keep in mind the principles discussed elsewhere in this book.

Step Four: Tell It to the Church (Church Accountability)

If your opponent professes to be a Christian and yet refuses to listen to the reconcilers' counsel, and if the matter is too serious to overlook, Jesus commands you to "tell it to the church" (Matt. 18:17). This does not mean standing up in a worship service and broadcasting the conflict to church members and visitors alike, since unwarranted publicity is totally inconsistent with the intent of Matthew 18. Instead, you should inform the leadership of the other person's church (and probably yours as well) of the problem and request their assistance in promoting justice and peace by holding both of you accountable to God's Word and to your commitments.[4]

Church leaders may consult with the reconcilers and confirm their counsel (especially if one of the reconcilers is a member of that church), or they may conduct an entirely independent investigation and give their own counsel. As with the decision of secular arbitrators, the church's opinion is intended to be binding on its own member, whether the party likes it or not. As Matthew

18:18–20 teaches, the church speaks with the authority of Christ himself when it acts pursuant to its biblical mandate to deal with sin (cf. Matt. 16:18; Heb. 13:17). First Corinthians 6:1–8 indicates that this authority extends not only to personal issues, but also to material issues. The only time a Christian may properly disobey his church is when its instructions are clearly contrary to what the Scriptures teach (see Matt. 23:1–3; Acts 4:18–20; 5:27–32).

If the other party's church gives advice that you will not follow, then your church must work in conjunction with the other church until a satisfactory solution is obtained. If either party adamantly refuses to listen to the advice of his respective church, other members of the church may need to be informed in a discreet and appropriate way so that they may also hold the stubborn party accountable to his responsibility to do what is right. Instead of associating with a stubborn brother (or sister) as though nothing were wrong, Christian friends should gently but firmly remind him that he has important business to take care of before he can properly worship God and take part in fellowship (2 Thess. 3:6, 14–15; 1 Cor. 5:9–11). If that does not resolve the problem, the church should proceed with step five.[5]

Step Five: Treat Him as a Nonbeliever

As I have shown repeatedly, God calls his people to act justly, seek peace, and be reconciled with others. If a Christian refuses to do these things, he is violating God's will. If he refuses to listen to his church's counsel to repent of this sin, Jesus says the church should "treat him *as* you would a pagan or a tax collector" (Matt. 18:17, emphasis added). Jesus' use of the word *as* is significant. Since only God can know a person's heart (1 Sam. 16:7; Rev. 2:23), the church has no power to decide whether a person *is* a believer. Instead, the church is called only to make a functional decision: If a person behaves like a nonbeliever would—by disregarding the authority of Scripture and of Christ's church—he should be treated as if he were a nonbeliever.

In other words, the church should not pretend that things are all right with people who claim to be Christians and yet refuse to listen to God as he speaks through the Scriptures and the church.

Treating unrepentant people as unbelievers is sometimes the only way to help them understand the seriousness of their sin. This may be accomplished by withdrawing various membership privileges, such as communion, church office, or teaching Sunday school, and may culminate in revoking their membership status altogether if they persist in their refusal to repent of sin.

But treating others as unbelievers also means that we look for every opportunity to evangelize them. We remind them again and again of the good news of salvation through Jesus Christ and urge them to receive his forgiveness by repenting of and turning from their sin. If they are behaving in a way that disrupts the peace of the church, it may be appropriate to exclude them from church property. Otherwise, we should welcome them to Sunday worship, as we do other nonbelievers. But instead of talking to them in superficial ways, we should graciously and repeatedly remind them of the gospel and urge them to repent of their wrongs. This treatment is designed to bring conviction to stubborn people, with the purpose of leading them to turn from their sinful ways and to be restored to fellowship with God and fellow believers. (This appears to have been the result of the discipline administered in the Corinthian church. Compare 1 Cor. 5:1–13 with 2 Cor. 2:5–11.)

Treating someone as a nonbeliever serves three important purposes. First, revoking the person's membership in the church prevents the Lord from being dishonored if that person continues to act in blatantly sinful ways (Rom. 2:23–24). Second, other believers are protected from being led astray by a bad example or divisive behavior (Rom. 16:17; 1 Cor. 5:1–6). Third, treating someone as a nonbeliever may help the rebellious person to realize the seriousness of his or her sin, turn from it, and be restored to God. This third purpose bears repeating. The intention in treating others as nonbelievers is not to injure them or punish them, but rather to help them see the seriousness of their sin and their need for repentance. Jesus loved people caught in sin enough to warn them of their sinful condition and its consequences and to urge them to repent (e.g., Mark 2:17; John 4:1–18). The church should do no less.[6]

Many Christians balk at this teaching. Some churches ignore or refuse to implement Matthew 18:17, even though the Bible teaches that God views accountability and discipline as an act of love and an important means to restore his wandering sheep and protect his people from being led astray by sinful examples. "My son, do not despise the LORD's discipline and do not resent his rebuke, because the LORD disciplines those he loves, as a father the son he delights in" (Prov. 3:11–12; see also Heb. 12:1–13; 1 Cor. 5:6; Rev. 3:19). By ignoring this teaching, a church is not only disobeying Jesus' specific commands, but also failing to face up to the seriousness of sin and its consequences (see Ezek. 34:4, 8–10). As Dietrich Bonhoeffer writes, "Nothing is so cruel as the tenderness that consigns another to his sin. Nothing can be more compassionate than the severe rebuke that calls a brother back from the path of sin."[7]

Consider this analogy. When a patient has cancer, it is not easy for his doctor to tell him, because it is a truth that is painful to hear and difficult to bear. Even so, any doctor who diagnoses cancer but fails to report it to a patient would be guilty of malpractice. After all, a patient can be properly treated only after the disease has been identified. Sin works in the same way; left undiagnosed and untreated, it causes increasing grief and spiritual deterioration (Prov. 10:17; 13:18; 29:1; Rom. 6:23). The church has a responsibility both to promote peace and unity and to help believers disentangle themselves from the terrible effects of sin (Gal. 6:1–2). Treating someone as an unbeliever is a serious and painful step, but it is also an act of obedience to God and a loving remedy for the person caught in sin.

This truth was powerfully illustrated when a man told his wife that he was filing for divorce and moving in with another woman. When the wife was unable to dissuade him, she went to their pastor for advice. He gave her several suggestions on how to persuade her husband to change his mind or at least to come in for counseling. Nothing she said to her husband during the next few days dissuaded him, and he began to pack his things.

In desperation, she returned to her pastor and asked him to talk with her husband. At first, the pastor declined to take an active role, saying that he "did not want to scare him away from the church." The wife asked the pastor how he could take such a position in the light of Matthew 18:15–20, Galatians 6:1–2, and many related passages. After a long discussion, the pastor finally realized that he was neglecting his responsibilities as a shepherd.

As a result, he went to visit the husband that evening and offered to help him work out his marital problems. When the husband adamantly refused to change his course, the pastor pleaded with him to change his mind and offered all of the resources of the church to help solve the problems in his marriage. When even that did not dissuade the husband, the pastor finally explained the Matthew 18 process and said, "I can't stop you from filing for divorce, but I must tell you that you may be removed from church membership if you deliberately violate Scripture as you are planning to do." After he got over his initial shock, the husband said, "You mean I'll be kicked out of the church for divorcing my wife?"

"Under these circumstances," the pastor replied, "yes." Hearing this, the husband lost his temper and ordered the pastor out of his home. Early the next morning, however, the pastor received a phone call from the husband, who wanted to talk with him again. They met an hour later, and by ten o'clock that morning the husband was on the telephone telling the "other woman" that he would not be moving in with her. Later that day the pastor began counseling with this couple, and together they started to work out the deep problems that had brought them to this crisis. Ten years later, they are still raising their family together and thanking God for a pastor who cared enough to get involved the way Jesus commanded.

I wish I could say that all interventions turn out this well, but obviously they don't. Even so, I know of many marriages that are together today because churches obeyed Jesus' teaching in Matthew 18:15–20. More importantly, even in those cases where one party proceeded on a sinful course in spite of efforts to hold him accountable, the churches at least knew that they had been faithful to the Lord. Such faithfulness can significantly increase the respect church members have for their leaders and for Scripture. At the same time, it sends a message that willful sin will not be casually overlooked, which encourages others in the church to work out their problems in a biblically faithful manner.

Is It Time to Go to Court?

When a dispute with another Christian cannot be resolved even through the intervention of your church or churches, you have only a few options left. One choice would be to drop the matter and give up any claims you have against the other person, which may be the best thing to do in some situations (see 1 Cor. 6:7–8). Another choice would be to try to persuade your opponent to accept some other form of alternative dispute resolution (see appendix B). A third choice would be to file a lawsuit. Since the Bible generally prohibits Christians from suing one another in civil court (1 Cor. 6:1–8), you should not file suit unless you have exhausted all other possible remedies and carefully weighed the cost of moving into litigation (see chapter 4). In appendix D you will find a detailed discussion on how to evaluate the advisability of litigation in various situations.

The World Needs Reconcilers!

If you think back on the last six months of your life, you can probably think of several people in your family, church, or work-place who were having difficulty resolving conflict. In most cases, they may only have needed someone to briefly explain a few of the basic peacemaking principles described in this book. In other situations, it would have been helpful to have another person sit down with both sides in the conflict to help them understand each other, admit and forgive personal offenses, and reach an agreement on material issues. In other words, they needed a reconciler to help them walk through the process described above.

Perhaps God is calling you to learn how to be a reconciler. If so, reconciler training can help you develop communication, counseling, and mediation skills that you could use to guide other people through conflict. You can use these skills on a personal level to serve friends, relatives, or coworkers who are struggling with the normal conflicts of daily life. If you are a church or ministry leader, you can teach and assist members of your church to resolve their differences biblically. And if you are a manager or professional, reconciler skills can improve your ability to lead employees or clients through conflict in a constructive manner.

If you would like to learn more about being a reconciler, I encourage you to read *Guiding People through Conflict*, a booklet that provides an introduction to basic reconciler skills. Appendix E describes Peacemaker Ministries' reconciler training program, and even more information is available on our web site. As you study this information, you could also be thinking about other people in your church who seem to have a gift for peacemaking and would benefit from further training. The church and the world need more reconcilers, so please pray about whether God is calling you to improve your skills and serve him by guiding others through conflict.

Developing a Culture of Peace in Your Church

I thank God that there is a growing number of churches that are committed and prepared to assist their members in following the process described in this chapter. They have built an environment in which their people are eager and able to resolve conflict and reconcile relationships in a way that clearly reflects the love and power of Jesus Christ. This environment, which I refer to as a "culture of peace," has the following characteristics:

Vision: The church is eager to bring glory to God by demonstrating the reconciling love and forgiveness of Jesus Christ, and therefore sees peacemaking as an essential part of the Christian life.

Training: The church knows that peacemaking does not come naturally, so it deliberately trains both its leaders and members to respond to conflict biblically in all areas of life.

Assistance: When members cannot resolve disputes privately, the church assists them through in-house trained reconcilers, even when conflicts involve financial, employment, or legal issues.

Perseverance: Just as God pursues us, the church works long and hard to restore broken relationships, especially when a marriage is at stake, and even when attorneys are involved.

Accountability: If members refuse to listen to private correction, church leaders get directly involved to hold members accountable to Scripture and to promote repentance, justice, and forgiveness.

Restoration: Wanting to imitate God's amazing mercy and grace, the church gladly forgives and fully restores members who have genuinely repented of serious and embarrassing sins.

Stability: Because relationships are valued and protected, leaders serve fruitfully year after year and members see the church as their long-term home.

Witness: Members are equipped and encouraged to practice peacemaking so openly in their daily lives that others will notice, ask why they do it, and hear about the love of Christ.

A culture of peace helps preserve marriages and other relationships. It also reduces conflict, membership turnover, and exposure to legal liability. Best of all, it improves a church's evangelistic witness. For more information on how to develop this kind of culture in your church, read appendix F. I hope your church will join the growing number of churches that are experiencing these benefits by equipping and assisting their people to respond to conflict biblically.

Summary and Application

By God's grace, most conflicts between Christians can be resolved by talking personally and privately with someone who has offended you. When personal efforts do not succeed, Jesus has given us a simple yet effective process for involving other people who can promote understanding and agreement. When this involvement is carried out with prayer, wisdom, and reliance on the power of the gospel, God is pleased to use our efforts to promote just settlements and preserve relationships that would otherwise have been lost.

If you are presently involved in a conflict and have not been able to resolve it privately, these questions will help you to apply the principles presented in this chapter.

1. Are the personal or material issues in this conflict too serious to overlook or walk away from? Why?

2. Why do you think your efforts to resolve this dispute in private have failed? Is there anything you could still do to resolve it in private?

3. If you must seek outside help to resolve this dispute, are there any persons who are likely to be trusted and respected by both you and your opponent?

4. What will you say to your opponent to encourage him or her to allow other people to meet with the two of you to help resolve this dispute? In particular, how would you describe the advantages of getting outside assistance?

5. If your opponent refuses to work voluntarily with others, would it be better to drop the matter or to ask the church to get involved? Why?

6. If all other avenues have failed to resolve this matter and you are considering filing a lawsuit, have you satisfied the conditions set forth in appendix D?

7. Go on record with the Lord by writing a prayer based on the principles taught in this chapter.

PART 4

GO AND BE RECONCILED

How can I demonstrate the forgiveness of God and encourage a reasonable solution to this conflict?

First go and be reconciled to your brother; then come and offer your gift.

Matthew 5:24

I just can't forgive Pam's adultery," Rick said. "She says she's sorry and she's begged for forgiveness, but I can't forget what she did. It's like a huge wall between us, and I can't get through it."

"So you think divorce is the answer?" I asked.

"I don't know what else to do! I told her that I forgive her, but I just can't be close to her again. She's depressed and has withdrawn even further from me. I'm afraid she's going to look for intimacy with someone else again. We're both in agony, and it seems like we'd be better off divorced."

I could see the weariness in his face. "I'm sure both of you are in terrible pain, Rick. But I don't think divorce is going to end it. You'll just trade one kind of pain for another. There is a way to keep your marriage together and to truly put the past behind you. But you won't find it with the empty forgiveness you've offered Pam."

"What do you mean, 'empty forgiveness'?"

"Rick, imagine that you had just confessed a serious sin to God, and for the first time in your life he spoke to you audibly: 'I forgive you, Rick, but I can't ever be close to you again.' How would you feel?"

After an awkward pause, he replied, "I guess I'd feel like God hadn't really forgiven me."

"But isn't that exactly the way you are forgiving Pam?" I asked.

Rick looked at the floor, wrestling for an answer.

In a softer voice, I continued, "Imagine instead that God said, 'Rick, I forgive you. I promise never to think about your sin again, or to dwell on it or brood over it. I promise never to bring it up and use it against you. I promise not to talk to others about it. And I promise not to let this sin stand between us or hinder our relationship.'"

After a long silence, tears began to fill Rick's eyes. "I would know I was completely forgiven . . . But I wouldn't deserve that kind of forgiveness after the way I've treated Pam."

"Would you ever deserve it?" I asked. "God's forgiveness is a free gift purchased for you by Jesus' death on the cross. He doesn't forgive you because you've earned it. He forgives you because he loves you. When you truly understand how precious and undeserved his forgiveness is, you will want to forgive Pam the same way he has forgiven you."

"I know I *should,* but how could I ever keep those promises? I can't imagine forgetting what Pam did! And I just don't feel like I could ever be close to her again."

"Hold on, Rick. Where in the Bible does it say that forgiveness is forgetting? Or that it depends on feelings? Forgiveness is a choice, a decision you make by God's grace in spite of your feelings. Of course it's hard, especially in a case like this. But if you ask for God's help as you make those promises to Pam, he will give you the grace to follow through on them."

We talked another thirty minutes about God's forgiveness. As Rick reflected on how much God had forgiven him, he discovered a longing to do the same with Pam. We prayed together, and then I called Pam and asked her to join us at my office. When she came in, doubt and fear were written all over her face.

As soon as she had sat down, Rick began. "Pam, I need to ask for your forgiveness. I have sinned so terribly against you. You asked me to forgive you, and I wouldn't give you real forgiveness. Instead, I have punished you with my bitterness and coldness. I have been so wrong. Will you please forgive me?"

Pam dissolved in tears. In between sobs, she poured out her own feelings of guilt and shame, along with her fear that Rick could never really forget what she had done.

Reaching out to take her hand, Rick responded, "I can understand your fear. I haven't handled this the way I should. I forgot how much God has forgiven me. But he has helped me today, and I want to forgive you the way he has forgiven me. With his help, I promise not to dwell on this anymore. I promise never to bring it up and use it against you. I promise not to talk to others about it. And I promise not to let it stand between us."

Rick wrapped his arms around Pam, and they cried together for several minutes. By offering her the redeeming forgiveness modeled by our Lord, Rick had brought life and hope back into their marriage. Although they would spend many hours of pastoral counseling to address the root causes of their marital problems, forgiveness had cleared a path through the rubble of the past. By God's grace, they could now deal with those problems in a way that could result in a completely restored marriage and a powerful testimony to the reconciling power of Jesus Christ.

10

FORGIVE
AS GOD FORGAVE YOU

Bear with each other and forgive whatever grievances
you may have against one another. Forgive as the Lord
forgave you.

Colossians 3:13

Christians are the most forgiven people in the world.
Therefore, we should be the most forgiving people in
the world. As most of us know from experience, however, it is often
difficult to forgive others genuinely and completely. We often find
ourselves practicing a form of forgiveness that is neither biblical
nor healing.

Perhaps you have said or thought the same thing Rick said to his
wife: "I forgive you—I just can't be close to you again." Think of
this statement in light of the prayer you have prayed many times,
"Forgive us our debts, as we also have forgiven our debtors" (Matt.
6:12). What would happen if God forgave you in exactly the same
way you are forgiving others at this time? To put it another way,
how would you feel if you had just confessed a sin to the Lord and

he responded, "I forgive you, but I can't be close to you again"? Like Rick, you probably would not feel forgiven.

As Christians, we cannot overlook the direct relationship between God's forgiveness and our forgiveness: "Be kind and compassionate to one another, forgiving each other, just as in Christ God forgave you" (Eph. 4:32). "Forgive as the Lord forgave you" (Col. 3:13b). God has given us an incredibly high standard to live up to when we have the opportunity to forgive someone. Fortunately, he also gives us the grace and the guidance we need to imitate him by forgiving others as he has forgiven us.

You Cannot Do It Alone

It is impossible to truly forgive others in your own strength, especially when they have hurt you deeply or betrayed your trust. You can try not to think about what they did or stuff your feelings deep inside and put on a false smile when you see them. But unless your heart is cleansed and changed by God, the memories and the feelings will still be lurking in the background, poisoning your thoughts and words, and preventing the rebuilding of trust and relationship.

There is only one way to overcome these barriers, and that is to admit that you cannot forgive in your own strength and that you desperately need God to come in and change your heart. There have been times when my honest prayer was,

God, I cannot forgive him in my own strength. In fact, I do not want to forgive him, at least until he has suffered for what he did to me. He does not deserve to get off easy. Everything in me wants to hold it against him and keep a high wall between us so he can never hurt me again. But your Word warns me that unforgiveness will eat away at my soul and build a wall between you and me. More importantly, you have shown me that you made the supreme sacrifice, giving up your own Son, in order to forgive me. Lord, please help me to *want* to forgive. Please change my heart and soften it so that I no longer want to hold this against him. Change me so that I can forgive and love him the way you have forgiven and loved me.

This kind of honesty and reliance on God is the key step in moving onto the path of forgiveness. As we will see later in this chapter, God is delighted to answer this call for help. As we receive and depend on his grace to us, we can breathe out the grace of forgiveness to others.

Neither a Feeling, nor Forgetting, nor Excusing

To understand what forgiveness is, we must first see what it is not. Forgiveness is not a feeling. It is an act of the will. Forgiveness involves a series of decisions, the first of which is to call on God to change our hearts. As he gives us grace, we must then decide (with our will) not to think or talk about what someone has done to hurt us. God calls us to make these decisions regardless of our feelings. As you will see, however, these decisions can lead to remarkable changes in our feelings.

Second, forgiveness is not forgetting. Forgetting is a *passive* process in which a matter fades from memory merely with the passing of time. Forgiving is an *active* process; it involves a conscious choice and a deliberate course of action. To put it another way, when God says that he "remembers your sins no more" (Isa. 43:25), he is not saying that he *cannot* remember our sins. Rather, he is promising that he *will not* remember them. When he forgives us, he chooses not to mention, recount, or think about our sins ever again. Similarly, when we forgive, we must draw on God's grace and consciously decide not to think or talk about what others have done to hurt us. This may require a lot of effort, especially when an offense is still fresh in mind. Fortunately, when we decide to forgive someone and stop dwelling on an offense, painful memories usually begin to fade.

Finally, forgiveness is not excusing. Excusing says, "That's okay," and implies, "What you did wasn't really wrong," or "You couldn't help it." Forgiveness is the opposite of excusing. The very fact that forgiveness is needed and granted indicates that what someone did was wrong and inexcusable. Forgiveness says, "We both know that what you did was wrong and without excuse. But since God has forgiven me, I forgive you." Because forgiveness deals honestly with sin, it brings a freedom that no amount of excusing could ever hope to provide.

Forgiveness Is a Decision

I once heard a joke that described a frequent failure in forgiving. A woman went to her pastor for advice on improving her marriage. When the pastor asked what her greatest complaint was, she replied, "Every time we get into a fight, my husband gets historical." When her pastor said, "You must mean *hysterical*," she responded, "I mean exactly what I said; he keeps a mental record of everything I've done wrong, and whenever he's mad, I get a history lesson!"

Tragically, this scenario is all too common. Having never learned the true meaning of forgiveness, many people keep a record of the wrongs of others and bring them up again and again. This pattern destroys their relationships and deprives them of the peace and freedom that come through genuine forgiveness.

To forgive someone means to release him or her from liability to suffer punishment or penalty. *Aphiemi,* a Greek word that is often translated as "forgive," means to let go, release, or remit. It often refers to debts that have been paid or canceled in full (e.g., Matt. 6:12; 18:27, 32). *Charizomai,* another word for "forgive," means to bestow favor freely or unconditionally. This word shows that forgiveness is undeserved and cannot be earned (Luke 7:42–43; 2 Cor. 2:7–10; Eph. 4:32; Col. 3:13).

As these words indicate, forgiveness can be a costly activity. When someone sins, they create a debt, and someone must pay it. Most of this debt is owed to God. In his great mercy, he sent his Son to pay that debt on the cross for all who would trust in him (Isa. 53:4–6; 1 Peter 2:24–25; Col. 1:19–20).

But if someone sinned against you, part of their debt is also owed to you. This means you have a choice to make. You can either *take* payments on the debt or *make* payments. You can take or extract payments on a debt from others' sin in many ways: by withholding forgiveness, by dwelling on the wrong, by being cold and aloof, by giving up on the relationship, by inflicting emotional pain, by gossiping, by lashing back or by seeking revenge against the one who hurt you. These actions may provide a perverse pleasure for the moment, but they exact a high price from you in the long run. As someone once said, "Unforgiveness is the poison we drink, hoping others will die."

Your other choice is to make payments on the debt and thereby release others from penalties they deserve to pay. Sometimes God will enable you to do this in one easy payment. You decide to forgive, and by God's grace the debt is quickly and fully canceled in your heart and mind. But when there has been a deep wrong, the debt it creates is not always paid at once. You may need to bear certain effects of the other person's sin over a long period of time. This may involve fighting against painful memories, speaking gracious words when you really want to say something hurtful, working to tear down walls and be vulnerable when you still feel little trust, or even enduring the consequences of a material or physical injury that the other person is unable or unwilling to repair.

Forgiveness can be extremely costly, but if you believe in Jesus, you have more than enough to make these payments. By going to the cross, he has already paid off the ultimate debt for sin and established an account of abundant grace in your name. As you draw on that grace through faith day by day, you will find that you have all that you need to make the payments of forgiveness for those who have wronged you.

God's grace is especially needed to release people from the ultimate penalty of sin. It is the same penalty that God releases us from when he forgives. Isaiah 59:2 says, "But your iniquities have separated you from your God; your sins have hidden his face from you, so that he will not hear" (cf. Rom. 6:23). When we repent of our sins and God forgives us, he releases us from the penalty of being separated from him forever, which is the worst penalty we could ever experience. He promises not to remember our sins any longer, not to hold them against us, not to let them stand between us ever again:

"I will forgive their wickedness and will remember their sins no more" (Jer. 31:34b; cf. Isa. 43:25).

"As far as the east is from the west, so far has he removed our transgressions from us" (Ps. 103:12).

"If you, O LORD, kept a record of sins, O Lord, who could stand?
  But with you there is forgiveness; therefore you are feared"
  (Ps. 130:3–4).

"[Love] keeps no record of wrongs" (1 Cor. 13:5).

Through forgiveness God tears down the walls that our sins have
built, and he opens the way for a renewed relationship with him.
This is exactly what we must do if we are to forgive as the Lord
forgives us: We must release the person who has wronged us from
the penalty of being separated from us. We must not hold wrongs
against others, not think about the wrongs, and not punish others
for them. Therefore, forgiveness may be described as a decision to
make four promises:

"I will not dwell on this incident."

"I will not bring up this incident again and use it against you."

"I will not talk to others about this incident."

"I will not let this incident stand between us or hinder our personal relationship."

By making and keeping these promises, you can tear down the
walls that stand between you and your offender. You promise not
to dwell on or brood over the problem or to punish by holding
the person at a distance. You clear the way for your relationship to
develop unhindered by memories of past wrongs. This is exactly
what God does for us, and it is what he calls us to do for others.

Corlette summarized these four promises in a little poem for her
children's curriculum, *The Young Peacemaker:*

> Good thought,
> Hurt you not.
> Gossip never,
> Friends forever.

Whenever I need to forgive my children for something they
have done, I pull them onto my lap, put my arms around them,
and remind them of the forgiveness we all have in Christ, which
enables me to forgive them. Then I recite Corlette's poem to them.

As I say the final words, I pull them close, give them a tight hug, and whisper "Friends forever" softly in their ears. I want them to know that no matter what they have done wrong, Jesus has opened the way for a complete restoration of our relationship. I want them to run quickly to me when they have done something wrong, instead of running away from me out of fear of punishment. I want them to know that repentance and confession will always lead to forgiveness and complete reconciliation, even if there are some consequences to accept along the way. I hope that as they experience genuine, affectionate reconciliation with me over and over again, they will come to know more fully the far better forgiveness they will always find when they run into the arms of God through prayer and faith.

Many people have never understood or experienced this kind of forgiveness. As a result, even when they hear the words "I forgive you," they continue to struggle with feelings of guilt and estrangement. Whenever others wrong you, you have an opportunity to introduce them to the wonderful world of true forgiveness. If another person admits that she has wronged you, do not just say, "I forgive you." Go on to describe the four promises that are packed into those three special words. And then take the opportunity to glorify God. Explain that the reason you are forgiving her in this way is because God has forgiven you in this way. Share the good news of what Jesus did on the cross and explain how his love is the model for your forgiveness. In addition to reassuring others about your intentions, this explanation may help them understand for the first time what God means when he says, "I forgive you."

When Should You Forgive?

Ideally, repentance should precede forgiveness (Luke 17:3). As we saw in chapter 4, however, minor offenses may be overlooked and put away even if the offender has not expressly repented. Your spontaneous forgiveness in these cases can put the matter behind you and save you and the other person from needless controversy.

When an offense is too serious to overlook and the offender has not yet repented, you may need to approach forgiveness as a two-stage process. The first stage requires *having an attitude of forgiveness,* and the second, *granting forgiveness.* Having an attitude of forgiveness is unconditional and is a commitment you make to God (see Mark 11:25; Luke 6:28; Acts 7:60). By his grace, you seek to maintain a loving and merciful attitude toward someone who has offended you. This requires making and living out the first promise of forgiveness, which means you will not dwell on the hurtful incident or seek vengeance or retribution in thought, word, or action. Instead, you pray for the other person and stand ready at any moment to pursue complete reconciliation as soon as he or she repents. This attitude will protect you from bitterness and resentment, even if the other person takes a long time to repent.

Granting forgiveness is conditional on the repentance of the offender and takes place between you and that person (Luke 17:3–4). It is a commitment to make the other three promises of forgiveness to the offender. When there has been a serious offense, it would not be appropriate to make these promises until the offender has repented (see chapter 6). Until then, you may need to talk with the offender about his sin or seek the involvement of others to resolve the matter (Matt. 18:16–20; see chapters 7 and 9). You could not do this if you had already made the last three promises. But once the other person repents, you can make these promises, closing the matter forever, the same way God forgives you.

Both stages of forgiveness were vividly demonstrated by God. When Christ died on the cross, he maintained an attitude of love and mercy toward those who put him to death. "Father, forgive them, for they do not know what they are doing" (Luke 23:34). At Pentecost, the Father's answer to Jesus' prayer was revealed. Three thousand people heard the apostle Peter's Pentecost message and were cut to the heart when they realized they had crucified the Son of God. As they repented of their sin, forgiveness was completed, and they were fully reconciled to God (Acts 2:36–41). This is exactly the pattern you should follow, "forgiving each other, just as in Christ God forgave you" (Eph. 4:32).

Can You Ever Mention the Sin Again?

The four promises are a human attempt to summarize the key elements of God's marvelous forgiveness for us. As a human device, they are limited and imperfect and should not be used in a rigid or mechanical fashion. In particular, the commitment not to bring up the offense again and use it against the offender should not be used to prevent you from dealing honestly and realistically with a recurring pattern of sin.

For example, you may know someone who has a problem with repeatedly losing his temper. Perhaps he confessed this to you a while ago, and you forgave him. Now he has done it again. Even though you are willing to forgive him for his latest outburst, you may believe that he needs to seek counseling from his pastor to deal with the heart issues that give rise to his anger. If all you can point to is the most recent incident, he might be able to shrug off your concern. For his sake, you may need to help him see that he is caught in an ongoing pattern of sin, which calls for counseling. In doing so, you are not breaking the second promise, because you are not bringing up his past wrong to use it against him. Rather, you are bringing it up for his good, to use it for his benefit.

Be careful, however, not to let this thinking become an excuse to brush the second promise aside and automatically bring up others' past wrongs to bolster your case against them. When someone has confessed a wrong and you have forgiven him, you should not bring it up again unless there is a very compelling reason to do so. Otherwise, you will rob people of hope that they can change or that you will ever give them another chance. The more you deal with each situation as a fresh and unique opportunity to grow and to experience the grace of God, the more open others will be to listen to your concerns.

What about the Consequences?

Forgiveness does not automatically release a wrongdoer from all the consequences of sin. Although God forgave the Israelites who rebelled against him in the wilderness, he decreed that they would die without entering the Promised Land (Num. 14:20–23). Even Moses was not shielded from this consequence (Deut. 32:48–52). Likewise, even though God forgave David for adultery and murder, God did not shield him from all the consequences that naturally flowed from his sin (2 Sam. 12:11–14; 13:1–39; 16:21–22; 19:1–4).

This is not to say that God is unmerciful; he is quick to remove the penalty of separation (2 Sam. 12:13) and often spares us from many of the consequences of our sins. When he does allow certain consequences to remain, it is always to teach us and others not to sin again.

Following God's example, you should remove any walls that stand between you and a repentant wrongdoer. It may also be appropriate to relieve that person from at least some of the consequences of his or her sin (Gen. 50:15–21; 2 Sam. 16:5–10; 19:18–23). For example, if someone negligently damaged your property and is truly unable to pay for needed repairs, you may decide to bear the cost yourself. Such mercy is especially appropriate when the offender seems to be sincerely repentant for his or her sin.

On the other hand, there may be times when you forgive someone but cannot afford to absorb the consequence of such wrongdoing. Or, even if you could bear the cost, doing so may not be the wisest and most loving thing for an offender, especially one caught in a pattern of irresponsibility or misconduct. As Proverbs 19:19 warns, "A hot-tempered man must pay the penalty; if you rescue him, you will have to do it again." Thus, a treasurer who secretly stole from your church may benefit from having to repay what he or she took. Likewise, a careless teenager may drive more safely in the future if he or she is made to pay for damages. An employee who repeatedly neglects his responsibilities may need to lose his job to learn needed lessons. (See appendix C for a detailed discussion of restitution.)

The important thing to remember is that once a person has expressed repentance, God calls you to truly forgive and to remove the penalty of personal separation. As you live out those four promises, ask God for grace to imitate his love and mercy and do only what will help to build up the other person. In other words, "forgive as the Lord forgave you."

Overcoming Unforgiveness

The promises of forgiveness can be difficult to make and even harder to keep. Fortunately, God promises to help us forgive others. He gives us this help through the Bible, which provides practical guidance and many examples of personal forgiveness. He also strengthens us through the Holy Spirit, who gives us the power and will to forgive others. Finally, for those times when we need extra help, he provides counsel and encouragement through pastors and fellow believers. As you draw on these resources, there are several steps you can take to overcome unforgiveness.

Confirm Repentance

It can be difficult to forgive a person who has failed to repent and confess clearly and specifically. When you find yourself in this situation, it may be wise to explain to the person who wronged you why you are having a difficult time forgiving. Corlette had to do this with me after I carelessly criticized her in front of several other people. When we were alone a while later, she let me know that I had hurt her. I quickly replied, "I'm sorry—that was wrong of me. Will you forgive me?" She said she would, but a few hours later she was still struggling with forgiveness. So she came to me and said, "I'm having a hard time forgiving you; could we talk about this some more?" When I agreed, she told me that she did not believe I realized how deeply I had hurt her. She then explained why my remarks had been so embarrassing and painful for her. She was right; I had not understood the effect my words had had on her. After hearing her explanation, I finally apologized specifically and sincerely for the effect my sin had had on her, and I made a commitment to be more sensitive toward her in the future. Once I repented and confessed properly, Corlette found it much easier to forgive me.

If you are having a difficult time forgiving someone, you may need to do what Corlette did. She helped me see where my confession was deficient (I had completely neglected four of the Seven A's!), and she encouraged me to take repentance more seriously. In doing so, she actually did me a service while removing a major hurdle to forgiveness.

Renounce Sinful Attitudes and Expectations

Forgiveness can also be hindered by sinful attitudes and unrealistic expectations. For example, either consciously or unconsciously, many of us withhold forgiveness because we believe the offender must earn or deserve our forgiveness or because we want to punish others or make them suffer. We may also withhold forgiveness because we want a guarantee that such an offense will never occur again.

These attitudes and expectations are utterly inconsistent with the command to forgive as God forgave us. There is no way we can earn or deserve God's forgiveness, which is why he gives it to repentant sinners as a free gift (Rom. 6:23). He calls us to grant forgiveness just as freely. Likewise, God does not withhold forgiveness in order to further punish people who have repented of their sins. As 1 John 1:9 promises, "If we confess our sins, he is faithful and just and will forgive us our sins" (cf. Ps. 103:9–12).

Furthermore, just as God demands no guarantee from us regarding our future conduct, we have no right to make such a demand of others. This fact is clearly revealed by Jesus' command in Luke 17:3–4: "If your brother sins, rebuke him, and if he repents, forgive him. If he sins against you seven times in a day, and seven times comes back to you and says, 'I repent,' forgive him." Forgiveness is based on repentance, not on guarantees. Therefore, once someone has expressed repentance for an action, we have no right to let our fears of the future delay forgiveness today.

Of course, if someone has expressed repentance but continues to behave in a hurtful manner, it may be appropriate to talk with the offender about *present* conduct. A pattern of sinful behavior may need to be addressed repeatedly before it is successfully overcome. Even so, we have no right to demand guarantees and withhold forgiveness from a repentant person.

Assess Your Contributions to the Problem

In some situations, your sins may have contributed to a conflict. Even if you did not start the dispute, your lack of understanding, careless words, impatience, or failure to respond in a loving manner may have aggravated the situation. When this has happened, it is easy to behave as though the other person's sins more than cancel yours. You then have a self-righteous attitude that can retard forgiveness. The best way to overcome this tendency is to prayerfully examine your role in the conflict and then write down everything you have done or failed to do that may have been a factor. Remembering your faults usually makes it easier to forgive others for theirs.

Recognize That God Is Working for Good

When someone has wronged you, it is also helpful to remember that God is sovereign and loving. Therefore, when you are having a hard time forgiving that person, take time to note how God may be using the offense for good. Is this an unusual opportunity to glorify God? How can you serve others and help them grow in their faith? What sins and weaknesses of yours are being exposed for the sake of your growth? What character qualities are you being challenged to exercise? When you perceive that the person who has wronged you is being used as an instrument in God's hand to help you mature, serve others, and glorify him, it may be easier for you to move ahead with forgiveness.

Remember God's Forgiveness

One of the most important steps in overcoming an unforgiving attitude is to focus your attention on how much God has forgiven you. The parable of the unmerciful servant vividly illustrates this principle (Matt. 18:21–35). In that story, a servant owed the king an enormous debt. When the king threatened to have the servant and his family sold as slaves to pay the debt, the servant begged for mercy. The king "took pity on him, canceled the debt and let him go" (v. 27). Moments later, the servant saw a man who owed him a debt that was tiny in comparison. When the servant demanded payment, the man asked for time to repay it. The servant refused and "had the man thrown into prison until he could pay the debt" (v. 30). When the king heard about this, he summoned the servant and said, "'You wicked servant . . . I canceled all that debt of yours because you begged me to. Shouldn't you have had mercy on your fellow servant just as I had on you?'" (vv. 32–33). Then, "In anger his master turned him over to the jailers to be tortured, until he should pay back all he owed" (v. 34). Jesus concludes the parable with these hard-hitting words, "This is how my heavenly Father will treat each of you unless you forgive your brother from your heart" (v. 35).

This parable illustrates an attitude that is all too common among Christians. We take God's forgiveness for granted, while we stubbornly withhold our forgiveness from others. In effect, we behave as though others' sins against us are more serious than our sins against God. Jesus teaches that this is a terribly sinful thing to do—it is an affront to God and his holiness, and it demeans the forgiveness Jesus purchased for us at Calvary. Until we repent of this sinful attitude, we will suffer unpleasant consequences. To begin with, we will feel separated from God and other Christians. We may also experience unusual hardships and lose blessings that would otherwise be ours (e.g., Ps. 32:1–5).[1]

If you are struggling with unforgiveness, take another look at the enormous debt for which God has forgiven you. Turning to the Bible and reminding yourself of God's holiness will help you see more clearly the seriousness of even your smallest sin (see Isa. 6:1–5; James 2:10–11). Make a list of some of the sins for which God has forgiven you. In particular, ask yourself whether you have ever treated God or others the same way you have been treated by the person you are trying to forgive. Take a long look at this list and remind yourself what you deserve from God because of your sins. Then rejoice in the wonderful promise of Psalm 103:8–11: "The LORD is compassionate and gracious, slow to anger, abounding in love. . . . He does not treat us as our sins deserve or repay us according to our iniquities. For as high as the heavens are above the earth, so great is his love for those who fear him."

The more you understand and appreciate the wonders of God's forgiveness, the more motivation you will have to forgive others. As Pat Morison notes in his excellent booklet on forgiveness, "We are not called to forgive others in order to earn God's love; rather, having experienced his love, we have the basis and motive to forgive others."[2]

Draw on God's Strength

Above all else, remember that true forgiveness depends on God's grace. If you try to forgive others on your own, you are in for a long

Go and Be Reconciled

and frustrating battle. But if you ask God to change your heart and you continually rely on his grace, you can forgive even the most painful offenses. God's grace was powerfully displayed in the life of Corrie ten Boom, who had been imprisoned with her family by the Nazis for giving aid to Jews early in World War II. Her elderly father and beloved sister, Betsie, died as a result of the brutal treatment they received in prison. God sustained Corrie through her time in a concentration camp, and after the war she traveled throughout the world, testifying to God's love. Here is what she wrote about a remarkable encounter in Germany:

> It was at a church service in Munich that I saw him, the former S.S. man who had stood guard at the shower room door in the processing center at Ravensbruck. He was the first of our actual jailers that I had seen since that time. And suddenly it was all there—the roomful of mocking men, the heaps of clothing, Betsie's pain-blanched face.
>
> He came up to me as the church was emptying, beaming and bowing. "How grateful I am for your message, Fraulein," he said. "To think that, as you say, he has washed my sins away!"
>
> His hand was thrust out to shake mine. And I, who had preached so often to the people in Bloemendall about the need to forgive, kept my hand at my side.
>
> Even as the angry, vengeful thoughts boiled through me, I saw the sin of them. Jesus Christ had died for this man; was I going to ask for more? "Lord Jesus," I prayed, "forgive me and help me to forgive him."
>
> I tried to smile, I struggled to raise my hand. I could not. I felt nothing, not the slightest spark of warmth or charity. And so again I breathed a silent prayer. "Jesus, I cannot forgive him. Give me Your forgiveness."
>
> As I took his hand the most incredible thing happened. From my shoulder along my arm and through my hand a current seemed to pass from me to him, while into my heart sprang a love for this stranger that almost overwhelmed me.
>
> So I discovered that it is not on our forgiveness any more than on our goodness that the world's healing hinges, but on him. When he tells us to love our enemies, he gives, along with the command, the love itself.[3]

Reconciliation and the Replacement Principle

Forgiveness is both an event and a process. Making the four promises of forgiveness is an event that knocks down a wall that stands between you and a person who has wronged you. Then a process begins. After you demolish an obstruction, you usually have to clear away debris and do repair work. The Bible calls this "reconciliation," a process involving a change of attitude that leads to a change in the relationship. More specifically, to be reconciled means to replace hostility and separation with peace and friendship. This is what Jesus had in mind when he said, "Go and be reconciled to your brother" (Matt. 5:24; cf. 1 Cor. 7:11; 2 Cor. 5:18–20).

Being reconciled does not mean that the person who offended you must now become your closest friend. What it means is that your relationship will be at least as good as it was before the offense occurred. Once that happens, an even better relationship may develop. As God helps you and the other person work through your differences, you may discover a growing respect and appreciation for each other. Moreover, you may uncover common interests and goals that will add a deeper and richer dimension to your friendship.

Reconciliation requires that you give a repentant person an opportunity to demonstrate repentance and regain your trust. This may be a slow and difficult process, especially when that person has consistently behaved in a hurtful and irresponsible manner. While you may proceed with some caution, you should not demand guarantees from a person who has expressed repentance. If the person stumbles, the process of loving confrontation, confession, and forgiveness may need to be repeated (Luke 17:3–4). In spite of setbacks and disappointments, for the Lord's sake the process of reconciliation should continue until your relationship has been fully restored.

Although reconciliation can sometimes take place with little or no special effort, in most cases you will need to remember the saying, "If you are coasting, you must be going downhill." In other words, unless a deliberate effort is made to restore and strengthen a relationship, it will generally deteriorate. This is especially true when you are recovering from intense and prolonged conflict. Moreover, unless you take definite steps to demonstrate your forgiveness, the other person may doubt your sincerity and withdraw from you.

These problems can be significantly reduced if you pursue reconciliation at three different levels.

In Thought

Even when we say, "I forgive you," many of us have a difficult time not thinking about what others have done to hurt us. Try as we might, memories of the offense keep popping back into our minds, and we find ourselves reliving all kinds of painful feelings.

I remember a time when this happened to me. When I woke up one morning, I immediately thought about what Jim (not his real name) had done to me the previous day. Since I had forgiven him, I tried to stop to thinking about it. Within fifteen minutes, however, the same thoughts were rolling through my mind. I pushed them aside once more, but before long, there they were again. After wrestling with these painful thoughts several more times, I realized I was stuck in a rut. When I asked God to change my heart and help me get rid of these thoughts and feelings, these two Bible passages came to my mind:

> "But I tell you who hear me: Love your enemies, do good to those who hate you, bless those who curse you, pray for those who mistreat you" (Luke 6:27–28).
>
> "Finally, brothers, whatever is true, whatever is noble, whatever is right, whatever is pure, whatever is lovely, whatever is admirable—if anything is excellent or praiseworthy—think about such things" (Phil. 4:8).

"Okay," I prayed, "but I'll need your help, Lord. I sure don't feel like doing any of this." By God's grace, I began to pray for Jim, asking God to be with him and to bless his day. My thoughts then turned to other matters. When I caught myself thinking about the offense an hour later, I prayed for Jim again, this time thanking God for some of Jim's admirable qualities. This process repeated itself many times during the next two days, and then I discovered something amazing. Whenever Jim came to my mind, my thoughts were usually positive and no longer gravitated toward the offense he had committed.

This was how I learned the *replacement principle*. It is very difficult simply to stop thinking about an unpleasant experience. Instead, we must replace negative thoughts and memories with positive ones. This principle is especially helpful when trying to keep the first promise of forgiveness. Every time you begin to dwell on or brood over what someone has done, ask for God's help and deliberately pray for that person or think of something about the offender that is "true, noble, right, pure, lovely, admirable, excellent, or praiseworthy." At first, you may struggle to come up with even one positive thought, but after you find one good thought or memory, others should come more easily. If you cannot think of a single good thing about the person you are trying to forgive, then use thankful thoughts about God and his work in this situation to replace unpleasant memories (see Phil. 4:4–7).

In Word

As Luke 6:27–28 implies, the replacement principle applies to your words as well as your thoughts. When talking to others about the person who offended you, make it a point to speak well of the person. Express appreciation for things he or she has done and draw attention to redeeming qualities. Do the same when talking to the offender. Praise, thank, or encourage!

Kind words are especially important if the other person is struggling with guilt or embarrassment. When Paul learned that a member of the church in Corinth had recently repented of a serious sin, he commanded the other members of the church to "forgive and comfort him, so that he will not be overwhelmed by excessive sorrow" (2 Cor. 2:7). As you verbally reaffirm your friendship and sincerely build up the other person, both of you should experience improved attitudes and feelings.

In Deed

If you really want to be reconciled to someone, apply the replacement principle to your actions as well (1 John 3:18). As C. S. Lewis noted, "Don't waste time bothering whether you 'love' your neighbor; act as if you did. As soon as we do this we find one of the great secrets. When you are behaving as if you loved someone, you will presently come to love him."[4]

When I first read Lewis's comment, I thought it was rather naive. But then I experienced exactly what he was describing. Corlette and I had quarreled about some petty thing, and I had not really forgiven her. My unhappiness was compounded by her request that I run to the grocery store to "pick up a few small items." (As you can guess, I dislike shopping for groceries.) As I grudgingly pushed my cart down the aisle, I noticed some special coffee that Corlette loves to drink. *If she hadn't been so unkind to me today, I would have surprised her with that.* Even as I thought these words, another part of me wanted to get her the coffee. I wrestled with conflicting feelings for a few moments and then decided to pick up the can, *just to check the price,* I told myself. The moment I touched it, my feelings began to change. My resentment soon melted away, and I was overwhelmed with love for my wife and a desire to see her face light up as I gave her this gift. Needless to say, we were completely reconciled shortly after I returned home.

Loving actions can do much more than change your feelings; they can also communicate in unmistakable terms the reality of your forgiveness and your commitment to reconciliation. Thomas Edison apparently understood this principle. When he and his staff were developing the incandescent light bulb, it took hundreds of hours to manufacture a single bulb. One day, after finishing a bulb, he handed it to a young errand boy and asked him to take it upstairs to the testing room. As the boy turned and started up the stairs, he stumbled and fell, and the bulb shattered on the steps. Instead of rebuking the boy, Edison reassured him and then turned to his staff and told them to start working on another bulb. When it was completed several days later, Edison demonstrated the reality of his forgiveness in the most powerful way possible. He walked over to the same boy, handed him the bulb, and said, "Please take this up to the testing room." Imagine how that boy must have felt. He knew that he didn't deserve to be trusted with this responsibility again. Yet, here it was, being offered to him as though nothing had ever happened. Nothing could have restored this boy to the team more clearly, more quickly, or more fully. How much more should those of us who have experienced reconciliation with God be quick to demonstrate our forgiveness with concrete actions.

Summary and Application

This is what reconciliation is all about. By thought, word, and deed, you can demonstrate forgiveness and rebuild relationships with people who have offended you. No matter how painful the offense, with God's help, you can make four promises and imitate the forgiveness and reconciliation that was demonstrated on the cross. By the grace of God, you can forgive as the Lord forgave you.

If you are presently involved in a conflict and have not been able to resolve it privately, these questions will help you apply the principles presented in this chapter.

1. How has your opponent sinned against you?
2. Which of these sins has your opponent confessed?
3. Which of the unconfessed sins can you overlook and forgive at this time? (Those that cannot be overlooked will have to be dealt with by applying the principles taught in chapters 7–9.)
4. Make the first decision of forgiveness: Admit that you cannot forgive on your own, and ask God to change your heart.
5. Now write out the four promises you will make to your opponent at this time to indicate your forgiveness.
6. What consequences of your opponent's sin will you take on yourself? What consequences will you expect your opponent to bear?
7. If you are having a hard time forgiving your opponent:
   a. Is it because you are not sure he or she has repented? If so, how could you encourage confirmation of repentance?
   b. Do you think your opponent must somehow earn or deserve your forgiveness? Are you trying to punish by withholding forgiveness? Are you expecting a guarantee that the offense will not happen again? If you have any of these attitudes or expectations, what do you need to do?

    c. How did your sins contribute to this problem? Which of these sins will God refuse to forgive if you repent? How can you imitate his forgiveness?

    d. Read Matthew 18:21–35. What is the point of this passage? How does it apply to you? How might God be working for good in this situation?

    e. What has God forgiven you for in the past? How serious are your opponent's sins against you when compared with your sins against God? How can you show God that you appreciate his forgiveness?

8. How can you demonstrate forgiveness or promote reconciliation:

    a. In thought?

    b. In word?

    c. In deed?

9. Go on record with the Lord by writing a prayer based on the principles taught in this chapter.

11

LOOK ALSO TO THE INTERESTS OF OTHERS

Each of you should look not only to your own interests, but also to the interests of others.

Philippians 2:4

So far we have focused primarily on how to resolve the personal issues that can arise during a conflict. As we all know, however, conflict may also involve material issues. Two friends may disagree on the cost of repairing damaged property, or two businesspeople may interpret a contract in entirely different ways. A couple may disagree on where to spend a vacation. Neighbors may differ on whether or not a fence needs to be replaced and who should bear the cost. Until these substantive matters are settled, peace will be hindered, even if the related personal issues are resolved. In this chapter we will look at five principles that can help you reach agreements on material issues in a biblically faithful manner.

Cooperative versus Competitive Negotiation

Many people automatically resort to a competitive style when negotiating material issues. They act like they are having a tug-of-war, with each person pulling aggressively to get what he or she wants and letting others look out for themselves.

Although this approach may be appropriate when prompt results are needed or when someone is defending important moral principles, it has three inherent weaknesses. First, a competitive approach often fails to produce the best possible solution to a problem. When people work against each other, they tend to focus on surface issues and neglect underlying desires and needs. As a result, they often reach inadequate solutions. Moreover, a competitive approach usually assumes that for one side to get more of the pie, the other side must get less. This "fixed pie" attitude discourages the openness and flexibility needed to develop creative and comprehensive solutions.

Second, competitive negotiation can also be quite inefficient. It usually begins with each side stating a specific position, and progress is made by successive compromises and concessions. Because each compromise typically is about half the size of the previous one and takes twice as long, this process can consume a great deal of time and generate significant frustration.

Finally, competitive negotiating can significantly damage personal relationships. This approach tends to be very self-centered and easily offends others. It also focuses on material issues rather than on personal concerns, perceptions, and feelings. At best, those involved in the process get the message that these relational matters are unimportant. At worst, the inherent contest of wills leads to overt intimidation, manipulation, and personal attacks. This competitive process often results in seriously damaged relationships.

Many of these problems can be avoided by negotiating in a cooperative rather than a competitive manner. People who practice cooperative negotiation deliberately seek solutions that are beneficial to everyone involved. By working with our opponents rather than against them, we are more likely to communicate and appreciate underlying needs and concerns. As a result, we are apt to develop wiser and more complete solutions. When carried out properly, cooperative negotiation is relatively efficient, because less time and energy is wasted on defensive posturing. Best of all, because attention is paid to personal concerns, this style of negotiation tends to preserve or even improve relationships.

Cooperative negotiation is highly commended by Scripture, which repeatedly commands us to have an active concern for the needs and well-being of others:

> "Love your neighbor as yourself" (Matt. 22:39).
>
> "[Love] is not self-seeking" (1 Cor. 13:5).
>
> "So in everything, do to others what you would have them do to you, for this sums up the Law and the Prophets" (Matt. 7:12).
>
> "Do nothing out of selfish ambition or vain conceit, but in humility consider others better than yourselves. Each of you should look not only to your own interests, but also to the interests of others" (Phil. 2:3–4; cf. 1 Cor. 10:24).

Having a loving concern for others does not mean always giving in to their demands. We do have a responsibility to look out for our own interests (Phil. 2:4). Furthermore, Jesus calls us to be "as shrewd as snakes and as innocent as doves" (Matt. 10:16). The Greek word *phronimos,* translated "shrewd" in this passage, means to be "prudent, sensible, and practically wise."[1] A wise person does not give in to others unless there is a valid reason to do so. After gathering all the relevant information and exploring creative options, a wise person works toward solutions that honor God and provide lasting benefits to as many people as possible. While this may sometimes lead to unilateral concessions, it usually requires that *both* sides contribute to a solution.

As these passages indicate, cooperative negotiation may be described as a combination of love and wisdom. I have found that this loving and wise process generally involves five basic steps, which may be summarized in this simple rule: When you need to negotiate, PAUSE. This acronym stands for the following steps:

Prepare

Affirm relationships

Understand interests

Search for creative solutions

Evaluate options objectively and reasonably

The more carefully you follow each of these steps, the more likely you will be to reach mutually beneficial agreements on material issues.

Prepare

Preparation is one of the most important elements of successful negotiation (Prov. 14:8, 22). This is especially true when significant issues or strong feelings are involved. Several activities are good preparation for negotiation:

Pray. Ask God for humility, discernment, and wisdom as you prepare.

Get the facts. Read relevant documents carefully (e.g., contracts, employment manuals, letters). Talk with key witnesses. Conduct necessary research.

Identify issues and interests (which I will define below). Try to discern the real cause of the disagreement. Carefully list the issues involved. Make a list of your interests as well as the interests of others as you understand them.

Study the Bible. Clearly identify the biblical principles involved, and make sure you know how to put them into practice.

Develop options. Do some brainstorming before you talk with your opponent so you can propose a few reasonable solutions to the problem. Be prepared to explain how each option will benefit your opponent.

Anticipate reactions. Put yourself in your opponent's shoes and try to predict a few likely reactions to your proposals. Develop a response to each of those reactions.

Plan an alternative to a negotiated agreement. Decide in advance what you will do if negotiations are not successful.

Select an appropriate time and place to talk. Consider your opponent's possible preferences.

Plan your opening remarks. In particular, plan how to set a positive tone at the outset of the meeting and how to encourage your opponent to enter into the discussion with an open mind.

Seek counsel. If you have doubts about how to proceed with negotiations, talk with people who can give you wise and biblically sound advice.

The Barking Dog. To make this discussion as practical and vivid as possible, I will show how the PAUSE approach to negotiation could be followed in an actual conflict. We will consider the following situation throughout this chapter.

Jim and Julie Johnson live on a two-acre tract of land outside of town. Their nearest neighbors, Steve and Sally Smith, have a similar acreage. The two houses are located within a hundred feet of each other on adjacent corners of the properties. The Smiths raise Border collies as a hobby and a small business. A few weeks ago they acquired a new dog named Molly, who barks sporadically several evenings a week. The annoying barking has been keeping the Johnsons awake at night, and their children are complaining about being tired in school. To make matters worse, the Smiths recently began to exercise and feed Molly at 5:00 A.M. This noisy activity robs the Johnsons of another hour of sleep.

A week or so ago, Jim noticed Sally working in her garden, and he went over to ask if she would do something about the barking. She said she was sorry, and for a few days the barking subsided. Within a week, however, it started again and seemed even worse than before. Yesterday another neighbor told Julie that Steve had called everyone in the subdivision to see whether the dog was bothering them. In the process, he had said some very critical things about Jim.

Julie has conducted her own survey and found out that only a few of her neighbors have been annoyed by Molly's barking. Two neighbors are hard of hearing, and some of the others live far enough away that they cannot hear the dog. Julie then checked with the county attorney and found out that it is a misdemeanor to keep a dog that disturbs a "considerable number of persons" in a neighborhood. Unfortunately, the county attorney does not seem to believe that Molly has disturbed enough people to justify misdemeanor charges. Therefore, Jim and Julie will need to negotiate a solution without the aid of the authorities.

Since the problem with the barking dog did not need to be resolved immediately, Jim and Julie took several days to prepare to negotiate with the Smiths. Each day they prayed for the Smiths and asked God for wisdom and discernment. They also spent some time discussing how to apply relevant biblical principles to this situation.

To verify their complaint and identify significant patterns, they began to keep a written log of when Molly barked. Jim read the subdivision covenants to see whether there were any rules against barking dogs, but there were none. Julie went to the library and looked in several books on dog training. They made a list of the suggestions that expert trainers gave regarding barking dogs.

Jim and Julie identified two issues that needed to be addressed: (1) Is it reasonable to expect the Smiths to do something about Molly's barking? (2) If it is, what is the best way to moderate her barking? They then made a preliminary list of the interests involved. They decided that they had the following interests: a desire for peace and quiet, sufficient rest for their children, and a comfortable relationship with the Smiths and with other neighbors. They speculated that the Smiths had these interests: an affection for dogs, a need for additional income, and possibly a resentment toward "being told what to do." (More interests are listed later in this chapter.)

The Johnsons then put together a preliminary list of options that might solve the problem, including the following: sell the dog, teach the dog not to bark, get a remote-controlled shock collar for the dog, muzzle the dog, get ear plugs for themselves, and so on. They tried to anticipate how the Smiths would respond to each option and listed the costs and benefits of the more viable ones.

Jim and Julie also spent some time discussing what they would do if the Smiths refused to do anything about the barking. Although they were tempted to find a way to retaliate and make life difficult for the Smiths, they knew that would not please or honor God. Therefore, they decided that if they could not stop the barking right away, they would simply work harder at cultivating a positive relationship with the Smiths. They would do this by inviting them over for meals, taking time to get to know their children, and looking for opportunities to help them or to be kind to them.

Since the Smiths seemed to relax more on Saturdays, Jim and Julie decided that would be a good time to approach them. They also decided that it would be wise to offer to talk at the Smiths' home, which would put them more at ease. They planned to request a meeting by having Jim go over to the Smiths in person and say something like this: "Molly seems to be barking a lot lately, and our children are having a difficult time getting enough sleep. Julie and I would appreciate it if you would be willing to take a few minutes to talk with us about this situation."

Jim and Julie also discussed three ways that Steve and Sally might react to this request, and they planned appropriate responses. Once their preparation was complete, they were ready to approach the Smiths.

This may seem like a lot of work, and it is. But in this real-life conflict, Jim and Julie wisely realized that they could either put their time into lying awake at night and grumbling throughout the day about the barking dog, or they could put their time into carefully negotiating with their neighbors to find a solution to this problem. You will need to make the same choice when you are faced with an issue that could affect you, your family, your church, or your employment in a significant or prolonged way. It will not be a question of *whether* you spend time on the problem; it will be a question of *where or how* you spend time on the problem. As Jim and Julie discovered, the sooner you devote your time to finding a solution to the problem, the less time you will spend stewing over it.

Affirm Relationships

A conflict generally involves two basic ingredients: people and a problem. All too often, we ignore the feelings and concerns of the people and focus all our attention on the problems that separate us. This approach often causes further offense and alienation, which only makes conflicts more difficult to resolve. One way to avoid these unnecessary complications is to affirm your respect and concern for your opponent throughout the negotiation process. For example, you may begin a conversation with words like these:

"You are one of my closest friends. No one in town has been more kind or thoughtful toward me. It's because I value our friendship so much that I want to find a solution to this problem."

"I admire how hard you have worked to pay this debt. I also appreciate your efforts to keep me informed about your financial situation. Since you have treated me with respect, I would like to do everything I can to find a workable payment plan."

"I appreciate your willingness to listen to my concerns about this project. Before I explain what they are, I want to make it clear that I will respect your authority to decide this matter, and I will do all that I can to make this project successful."

Obviously, these affirming words must be backed up with comparable actions. If they are not, your opponent will rightfully conclude that you are a flatterer and a hypocrite. Here are a few ways to demonstrate concern and respect during the negotiation process:

Communicate in a courteous manner. Listen respectfully to what others have to say. Use words like "please," "May I explain?" "Would it be all right with you if . . .?" and "I don't think I explained my reasons very clearly."

Spend time on personal issues. Instead of moving directly to material issues, try to understand your opponent's personal concerns. Deal with personal offenses and frustrations as soon as possible.

Submit to authority. Offer clear and reasonable advice, and be as persuasive as possible, but respect the authority of leaders and support their decisions to the best of your ability.

Earnestly seek to understand. Pay attention to what others are thinking and feeling. Ask sincere questions. Discuss their perceptions.

Look out for the interests of others. Seek solutions that really satisfy others' needs and desires.

Address sin in a gracious manner. If you must talk to others about their wrongs, use the skills described in chapter 8.

Allow face-saving. Don't back others into a corner. Develop solutions that are consistent with others' values and with God's.

Give praise and thanks. When someone makes a valid point or a gracious gesture, acknowledge it or express your appreciation for it.

If you sincerely and consistently affirm your concern and respect for the other person, you will generally have more freedom to discuss material issues honestly and frankly. Even if you are not entirely satisfied with an agreement, it is wise to affirm your relationship with the other person at the end of the negotiation process. This protects your relationship from residual damage and may improve your ability to negotiate subsequent issues in a more satisfactory manner.

The Barking Dog. Affirming their relationship with the Smiths was a basic part of the Johnsons' initial request for a meeting with them. By *asking* for a meeting instead of demanding it, Jim conveyed courtesy and respect. This process continued during their first meeting with the Smiths the next day. Jim began the meeting by saying: "We really appreciate your willingness to talk with us. In fact, we're hoping that this situation will give us a chance to get to know one another better and to be better neighbors than before."

After allowing Steve and Sally to respond, Julie asked if it would be all right for her to explain some of the Johnsons' concerns. She chose her words carefully and used "I" (or "we") statements as much as possible. She was careful not to accuse the Smiths of deliberately bothering anyone, and she made it clear that she and Jim were assuming the best about them. She then asked Steve and Sally to explain some of their feelings and concerns. As they did so, Jim and Julie asked questions at appropriate times and responded with statements like, "I see," "I didn't realize that," and "That helps me to understand your situation." Although the Smiths were somewhat defensive when the conversation began, they eventually began to relax. As their relationship with the Johnsons was affirmed, they became increasingly willing to talk about the problem that had brought them together.

Understand Interests

The third step in the PAUSE strategy is to understand the interests of those involved in the disagreement. Only then can you properly respond to the command to "look not only to your own interests, but also to the interests of others." In order to identify interests, it is important to understand how they differ from issues and positions.

An *issue* is an identifiable and concrete question that must be addressed in order to reach an agreement. For example: "Should the Smiths do something to stop Molly's barking?" or "How can the Smiths stop Molly's barking?"

A *position* is a desired outcome or a definable perspective on an issue. For example: "If the dog keeps barking, you should get rid of her," or "She's my dog, and you have no right to tell me what to do with her."

An *interest* is what motivates people. It is a concern, desire, need, limitation, or something a person values. Interests provide the basis for positions. Some interests are concrete and easy to identify. For example: "I like breeding and training dogs, and I need the extra income," or "My kids need sleep." Other interests are abstract, hidden, and difficult to measure. For example: "I don't want my family to think I can be pushed around," or "This is the only thing I've ever done that made me feel like a success."

As these examples demonstrate, positions are frequently incompatible. One person's desired result often conflicts with the other person's desired result. While interests may sometimes clash as well, in many situations the parties' primary interests are surprisingly compatible. (For example, both the Smiths and the Johnsons probably want their children to enjoy living in this neighborhood.) Therefore, when people focus on interests rather than positions, it is usually easier to develop acceptable solutions.

The Bible is filled with stories that illustrate the wisdom of identifying and focusing on interests rather than positions. One of my favorite negotiation stories is described in 1 Samuel 25:1–44. David's popularity among the people of Israel had become so great that King Saul was jealous and tried to kill him. David and several hundred of his supporters fled into the desert, where they lived as mercenaries. During this time, they protected the flocks and herds of the local inhabitants from marauders. One of the people who had benefited from David's protection was a wealthy landowner named Nabal. Therefore, when David's provisions ran low, he sent ten young men to ask Nabal for food. In spite of the benefit that he had received from David, Nabal denied the request and hurled insults at the young men. When David learned of this, he was furious. He immediately set out with four hundred armed men, determined to kill Nabal and all his men.

In the meantime, Nabal's wife, Abigail, learned what Nabal had done. Seeing the danger her husband was in, she set out to negotiate a peace treaty with David. First she loaded a large amount of food on several donkeys and instructed her servants to take it to David. (Very wise preparation!) She then mounted her own donkey and set out to intercept him before he had time to launch his attack. When Abigail met David at the foot of the mountains, she dismounted and bowed down before him. Then she said:

> My lord, let the blame be on me alone. Please let your servant speak to you; hear what your servant has to say. . . . *[T]he LORD has kept you, my master, from bloodshed and from avenging yourself with your own hands.* . . . Please forgive your servant's offense, for the LORD will certainly make a lasting dynasty for my master, because he fights the LORD's battles. *Let no wrongdoing be found in you as long as you live.* Even though someone is pursuing you to take your life, the life of my master will be bound securely in the bundle of the living by the LORD your God. But the lives of your enemies he will hurl away as from the pocket of a sling. When the LORD has done for my master every good thing he promised concerning him and has appointed him leader over Israel, *my master will not have on his conscience the staggering burden of needless bloodshed or of having avenged himself.*
>
> verses 24–31, emphasis added

This is an insightful and shrewdly crafted appeal. Abigail clearly affirmed her concern and respect for David (saying "please," asking to talk, and repeatedly referring to him as "master"). She used words and metaphors that would be pleasing to his ears: "The LORD will certainly make a lasting dynasty for my master" reminded him of Samuel anointing him as future king, and "the pocket of a sling" touched on the most glorious moment of David's life, when he killed Goliath with his sling. More importantly, instead of lecturing him or talking directly about her own concerns, Abigail focused on David's primary interest in this situation. She had probably heard about King Saul's recent massacre of an entire town of people who had innocently given assistance to David (1 Sam. 22:6–19). She also appeared to know that David had recently passed up an opportunity to kill Saul (1 Sam. 24:1–22). Abigail must have seen that David's clean record and honorable reputation was of great value to him, especially when compared to Saul's bloody record. She realized that if David stained his hands with innocent blood, he would lose God's blessing as well as the love and respect of the people of Israel. David's rage had blinded him to his own interests, but Abigail's brilliant appeal brought him to his senses, and he expressed his gratitude:

> David said to Abigail, "Praise be to the LORD, the God of Israel, who has sent you today to meet me. May you be blessed for your good judgment and for keeping me from bloodshed this day and from avenging myself with my own hands. Otherwise, as surely as the LORD, the God of Israel, lives, who has kept me from harming you, if you had not come quickly to meet me, not one male belonging to Nabal would have been left alive by daybreak. . . . Go home in peace. I have heard your words and granted your request."
>
> 1 Samuel 25:32–35

This dramatic incident shows that "wisdom is better than strength" (Eccles. 9:16). It also illustrates one of the most important principles of cooperative negotiation: The more fully you understand and look out for your opponent's interests, the more persuasive and effective you can be in negotiating an agreement.

Before you attempt to understand the interests of other people, it is wise to make a written list of your own interests. Remembering the three opportunities provided by conflict, you might begin by listing interests related to glorifying God, serving others, and growing to be like Christ. This part of your list is primarily for your own benefit, and it may not be appropriate to reveal these interests to your opponent, especially at the outset of negotiations.

You should also note any personal concerns, desires, needs, or limitations that are not included in one of the categories described above. Your list should include everything that is of value to you or that might be motivating you in this particular situation. Once this list is fairly complete, it often helps to note which interests have the greatest priority. This will help you make wise decisions if you later have to choose between several interests.

You should then try to discern your opponent's interests. Before you meet together, you may analyze information you already have or do some discreet research to develop a list of possible interests. When you are actually talking with your opponent, you should carefully note anything he says and does that reveals hidden interests. Asking "Why?" and "Why not?" and "How?" at appropriate times can provide additional insights.

It is often helpful to get each side's interests out in the open. One way to do this is to take out a sheet of paper and write down all the interests that have already come to the surface. Explain to your opponent what you are doing, and read the items you are listing. Then ask what other concerns, goals, or interests your opponent has. As much as possible, acknowledge them as being reasonable and significant. Ask questions to clarify your understanding. Set a positive tone by drawing attention to similar interests and areas of agreement.

Once you and the other party understand each other's interests, you can redefine and set priorities for the *issues* you will need to resolve to reach an agreement. Place the easiest issues at the beginning of your list. If you work on those first, you should see some positive results more quickly. This tends to encourage further cooperation and builds momentum as you move on to the more difficult issues.

The Barking Dog. By the time they sat down to talk with the Smiths, Jim and Julie had developed a more thorough list of the interests they thought were involved in this situation. It included the following items:

1. Personal interests that are confidential for now
   a. Glorify God
      i. Trust, obey, imitate, and acknowledge him
      ii. Show the power of the gospel in our lives
      iii. Overlook minor offenses

       iv. Do all we can to live at peace

       v. Do what is just and right

      vi. Exercise compassion and mercy

     vii. Speak the truth in love

  b. Serve others

       i. Teach our children by example what it means to be a Christian

      ii. Do good to the Smiths; try to help them in concrete ways

     iii. Demonstrate and, if possible, describe the difference Jesus has made in our lives, in the hope that the Smiths may be encouraged to follow him (if they are not already Christians)

      iv. Help the Smiths see where they may need to change, and give them all the encouragement and help we can

  c. Grow to be like Christ

       i. See our weaknesses more clearly so that we will learn to depend on God more consciously and consistently

      ii. See our sins and idols more clearly so that with God's help we can repent and change

     iii. Practice the character traits we see in our Lord, such as love, joy, peace, patience, kindness, goodness, faithfulness, gentleness, self-control, discernment, wisdom, and perseverance

2. Personal interests we should reveal

  a. A desire for peace and quiet (which is the reason we moved to the country)

  b. Sufficient rest for us and for our children

  c. A comfortable relationship with the Smiths and with other neighbors

  d. Having our children get along with the Smiths' children so they can have good playmates nearby

3. Interests the Smiths may have that may be mentioned when it seems appropriate

  a. Affection for dogs

  b. A need for additional income

  c. A comfortable relationship with their neighbors

  d. Having their children get along with our children

4. Interests the Smiths may have that we should be sensitive to but should not mention
   a. Tension within their marriage or family that makes them more irritable or less thoughtful toward others
   b. Not enough money to pursue expensive solutions (e.g., building a new kennel)
   c. A resentment toward "being told what to do"

Shortly after they sat down with the Smiths, Jim and Julie suggested that they try to understand one another's interests in the situation. After the Johnsons explained what an interest is and how this step would help understand them, Steve and Sally jumped right to their position and said they were not willing to get rid of Molly. Jim reflected this back as an interest: "You value her a lot, don't you?" Jim and Julie explained a few of their own interests and then paused to allow the Smiths to explain more of theirs. By reflecting and paraphrasing the Smiths' words, the Johnsons showed they were really listening to them and trying to understand their perspective. This drew the Smiths out further. As they talked, Jim and Julie learned that their preliminary appraisal of the Smiths' interests was fairly accurate, but it was not complete. They learned that the Smiths had these additional interests:

Steve and Sally both came from families that loved dogs and invested a lot of time and energy in them; Molly was descended from one of Sally's father's favorite dogs.

Steve didn't feel very successful in his occupation as an accountant, but he derived a great deal of satisfaction and a sense of accomplishment from his success as a breeder and trainer.

One of the main reasons Steve and Sally valued their dogs so highly was that showing them provided an opportunity for their entire family to work and travel together; also, by assigning the care of the dogs to their children, they were teaching them to be responsible.

When they left town for family trips, Steve and Sally worried about their dogs because they had not found anyone they really trusted to take proper care of them.

Their house had been burglarized several years ago, and Sally was fearful of its happening again. Therefore, having a dog that barked at disturbances was very reassuring to her.

As Jim and Julie considered these additional interests, they realized that getting rid of Molly would not be an option for the Smiths. Solving this problem was going to take some careful thinking.

Search for Creative Solutions

The fourth step in the PAUSE strategy is to search for solutions that will satisfy as many interests as possible. This process should begin with spontaneous inventing. Everyone should be encouraged to mention *any* idea that comes to mind. Imagination and creativity should be encouraged, while evaluating and deciding should be postponed. As you are searching for possible solutions, avoid the assumption that there is only one answer to your problem. The best solution may involve a combination of several options, so feel free to use parts of several ideas to form a variety of choices.

During this stage, make a conscious effort to "expand the pie." Try to bring in additional interests that could be satisfied as part of your agreement. For example, if the primary issue being negotiated is whether your neighbor will replace his broken fence, you might offer to help him remove some diseased trees that threaten to fall on your garage. By focusing on shared interests and developing options that provide mutual gains, you can create incentives for agreement on the more difficult points of contention.

As you begin to identify possible solutions that seem wise to you, you should make an effort to "sell" these options to your opponent. In other words, explain how these solutions would benefit your opponent.

The Barking Dog. After discussing their interests, the Johnsons and the Smiths began to search for some creative solutions to their problem. As the Smiths began to believe that the Johnsons were really trying to be reasonable, they relaxed more and were willing to do some "wild brainstorming" (as Jim put it). Here were some of the ideas they came up with:

The Johnsons and their children could get earplugs, or they could purchase a "white noise" box (a device that tends to mask other noise).

Teach Molly not to bark at night by using a remote-controlled shock collar.

Put a fence or row of trees between the houses to muffle the noise.

Exercise the dogs a little later in the morning.

The Johnsons could change their sleep schedule so that they are not in bed when Molly normally barks.

Get an electronic burglar alarm for the Smiths' home.

Move the Johnson children's bedrooms to the far side of the house where they wouldn't hear the barking so much.

Partway through their discussion, Sally suggested that they think for a moment about the times that Molly barked the most. As they compared records, they discovered that most of the nighttime barking occurred when the Smiths were out of town for several days and Molly had not been out of her kennel for any exercise. (The person who took care of the dogs in the Smiths' absence merely came by to give them food and fresh water.) Realizing that Molly was probably getting tired of being confined, Julie offered to have her oldest daughter, Karen, feed and water Molly and take her for a walk each day when the Smiths were gone. Sally knew Karen to be responsible and conscientious, so she was open to the idea and even said that they could pay Karen. However, Steve doubted that Karen could handle Molly, so he was not willing to agree to this proposal.

Trying to change the focus of the conversation, Sally noted that Molly sometimes barked even when they were at home. Jim then asked, "What do you think Molly is barking at?" Several possibilities came to mind. The one that seemed most likely was that she was barking at people walking along a nearby highway. Jim asked whether Steve would be willing to move the kennel to the other side of his house where Molly couldn't see the highway. Steve rejected the idea because he didn't have time to do the work, and it would be too expensive to hire someone to do it. "Besides," he said, "I'm not convinced that she's barking at people along the road, so mov-

242 Go and Be Reconciled

ing the kennel may be a total waste of time. Furthermore, there's no shade on that side of the house in the afternoon, and I don't want my dogs getting baked by the sun."

After discussing a few more possibilities, Jim sensed that Steve's patience was wearing thin, so he suggested that they take a few days to think about the situation and talk again on Wednesday evening. The Smiths agreed. As they left, Jim and Julie expressed their appreciation for the Smiths' willingness to meet with them.

Evaluate Options Objectively and Reasonably

The final step in the PAUSE strategy is to evaluate possible solutions objectively and reasonably so you can reach the best possible agreement. Even if the previous steps have gone well, you may encounter significant differences of opinion when you get to this stage. If you allow negotiations to degenerate into a battle of wills, your previous work will have been wasted. Therefore, instead of relying on personal opinions, insist on using objective criteria to evaluate the options before you. If you are dealing with Christians, refer to relevant biblical principles. Whenever possible, introduce appropriate facts, official rules and regulations, or professional reports. In addition, you may seek advice from experts or respected advisors.

The Book of Daniel contains an outstanding example of an objective evaluation. When Nebuchadnezzar attacked Jerusalem in 605 B.C., he captured many Israelites from noble families and brought them back to Babylon. He instructed the chief of his court officials to bring in "young men without physical defect, handsome, showing aptitude for every kind of learning, well informed, quick to understand, and qualified to serve in the king's palace" (Dan. 1:4). Among these were Daniel, Hananiah, Mishael, and Azariah.

When Daniel learned that he and his companions would be provided with food and wine that was ceremonially unclean, he asked the chief official for permission to eat different food. Although the official was sympathetic, he refused Daniel's request, saying, "I am afraid of my lord the king. . . . Why should he see you looking worse than the other young men your age? The king would then have my head because of you" (v. 10). This left Daniel with two interesting choices. He could eat the food and defile himself, or he could refuse to eat and either starve to death or be killed for disobedience. Instead, he chose to PAUSE.

> Daniel then said to the guard whom the chief official had appointed over Daniel, Hananiah, Mishael and Azariah, "Please test your servants for ten days: Give us nothing but vegetables to eat and water to drink. Then compare our appearance with that of the young men who eat the royal food, and treat your servants in accordance with what you see." So he agreed to this and tested them for ten days.
>
> At the end of the ten days they looked healthier and better nourished than any of the young men who ate the royal food. So the guard took away their choice food and the wine they were to drink and gave them vegetables instead.
>
> Daniel 1:11–16

As you can see, Daniel carefully prepared his negotiation strategy. He affirmed his respect for those who were in authority over him. By God's grace, he understood the interests of the people with whom he was dealing. The king probably wanted healthy and productive workers. The chief official wanted to keep his head. Instead of focusing exclusively on his own interests, Daniel searched for a solution that would meet their interests as well as his own. Then, rather than offering his personal opinions, he suggested a way that the guard could evaluate his proposal objectively. When the test results showed that Daniel's proposed solution was valid and reasonable, a permanent agreement was quickly reached.

In addition to using objective criteria, you should make every effort to negotiate in a reasonable manner. Listen carefully to your opponent's concerns and suggestions, showing respect for his or her values and interests. Try to discern the hidden reasons behind objections and positions. Continue to put yourself in the other person's shoes and try to see things from that perspective. In your responses, build on the other person's ideas and words. Invite specific criticism, alternatives, and advice. Whenever your opponent tries to put pressure on you, move the discussion back to objective principles. Throughout your discussions, treat the other person as you would like to be treated.

If your evaluations result in an agreement, it is often wise to put it in writing. This will help to prevent misunderstandings and subsequent disputes on the details. At the very least, your agreement should cover these items:

What issues were resolved

What actions will be taken

Who is responsible for each action

Dates by which each action should be completed

When and how the results of the agreement will be reviewed

If you are unable to reach an agreement, don't give up too quickly. It may be that you need to return to one of the earlier steps to identify overlooked interests or to invent new options. On the other hand, it may be wise to summarize what you have accomplished and what remains to be done, and then take a few hours or days to think about the matter. If you believe that further private negotiations will be ineffective, you may suggest that the unresolved issues be discussed with the assistance of one or more objective advisors (see chapter 9).

The Barking Dog. When Jim and Julie got home that night, they made sure their windows were open so they could hear Molly the moment she began to bark. Sure enough, an hour later she began barking insistently. Jim ran outside and saw that two people on bicycles had just ridden by. He kept a journal for the next two evenings and noted three other barking episodes that coincided with people walking or riding by on the highway. He and Julie also prayed and talked some more about possible solutions. As a result, when they met with the Smiths on Wednesday night, they were prepared to offer some objective information and some creative proposals.

First they showed Steve their journal, indicating the relationship between Molly's barking and people passing by on the highway. Steve acknowledged that Molly was probably barking at those people, but he repeated his concerns about the lack of shade and his lack of time to move the kennel. Jim countered by saying, "I've been looking for a way to give my son some experience in construction work. How about if he and I come over next Saturday and help you dismantle and move your kennel? I'll bet it would only take us three or four hours. As far as needing shade, my father-in-law has got dozens of young trees on his land north of town. We could take your pickup truck out there and bring back all the trees you'd need to put in a great shelter belt around the kennel. Dad gets his land cleared, my son learns about carpentry and transplanting trees, and you have a new kennel."

Jim's proposal was so reasonable that Steve couldn't think of a way to say no. That's when Julie added her suggestion: "I have an idea about the problem of your going out of town. I talked with Karen, and she said she'd be delighted to take care of your dogs. I can understand your reluctance to trust them to a stranger, so why not have her come over to your house every day for the next week to help you work your dogs? If she proves she can handle them, then maybe you'll feel more comfortable trusting her with them. If not, we can look for another solution. Also, I should tell you that if you let her care for them, she would prefer not to be paid in cash. What she would really like is a puppy out of one of Molly's litters next year."

Once the conversation turned to puppies, Steve's heart really softened. The more he thought about the suggestions Jim and Julie were making, the more he liked them. It took a while to work out all of the details, but later conversations became even easier as the two families learned to cooperate more and more.

Summary and Application

Negotiation does not have to be a painful tug-of-war. If approached properly, many people will respond favorably to cooperative negotiation, which can allow you to find mutually beneficial solutions to common problems. Sometimes all it takes is a willingness to "look not only to your own interests, but also to the interests of others."[2]

If you are presently involved in a conflict, these questions will help you apply the principles presented in this chapter.

1. Which style of negotiation is most appropriate in your situation: competitive or cooperative? Why?

2. How can you prepare to negotiate a reasonable agreement in this situation?

3. How can you affirm your concern and respect for your opponent?

4. Understand the interests by answering these questions:

   a. Which material issues need to be resolved in order to settle this conflict? What positions have you and your opponent already taken on these issues?

   b. What are your interests in this situation?

   c. What are your opponent's interests in this situation?

5. What are some creative solutions or options that would satisfy as many interests as possible?

6. What are some ways that these options can be evaluated objectively and reasonably?

7. Go on record with the Lord by writing a prayer based on the principles taught in this chapter.

12

OVERCOME EVIL
WITH GOOD

Do not be overcome by evil, but overcome evil with
good.

Romans 12:21

Peacemaking does not always go as easily as we would like it
to. Although some people will readily make peace, others will
be stubborn and defensive and resist our efforts to be reconciled.
Sometimes they will become even more antagonistic and find new
ways to frustrate or mistreat us. Our natural reaction is to strike
back at such people, or at least to stop doing anything good to them.
As we have seen throughout this book, however, Jesus calls us to
take a remarkably different course of action: "But I tell you who
hear me: Love your enemies, do good to those who hate you, bless
those who curse you, pray for those who mistreat you. . . . Then
your reward will be great, and you will be sons of the Most High,
because he is kind to the ungrateful and wicked. Be merciful, just
as your Father is merciful" (Luke 6:27–28, 35–36).

From a worldly perspective, this approach seems naive and appears to concede defeat, but the apostle Paul knew better. He had

learned that God's ways are not the world's ways. He also understood the profound power we have through Christ. When he was subjected to intense and repeated personal attacks, he described his response with these words: "For though we live in the world, we do not wage war as the world does. The weapons we fight with are not the weapons of the world. On the contrary, they have divine power to demolish strongholds. We demolish arguments and every pretension that sets itself up against the knowledge of God, and we take captive every thought to make it obedient to Christ" (2 Cor. 10:3–5).

Paul realized that a true peacemaker is guided, motivated, and empowered by his or her identity in Christ. This identity is based on faith in the most amazing promise we could ever hear: God has forgiven all our sins and made peace with us through the death and resurrection of his Son. And he has given us the freedom and power to turn from sin (and conflict), to be conformed to the likeness of Christ, and to be his ambassadors of reconciliation (2 Cor. 5:16–20). It is the realization of who we are in Christ that inspires us to do the unnatural work of dying to self, confessing sin, addressing others' wrongs graciously, laying down rights, and forgiving deep hurts—even with people who persist in opposing or mistreating us.

Paul also understood that God has given us divine weapons to use in our quest for peace. These weapons include Scripture, prayer, truth, righteousness, the gospel, faith, love, joy, peace, patience, kindness, goodness, faithfulness, gentleness, and self-control (Eph. 6:10–18; Gal. 5:22–23). To many people, these resources and qualities seem feeble and useless when dealing with "real" problems. Yet these are the very weapons Jesus used to defeat Satan and to conquer the world (e.g., Matt. 4:1–11; 11:28–30; John 14:15–17). Since Jesus chose to use these weapons instead of resorting to worldly weapons, we should do the same.

Romans 12:14–21 describes how we should behave as we wield these spiritual weapons, especially when dealing with people who oppose or mistreat us:

> Bless those who persecute you; bless and do not curse. Rejoice with those who rejoice; mourn with those who mourn. Live in harmony

with one another. Do not be proud, but be willing to associate with people of low position. Do not be conceited. Do not repay anyone evil for evil. Be careful to do what is right in the eyes of everybody. If it is possible, as far as it depends on you, live at peace with everyone. Do not take revenge, my friends, but leave room for God's wrath, for it is written: "It is mine to avenge; I will repay," says the Lord. On the contrary: "If your enemy is hungry, feed him; if he is thirsty, give him something to drink. In doing this, you will heap burning coals on his head." Do not be overcome by evil, but overcome evil with good.

This passage shows that Paul understood the classic military principle that the best defense is an effective offense. He did not encourage a passive response to evil. Instead, he taught that we should go on the offensive—not to beat down or destroy our opponents, but to win them over, to help them see the truth, and to bring them into a right relationship with God. As this passage indicates, there are five basic principles that contribute to a victorious offensive. We have already referred to most of these principles in previous chapters, but now we will look at them again to see how we can use them with people who have persistently resisted our efforts to make peace.[1]

Control Your Tongue

The more intense a dispute becomes, the more important it is to control your tongue (Rom. 12:14). When you are involved in prolonged conflict, you may be sorely tempted to indulge in gossip, slander, and reckless words, especially if your opponent is saying critical things about you. But if you react with harsh words or gossip, you will only make matters worse. Even if your opponent speaks maliciously against you or to you, do not respond in kind. Instead, make every effort to breathe grace by saying only what is both true and helpful, speaking well of your opponent whenever possible, and using kind and gracious language. As Peter wrote, "Do not repay evil with evil or insult with insult, but with blessing, because to this you were called so that you may inherit a blessing" (1 Peter 3:9; cf. 1 Cor. 4:12–13).

In addition to preventing further offenses, controlling your tongue can help you to maintain a loving attitude and an accurate perspective of your situation (see chapters 4 and 8). As a result, you are likely to think and behave more wisely and constructively than you would if you indulged in all kinds of critical talk. Instead of undermining further progress, you will be prepared to take advantage of new opportunities for dialogue and negotiation.

Seek Godly Advisors

As Paul says, it is difficult to battle evil alone (Rom. 12:15–16). This is why it is important to develop relationships with people who will encourage you and give you biblically sound advice. These friends should also be willing to correct and admonish you when they see that you are in the wrong (Prov. 27:5–6).

Godly advisors are especially helpful when you are involved in a difficult conflict and are not seeing the results you desire. If a lack of noticeable progress causes you to doubt the biblical principles you are following, you may be tempted to abandon God's ways and resort to the world's tactics. One of the best ways to avoid straying from the Lord is to surround yourself with wise and spiritually mature people who will encourage you to stay on a biblical course, even when the going is tough.

Keep Doing What Is Right

Romans 12:17 emphasizes the importance of continuing to do what is right even when it seems that your opponent will never cooperate. When Paul says, "Be careful to do what is right in the eyes of everybody," he does not mean that we should be slaves to the opinions of others. The Greek word that is translated "be careful" (*pronoeo*) means to give thought to the future, to plan in advance, or to take careful precaution (cf. 2 Cor. 8:20–21). Therefore, what Paul is saying is that you should plan and act so carefully and so properly that any reasonable person who is watching you will eventually acknowledge that what you did was right. Peter taught the same principle when he wrote:

Live such good lives among the pagans that, though they accuse you of doing wrong, they may see your good deeds and glorify God on the day he visits us. . . . For it is God's will that by doing good you should silence the ignorant talk of foolish men. . . . But do this with gentleness and respect, keeping a clear conscience, so that those who speak maliciously against your good behavior in Christ may be ashamed of their slander.

1 Peter 2:12, 15; 3:15b–16

This principle is dramatically illustrated in 1 Samuel 24:1–22. When King Saul was pursuing David relentlessly through the desert, intending to murder him, Saul carelessly entered a cave where David and his men were hiding deep inside. David's men urged him to kill the king, but David refused, saying, "I will not lift my hand against my master, because he is the LORD's anointed" (v. 10b). After Saul left the cave and walked away, David emerged and called after him. When Saul realized that David could have killed him, he was deeply convicted of his sin and said:

You are more righteous than I. . . . You have treated me well, but I have treated you badly. You have just now told me of the good you did to me; the LORD delivered me into your hands, but you did not kill me. When a man finds his enemy, does he let him get away unharmed? May the LORD reward you well for the way you treated me today. I know that you will surely be king and that the kingdom of Israel will be established in your hands.

verses 17–20

Years later Saul's prediction came true, and David ascended the throne of Israel. David's determination to obey God and to keep doing what was right helped him avoid saying and doing things he would have later regretted. As a result, all of his enemies were eventually won over or defeated. Thousands of years later people are still taking note of David's righteousness.

I have seen many others who resolved to keep doing what was right even in terribly painful situations. When John's wife, Karen, divorced him and moved in with her high school sweetheart, John was devastated, especially when his church refused to do anything to try to save their marriage. But he drew on God's grace and resisted the temptation to give in to self-pity or bitterness. He refused to criticize Karen, especially in front of their children. He bent over backwards to accommodate their ever-changing visitation schedule. Most of all, he continued to pray for Karen, and whenever they talked with each other, he asked God to help him speak to her with genuine love and gentleness.

After about a year, Karen and her boyfriend were fighting continually. As she compared his behavior to John's unfailing kindness in the face of her betrayal, she began to realize what a terrible mistake she had made. With great trepidation she asked John if there was any chance they could get together again. To her amazement, he said yes and suggested that they start counseling with the pastor at his new church. Eight months later, their children had the joy of seeing their parents renewing their vows and reuniting their family.

Whether Karen came back to him or not, John's decision to keep doing what was right honored God. His behavior was also a powerful witness to his children about the love and forgiveness of Christ. And he later learned that his example had helped some other divorced people respond to their ex-spouses graciously, even though none of them came back. As John showed, doing what is right—even in the face of unjust treatment—is always the safest path to walk.

Recognize Your Limits

When dealing with difficult people, it is also important to recognize your limits. Even when you continue to do what is right, some people may adamantly refuse to admit you are right or to live at peace with you. This is why Paul wrote, "If it is possible, as far as it depends on you, live at peace with everyone" (Rom. 12:18). In other words, do all you can to be reconciled to others, but remember that you cannot force others to do what is right. If you have done everything within your power to resolve a conflict, you have fulfilled your responsibility to God and may stop actively trying to solve the problem. If circumstances change and you have new opportunities to seek peace with an opponent, you should certainly try to do so. In the meantime, however, it is not necessary or wise to waste time, energy, and resources fretting about someone who stubbornly refuses to be reconciled.

It is easier to accept your limits if you have a biblical view of success. The world defines success in terms of what a person possesses, controls, or accomplishes. God defines success in terms of faithful obedience to his will. The world asks, "What results have you achieved?" God asks, "Were you faithful to my ways?" As we saw in chapter 3, the Lord controls the ultimate outcome of all you do. Therefore, he knows that even your best efforts will not always accomplish the results you desire. This is why he does not hold you accountable for specific results. Instead, he asks for only one thing—obedience to his revealed will. "Fear God and keep his commandments, for this is the whole duty of man" (Eccles. 12:13b). If you have done all that you can to be reconciled to someone, you have fulfilled your duty and are a success in God's eyes. Let him take it from there.

An essential aspect of recognizing your limits is rejecting the temptation to take personal revenge on someone who is doing wrong (or even dream about it). Paul reminds us that God is responsible for doing justice and for punishing those who do not repent (Rom. 12:19). Proverbs 20:22 commands, "Do not say, 'I'll pay you back for this wrong!' Wait for the LORD, and he will deliver you" (cf. 24:29). God has many instruments that he can use to bring evil people to justice and deliver you from them. Among other things, he can use the church (Matt. 18:17–20), the civil courts (Rom. 13:1–5), or even Satan (1 Cor. 5:5; 1 Tim. 1:20) to deal with unrepentant people.

Instead of taking justice into your own hands, respect and cooperate with God's methods for dealing with people who persist in doing wrong. Sometimes this may involve church discipline, and in other cases it may be appropriate for you to pursue litigation (see appendix D). In some cases, however, all you are to do is wait for God to deal with people in his own way (see Psalms 37 and 73). Although his results may come more slowly than you desire, they will always be better than anything you could bring about on your own.

Use the Ultimate Weapon

The final principle for responding to a stubborn opponent is described in Romans 12:20–21: "On the contrary: 'If your enemy is hungry, feed him; if he is thirsty, give him something to drink.

In doing this, you will heap burning coals on his head.' Do not be overcome by evil, but overcome evil with good." Here is the ultimate weapon: *deliberate, focused love* (cf. Luke 6:27–28; 1 Cor. 13:4–7). Instead of reacting spitefully to those who mistreat you, Jesus wants you to discern their deepest needs and do all you can to meet those needs. Sometimes this will require going to them to show them their faults. At other times there may be a need for mercy and compassion, patience, and words of encouragement. You may even have opportunities to provide material and financial assistance to those who least deserve it or expect it from you.

Paul's reference to "burning coals on his head" indicates the irresistible power of deliberate, focused love. Ancient armies often used burning coals to fend off attackers (Ps. 120:4). No soldier could resist this weapon for long; it would eventually overcome even the most determined attacker. Love has the same irresistible power. At the very least, actively loving an enemy will protect you from being spiritually defeated by anger, bitterness, and thirst for revenge. And, in some cases, your active and determined love for your opponent may be used by God to bring that person to repentance.[2]

This powerful love is vividly described in Ernest Gordon's marvelous book, *To End All Wars* (formerly titled *Through the Valley of the Kwai*). Gordon was captured by the Japanese during World War II and forced, with other British prisoners, to endure years of horrible treatment while building the notorious "Railroad of Death" through Thailand. Faced with the starvation and disease of the prison camps and the brutality of his captors, who killed hundreds of his comrades, Gordon survived to become an inspiring example of the triumph of Christian love against human evil.

This love shone especially bright one day when Gordon and his fellow prisoners came upon a trainload of wounded Japanese soldiers who were being transported to Bangkok. Here is how Gordon describes God's work of grace:

> They were on their own and without medical care. . . . Their uniforms were encrusted with mud, blood, and excrement. Their wounds, sorely inflamed and full of pus, crawled with maggots. We could understand now why the Japanese were so cruel to their prisoners. If they didn't care for their own, why should they care for us?

The wounded men looked at us forlornly as they sat with their heads resting against the carriages waiting fatalistically for death. They were the refuse of war; there was nowhere to go and no one to care for them. . . .

Without a word, most of the officers in my section unbuckled their packs, took out part of their ration and a rag or two, and, with water canteens in their hands went over to the Japanese train to help them. Our guards tried to prevent us . . . but we ignored them and knelt by the side of the enemy to give them food and water, to clean and bind up their wounds, to smile and say a kind word. Grateful cries of *"Aragatto!"* ("Thank you!") followed us when we left. . . .

I regarded my comrades with wonder. Eighteen months ago they would have joined readily in the destruction of our captors had they fallen into their hands. Now these same men were dressing the enemy's wounds. We had experienced a moment of grace, there in those blood-stained railway cars. God had broken through the barriers of our prejudice and had given us the will to obey his command, "Thou shalt love."[3]

Most of us will never be subjected to this kind of abuse or have to reach across so great a chasm to love those who have wronged us. Therefore we need to keep stories like Ernest Gordon's and Corrie ten Boom's in mind when we are challenged with loving an enemy. The same principles apply no matter how great or small the conflict. As we love our enemies and seek to meet their needs, we can glorify God and protect our souls from the acid of bitterness and resentment, just as Gordon and his comrades did. And in some cases, God may use our loving acts to soften the hearts of our opponents.

I am blessed to have a wife who has loved me like this time after time. One night we had such a strong disagreement that we went to bed unreconciled. (Yes, we broke the command not to let the sun go down on our anger.) As we lay there facing away from each other, a bizarre contest developed. Without either one of us saying a word, we tacitly agreed that "he who moves first is weak." I was not going to budge an inch until Corlette moved. She was just as determined not to move until I did. So we lay there like two frozen bodies.

I was soon more frozen than I wanted to be. I had been so distracted when I crawled into bed that I had not pulled the covers over me. It was wintertime, and we usually slept with our bedroom window open, so the room was soon very cold, as was I. But I was so caught up in my stubborn pride that I refused to move and pull up the covers.

After a few minutes, I began to tremble from the cold. Corlette felt it through the mattress and slowly turned her head (so I could not tell she was moving!) to see what was going on. She understood my predicament in a moment: Her silly, stubborn husband had backed himself into a corner and needed help to get out. Giving up her desire to win the ridiculous contest of wills, Corlette made the first move. She reached down, took hold of the blankets at my feet, and pulled them gently over my shoulders.

In a few moments I was trembling even more, but not from the cold. Her loving gesture was so entirely undeserved that it melted my heart. My anger and pride dissolved, and I finally saw how much I had sinned against her. With tears of regret, I turned to Corlette and experienced the joy and freedom that comes from making peace.

There is such wisdom and power in these simple words: "'If your enemy is hungry, feed him; if he is thirsty, give him something to drink. In doing so you will heap burning coals on his head.' Do not be overcome by evil, but overcome evil with good."

Summary and Application

The principles described in Romans 12:14–21 are applicable at every stage of a conflict, and they are echoed throughout the Bible—"Love your neighbor as yourself." "Do to others what you would have them do to you." "Overlook an offense." "If someone is caught in a sin, restore him gently." "Speak the truth in love." "Look out for the interests of others." "Forgive as the Lord forgave you." "Do not be overcome by evil, but overcome evil with good."

Applying these principles can be difficult, but it is always worth the effort, because God delights to work in and through us as we serve him as peacemakers. As Paul promises: "Therefore, my dear brothers, stand firm. Let nothing move you. Always give yourselves fully to the work of the Lord, because you know that your labor in the Lord is not in vain" (1 Cor. 15:58).

If you are presently involved in a conflict, these questions will help you apply the principles presented in this chapter.

1. On whom are you relying to guide your responses to this conflict?
2. Which worldly weapons have you been using, or are you tempted to use, in this situation?
3. How can the gospel of Jesus Christ guide, motivate, and empower you from this point forward?
4. Have you been using your tongue to bless your opponents or to speak critically of them? How could you breathe grace to them in the days ahead?
5. To whom can you turn for godly advice and encouragement?
6. What can you keep on doing in this situation that is right?
7. Have you done everything in your power to live at peace with your opponent? Is it appropriate to turn to church or civil authorities to seek assistance in resolving this dispute?
8. What needs does your opponent have that God may want you to try to meet? In other words, how can you love your opponent in a deliberate and focused way?
9. Go on record with the Lord by writing a prayer based on the principles taught in this chapter.

CONCLUSION

The Peacemaker's Pledge

Peacemaking can involve a wide variety of activities, all of which may be summarized in four basic principles drawn directly from Scripture. Taken together, these principles could be called "The Peacemaker's Pledge."

The Peacemaker's Pledge

As people reconciled to God by the death and resurrection of Jesus Christ, we believe that we are called to respond to conflict in a way that is remarkably different from the way the world deals with conflict (Matt. 5:9; Luke 6:27–36; Gal. 5:19–26). We also believe that conflict provides opportunities to glorify God, serve other people, and grow to be like Christ (Rom. 8:28–29; 1 Cor. 10:31–11:1; James 1:2–4). Therefore, in response to God's love and in reliance on his grace, we commit ourselves to responding to conflict according to the following principles.

Glorify God

Instead of focusing on our own desires or dwelling on what others may do, we will rejoice in the Lord and bring him praise by depending on his forgiveness, wisdom, power, and love as we seek to faithfully obey his commands and maintain a loving, merciful, and forgiving attitude (Ps. 37:1–6; Mark 11:25; John 14:15; Rom. 12:17–21; 1 Cor. 10:31; Phil. 4:2–9; Col. 3:1–4; James 3:17–18; 4:1–3; 1 Peter 2:12).

Get the Log Out of Your Own Eye

Instead of blaming others for a conflict or resisting correction, we will trust in God's mercy and take responsibility for our own contribution to conflicts—confessing our sins to those we have wronged, asking God to help us change any attitudes and habits that lead to conflict, and seeking to repair any harm we have caused (Prov. 28:13; Matt. 7:3–5; Luke 19:8; Col. 3:5–14; 1 John 1:8–9).

Gently Restore

Instead of pretending that conflict doesn't exist or talking about others behind their backs, we will overlook minor offenses or we will talk personally and graciously with those whose offenses seem too serious to overlook, seeking to restore them rather than condemn them. When a conflict with a Christian brother or sister cannot be resolved in private, we will ask others in the body of Christ to help us settle the matter in a biblical manner (Prov. 19:11; Matt. 18:15–20; 1 Cor. 6:1–8; Gal. 6:1–2; Eph. 4:29; 2 Tim. 2:24–26; James 5:9).

Go and Be Reconciled

Instead of accepting premature compromise or allowing relationships to wither, we will actively pursue genuine peace and reconciliation—forgiving others as God, for Christ's sake, has forgiven us, and seeking just and mutually beneficial solutions to our differences (Matt. 5:23–24; 6:12; 7:12; Eph. 4:1–3, 32; Phil. 2:3–4).

By God's grace, we will apply these principles as a matter of stewardship, realizing that conflict is an opportunity, not an accident. We will remember that success in God's eyes is not a matter of specific results, but of faithful, dependent obedience. And we will pray that our service as peacemakers will bring praise to our Lord and lead others to know his infinite love (Matt. 25:14–21; John 13:34–35; Rom. 12:18; 1 Peter 2:19; 4:19).

This pledge is available in a poster and in a brochure that also contains the Slippery Slope diagram, the Seven A's of Confession, the Four Promises of Forgiveness, and the PAUSE Principle of Negotiating. I encourage you to acquire one of these pamphlets through Peacemaker Ministries and use the Pledge in three ways. First, use it as a personal commitment and guide for resolving the conflicts that God allows in your life. In doing so, you can experience the joy of bringing glory to God, serving other people, and growing to be like Christ.

Second, use the Pledge as a teaching tool to help others understand and follow the marvelous peacemaking principles God has given us in Scripture. As people learn from you, they too can model and teach these principles, and eventually influence an ever-growing circle of people.

Finally, use the Pledge as a standard for conflict resolution in your church, ministry, or business. As more and more groups of Christians learn and commit themselves to what the Bible teaches about peacemaking, the church as a whole will be able to deal with conflict in a more biblically consistent manner. Such a trend would help to reestablish the church as the effective peacemaking body God intended it to be and exalt the Lord Jesus Christ, the greatest peacemaker of all.

APPENDIX A

A PEACEMAKER'S CHECKLIST

Whenever you are involved in a conflict, you may apply the four basic principles of peacemaking by asking yourself these questions:

Glorify God: How can I please and honor the Lord in this situation?

Get the log out of your eye: How can I show Jesus' work in me by taking responsibility for my contribution to this conflict?

Gently restore: How can I lovingly serve others by helping them take responsibility for their contribution to this conflict?

Go and be reconciled: How can I demonstrate the forgiveness of God and encourage a reasonable solution to this conflict?

The following checklist summarizing the principles presented in this book is designed to help you answer the four questions.

Glorify God

With God's help, I will seek to glorify him by:

☐ Depending on and drawing attention to his grace—that is, his undeserved love, mercy, forgiveness, strength, and wisdom that he gives to us through Jesus Christ

☐ Doing everything in my power to live at peace with those around me

☐ Remembering that Jesus' reputation is affected by the way I get along with others

☐ Asking God to help me to trust him, obey him, imitate him, and acknowledge him in the midst of conflict

☐ Guarding against Satan's schemes and false teachings, which are designed to promote selfishness and incite conflict

☐ Using conflict as an opportunity to serve others

☐ Cooperating with God as he prunes me of sinful attitudes and habits and helps me grow to be more like Christ

☐ Seeing myself as a steward and managing myself, my resources, and my situation in such a way that God would say, "Well done, good and faithful servant!"

Get the Log Out of Your Eye

To decide whether something is really worth fighting over, with God's help I will:

☐ Define the issues (personal and material), decide how they are related, deal only with issues that are too important to be overlooked, and begin usually with personal issues

☐ Overlook minor offenses

☐ Change my attitude by rejoicing in the Lord and remembering how much he has forgiven me, being gentle toward others, replacing anxiety with prayer and trust, deliberately thinking about what is good and right in others, and putting into practice what God has taught me through the Bible

☐ Carefully consider how much it will cost (emotionally, spiritually, and financially) to continue a conflict instead of simply settling it

☐ Use my rights only to advance God's kingdom, to serve others, and to enhance my ability to serve and grow to be like Christ

To identify desires that may have turned into idols and contributed to this conflict, I will examine my heart by asking myself the following X-ray questions:

- ☐ What am I preoccupied with? (What is the first thing on my mind in the morning and/or the last thing at night?)
- ☐ How would I fill in this blank? "If only _____, then I would be happy, fulfilled, and secure."
- ☐ What do I want to preserve or avoid at any cost?
- ☐ Where do I put my trust?
- ☐ What do I fear?
- ☐ When a certain desire is not met, do I feel frustration, anxiety, resentment, bitterness, anger, or depression?
- ☐ Is there something I desire so much that I am willing to disappoint or hurt others in order to have it?

Before talking to others about their wrongs, with God's help I will examine myself by asking:

- ☐ Am I guilty of reckless words, falsehood, gossip, slander, or any other worthless talk?
- ☐ Have I tried to control others?
- ☐ Have I kept my word and fulfilled all of my responsibilities?
- ☐ Have I abused my authority?
- ☐ Have I respected those in authority over me?
- ☐ Have I treated others as I would want to be treated?
- ☐ Am I being motivated by lusts of the flesh, pride, love of money, fear of others, or wanting good things too much?

When I see that I have sinned, I will ask for God to help me:

- ☐ Repent—that is, change the way I have been thinking so that I turn away from my sin and turn toward God
- ☐ Confess my sins by using the Seven A's: addressing everyone I have affected; avoiding *if, but,* and *maybe;* admitting specifically what I did wrong; acknowledging how I have hurt others; accepting the consequences of my actions; explaining how I will alter my attitudes and behavior in the future; and asking for forgiveness

☐ Change my attitudes and behavior by praying for God's help, delighting myself in the Lord so that I can overcome my personal idols, studying the Bible, and practicing godly character

Gently Restore

☐ When I am estranged from someone else, I will ask God to help me discern the most effective way to approach him to confess my sins or show him his fault

☐ Even if I work through other people at first, I will do all I can to talk face-to-face eventually so we can both express and confirm repentance, confession, and forgiveness

☐ When I learn that someone has something against me, I will go to that person to talk about it, even if I don't believe I have done anything wrong

I will consider a sin too serious to overlook if it:

☐ Is dishonoring God
☐ Has damaged our relationship
☐ Is hurting or might hurt other people
☐ Is hurting the offender and diminishing his or her usefulness to God

When I need to show others their fault, with God's help I will:

☐ Draw on God's grace so that I can breathe grace to others

☐ Do everything I can to bring hope through the gospel by focusing on what God has done and is doing for us through Christ

☐ Listen responsibly by waiting patiently while others speak, concentrating on what they say, clarifying their comments through appropriate questions, reflecting their feelings and concerns with paraphrased responses, and agreeing with them whenever possible

☐ Make charitable judgments by believing the best about others until I have facts to prove otherwise

☐ Speak the truth in love

☐ Talk from beside people, not from above them, as a fellow sinner who needs forgiveness and grace as much as they do

☐ Help others examine the desires that may be ruling their hearts

- [ ] Choose a time and place that will be conducive to a productive conversation
- [ ] Talk in person whenever possible
- [ ] Engage others by using stories, analogies, and metaphors that touch their hearts
- [ ] Communicate so clearly that I cannot be misunderstood
- [ ] Plan my words in advance and try to anticipate how others will respond to me
- [ ] Use "I" statements when appropriate
- [ ] State objective facts rather than personal opinions
- [ ] Use the Bible carefully and tactfully
- [ ] Ask for feedback
- [ ] Offer solutions and preferences
- [ ] Recognize my limits and stop talking once I have said what is reasonable and appropriate

If I cannot resolve a dispute with someone in private and the matter is too serious to overlook, with God's help I will:

- [ ] Suggest that we seek help from one or more spiritually mature advisors who can help both of us see things more objectively
- [ ] If necessary, ask one or two others to talk with us
- [ ] If necessary, seek help from our respective churches and respect their authority
- [ ] Go to court only if I have exhausted my church remedies, if the rights I am seeking to enforce are biblically legitimate, and if my action has a righteous purpose

Go and Be Reconciled

When someone has wronged me, I will ask God to change my heart so that I want to forgive him.

When I forgive someone, with God's help I will make these promises:

- [ ] I will not dwell on this incident.
- [ ] I will not bring up this incident again and use it against you.
- [ ] I will not talk to others about this incident.
- [ ] I will not allow this incident to stand between us or to hinder our personal relationship.

When I am having a difficult time forgiving someone, with God's help I will:

- ☐ Renounce the desire to punish the other person, to make that person earn my forgiveness, or to demand guarantees that I will never be wronged again
- ☐ Assess my contributions to the problem
- ☐ If necessary, talk with that person to address any unresolved issues and to confirm repentance
- ☐ Recognize the ways that God is using the situation for good
- ☐ Remember how much God has forgiven me, not only in this situation but also in the past
- ☐ Draw on God's strength through prayer, Bible study, and, if necessary, Christian counseling

With God's help I will demonstrate forgiveness and practice the replacement principle by:

- ☐ Replacing painful thoughts and memories with positive thoughts and memories
- ☐ Saying positive things to and about the person whom I have forgiven
- ☐ Doing loving and constructive things to and for the person whom I have forgiven

When I need to negotiate an agreement on material issues, with God's help I will PAUSE:

- ☐ Prepare thoroughly for our discussions
- ☐ Affirm my respect and concern for my opponent
- ☐ Understand my opponent's interests
- ☐ Search for creative solutions that will satisfy as many of our interests as possible
- ☐ Evaluate various options objectively and reasonably

When others continue to mistreat or oppose me, with God's help I will:

☐ Control my tongue and continue to say only what is helpful and beneficial to others

☐ Seek counsel, support, and encouragement from spiritually mature advisors

☐ Keep doing what is right no matter what others do to me

☐ Recognize my limits by resisting the temptation to take revenge and by remembering that being successful in God's eyes depends on faithfulness, not results

☐ Continue to love my enemy by striving to discern and address his or her spiritual, emotional, and material needs

Appendix B

Alternative Ways to Resolve Disputes

Since the early '80s, a great deal of attention has been devoted to developing alternative ways to settle conflicts. In this appendix, I will describe and compare several of the more common dispute resolution processes, including negotiation, mediation, arbitration, litigation, and Christian conciliation.

Negotiation

Negotiation is a personal bargaining process in which parties seek to reach a mutually agreeable settlement of their substantive differences. Although some people are able to negotiate for themselves, many rely on attorneys or other professionals to advise them or act on their behalf.

Negotiation has several advantages when compared to more formal methods of resolving disputes. It is usually faster, less expensive, and less time-consuming, and more private and flexible than arbitration or litigation. Because it is entirely voluntary, negotiation also reduces the likelihood that one party will lose everything while the other party wins.

The primary disadvantage of negotiation is that it sometimes allows a more knowledgeable or powerful person to take advantage of a weaker person, thus resulting in injustice. In addition, if attorneys are involved, negotiation may still cost thousands of dollars. Also, some parties may use negotiation to resolve urgent money and property issues without considering the deeper personal problems that may continue to cause conflict and alienation.

Mediation

Mediation is similar to negotiation, except that it involves the assistance of one or more neutral mediators who work to facilitate communication and understanding between the parties. The mediator may initially act as an intermediary between the parties, but the ultimate goal is usually to arrange a conference at which all of the parties and the mediator are present. A mediator helps the parties explore various solutions to their differences, but the parties retain control of the results and are not obligated to follow the mediator's advice. A mediator may be a paid professional, a respected individual from the community, or a personal acquaintance of the parties who agrees to help them without charge.

The presence of a neutral mediator tends to reduce the possibility that one party will take advantage of the other. Mediation has several other advantages when compared to arbitration and litigation. Because of its informal nature, mediation is relatively flexible, private, inexpensive, and time efficient. It facilitates understanding and allows parties to maintain their dignity while dealing with sensitive issues. Consequently, it is less likely to damage a relationship than is a more adversarial process. As a voluntary process, it is also likely to allow both parties to win on some of their concerns and arrive at a settlement that both sides will be inclined to preserve.

Mediation does have several disadvantages, however. Either party may refuse to participate in the process. Imbalances of power may still affect the results. The process may become deadlocked, thus wasting the previous investment of time and money. Also, the results of mediation are not legally enforceable unless the parties incorporate their settlement into a legal contract.

Arbitration

In arbitration, the parties agree to present each side of their dispute before one or more neutral arbitrators and, in most cases, to be legally bound by the arbitrator's decision on the matter. Unlike mediators, arbitrators do not attempt to help the parties communicate with each other or assist them in negotiating a settlement. Instead, like judges, they gather evidence and render a binding decision. Most states have laws that allow parties to appoint their own arbitrators; these may be unpaid volunteers or trained professionals from organizations like Peacemaker Ministries or the American Arbitration Association.

The primary advantage of arbitration when compared to negotiation and mediation is that it always produces a resolution to a dispute, even if one or both of the parties do not like it. In contrast to litigation, arbitration is relatively private and informal and is usually less expensive. Also, because most laws allow only limited grounds for appealing an arbitration decision, arbitration has the capability to produce a final, legally enforceable result more quickly than litigation.

When compared to negotiation and mediation, the primary disadvantage of arbitration is that relationship problems are ignored, which often perpetuates or aggravates personal estrangement. Arbitration also has disadvantages when compared to litigation. It is less guarded by procedural rules. Because many arbitrators lack formal legal training, arbitrated decisions are sometimes less consistent and predictable than courtroom decisions. Also, if one party refuses to abide by the arbitrators' decision, the other party may still need to resort to the courts to enforce it.

Litigation

Litigation utilizes the judges, juries, and procedural rules of the civil court system. Compared to other methods of resolving a dispute, litigation has several advantages. A court has the authority to require all parties to appear and to abide by its decisions. With its foundation of statutes and case law, a court is also able to render more predictable decisions on many issues. In addition, court decisions are a matter of public record, recognized in other jurisdictions and subject to full appellate review.

Litigation has many disadvantages, however. In addition to being expensive and time-consuming, litigation is constrained by formal procedures, encourages public attention, offers limited remedies (usually money or injunctions), and often allows one party to win completely while the other party loses everything. Court technicalities restrict communication and understanding between parties, often leaving them frustrated and angry. A court is usually forced to deal with the symptoms of a problem rather than its real causes, leaving the parties in an ongoing state of antagonism. As a result of these factors, litigation is likely to increase bitterness between the parties and further damage any personal relationship they had previously enjoyed.

The side effects of litigation and, to a lesser degree, of the other secular methods of conflict resolution are even more serious when viewed from a spiritual perspective. The more adversarial a process is, the more likely it is to provide a poor witness of Christian love and obedience to God. The adversarial process aggravates critical attitudes and encourages complaining and self-justification. It obstructs confession and repentance, thus prolonging destructive habit patterns. Moreover, as the parties' hearts are hardened by these factors, they are likely to experience more conflict in the future. This is why Supreme Court justice Antonin Scalia said, "Judges can also tell you of brothers and sisters permanently estranged by litigation over a will, or of once-friendly neighbors living in undying enmity because of a boundary dispute that is, in financial terms, inconsequential. Whatever the legal rights and wrongs of such matters, these results are not worth it."[1]

As Justice Scalia noted, the spiritual, emotional, financial, and time costs of resolving a dispute through the adversarial process often negate whatever else might be gained. Therefore, whenever possible, a Christian should exhaust the principles of conflict resolution set forth in the Bible before resorting to other means.

Christian Conciliation

Christian conciliation is a process for reconciling persons and resolving disputes out of court in a biblically faithful manner.[2] Ideally, this process is carried out by reconcilers who serve under the guidance and authority of the parties' churches as described in chapter 9, but it can also be conducted by professional conciliators who serve the parties on a contract basis. The process is conciliatory rather than adversarial in nature—that is, it encourages honest communication and reasonable cooperation rather than unnecessary contention and manipulation.

Conciliation may involve three steps. First, one or both parties may receive *individual counseling* or *conflict coaching* on how to resolve the dispute in private, without a third party. Second, if private efforts are unsuccessful, the parties may submit their dispute to biblical *mediation,* a process in which one or more Christian conciliators meet with them to promote constructive dialogue and encourage a voluntary and biblically faithful settlement of their personal and substantive differences. Third, if mediation is unsuccessful, the parties may proceed to biblical *arbitration,* which means that one or more arbitrators will hear their case and render a legally binding decision that is consistent with Scripture.

Christian conciliation is more values-oriented than most types of mediation. While secular mediators will work to help the parties come to a voluntary settlement, they will often be reluctant to go beyond this, especially if doing so would require that they evaluate others' attitudes and behavior from a moral perspective. In contrast, Christian conciliators make it a point to draw out the underlying reasons for a dispute, which are sometimes referred to as "matters of the heart." Believing that God has established timeless moral principles, which he has recorded in Scripture and written in our hearts, Christian conciliators will draw the parties' attention to attitudes, motives, or actions that appear to be inconsistent with those standards. This will be especially true with parties who profess to be Christians; anyone who claims to be a follower of Christ will be encouraged to obey God's commands and behave in a manner that will please and honor him.

When compared to secular means of resolving disputes, Christian conciliation has many advantages. It promotes traditional values, preserves relationships, encourages meaningful change, avoids negative publicity, provides a positive Christian witness, and is relatively inexpensive. In addition, when compared to litigation, Christian conciliation is less constrained by rigid procedures and, therefore, allows more creative remedies and faster results. Another benefit is that Christian conciliators have much more flexibility than do civil judges when it comes to hearing testimony or reviewing evidence. Thus, if a dispute involves defects in the construction of a building or the repair of an automobile, a conciliator may personally inspect the building or drive the car. As a result of this flexibility, parties often feel that the facts and issues in the case are given a more thorough review than could occur in a court of law.

People who sincerely want to do what is right and are open to learning where they have been wrong can receive great benefits from the conciliation process. Conciliators can help them to identify improper attitudes or unwise practices, to understand more fully the effects of their decisions and policies, and to make improvements in their lives and businesses that will help them avoid unnecessary conflict in the future.

Christian conciliation does have limitations, however. Conciliators do not have the same authority as civil judges and, therefore, cannot force parties to cooperate with conciliation or abide by its results. (However, signed agreements reached through mediation and arbitration awards can be enforced by a civil court.) Conciliation can be less predictable than litigation, because each case has different conciliators and because the process is less constrained by procedures, statutes, and case precedents. Finally, there are only limited grounds for appealing arbitrated decisions, which means parties will have little opportunity to have an unfavorable decision reviewed by a higher authority. (On the other hand, this means they will be spared from the expenses and delays inherent in the appeal process.)

In spite of these limitations, Christian conciliation usually provides more thorough and satisfying solutions to conflict than can be obtained through secular processes. As a couple wrote after their dispute was resolved:

> I believe that the most valuable thing we received from [Christian conciliation] was sound advice, seasoned with good Christian ethics and godly wisdom. I really believe that the right answer was attained. Understand please that the answers you gave were not what I came to hear, but I knew that this was right and it was confirmed as the neighbors were pacified. You could not have been more helpful. Our only regret was that we waited much too long to come to you.

As I mentioned above, whenever possible, Christian conciliation should be pursued within a local church with the help of spiritually mature Christians. If this kind of conflict resolution is not available within a church, parties can seek assistance from other godly people who are capable of serving in this way. When needed, parties or church leaders may obtain printed resources (such as "Rules of Procedure," various model forms, or *Guiding People through Conflict*) and specialized assistance through Peacemaker Ministries (see appendix E).

Appendix C

Principles
of Restitution

Restitution is an important biblical concept. When a person has injured someone else, God says that he "must confess the sin he has committed . . . [and] make full restitution for his wrong" (Num. 5:7). This is what Zacchaeus did when he was led to repentance by the Lord Jesus. Zacchaeus did not merely ask for forgiveness and go on about his business. Instead, he stood up in front of Jesus and the people he had wronged and said, "Look, Lord! Here and now I give half of my possessions to the poor, and if I have cheated anybody out of anything, I will pay back four times the amount" (Luke 19:8).

Restitution produces several benefits. As much as possible, it restores the injured party to his or her former position. Restitution also benefits society by making destructive behavior unprofitable. In addition, it gives the offender an opportunity to make amends for sin and to demonstrate by actions that he or she wishes to be restored to the injured person and to society in general.

Much of what the Bible teaches about restitution is given in the form of case law. In other words, instead of presenting a multitude of specific rules to cover every conceivable situation, the Bible provides a few examples from which we can derive general principles that carry over into similar situations. For example, the principles taught in Exodus 21:18–23 apply to all kinds of personal injuries directly caused by people. These principles would also apply to injuries resulting from various forms of negligence, such as failing to install adequate railings on balconies or fences around swimming pools (see Deut. 22:8). Likewise, the principles set forth in Exodus 22:1–15 apply to all types of property damage, such as theft or accidental damage to borrowed property.

According to Exodus 21:19, when a person is deliberately injured, the offender is liable for all actual damages—that is, for medical expenses and for time lost from work. An offender is also liable for actual damages resulting from negligence (Exod. 21:22–35; cf. vv. 28–29). Exodus 21:22 implies that the injured party should assess damages and report them to the offender. If the offender believes the assessment is too high, the matter should be arbitrated by an appropriate authority (cf. 1 Cor. 6:1–8). Although the Bible gives clear support for *actual damages,* it does not provide any explicit guidance on making restitution for pain and suffering or for intentional infliction of emotional distress. The primary biblical remedy for these wrongs is confession, repentance, and forgiveness.

When property has been damaged unintentionally, the Bible says that the offender must make "simple restitution," that is, repair or replace the property (Exod. 22:5–6). If the theft or damage was intentional but the offender has truly repented and was determined to make restitution even before the crime was discovered, the offender must pay for the property plus a penalty of twenty percent (Lev. 6:1–5; cf. Num. 5:5–10). If the offense was intentional and the offender is apprehended along with the undamaged property, the offender must return it along with its equivalent value (Exod. 22:4). If the offender is caught after the property has been disposed of, the offender must pay at least four times its value. If the property is difficult to replace, the offender must repay five times its value (Exod. 22:1).[1] These penalties are obviously designed to discourage deliberate wrongs and to encourage prompt repentance and confession.

Some people argue that restitution is not a valid concept in the New Testament age. I disagree. Nothing in the New Testament explicitly repeals the concept (see Matt. 5:17–20). In fact, restitution is implicitly endorsed by Jesus in Luke 19:1–10. Moreover, restitution is a sign of taking responsibility for one's actions, and nothing in the Bible indicates that God wants believers to be less responsible in this age than they were before the advent of Christ.

Furthermore, restitution is not inconsistent with forgiveness. Believers in Old Testament times were called to forgive others' offenses, yet they were entitled to receive restitution (Num. 5:5–8). Forgiving another person's wrong means you will not dwell on it, use it against the person, talk to others about it, or let it stand between you. But being forgiven does not necessarily release the offender from responsibility to repair the damage. Certainly, an injured party may exercise mercy, and in some cases it is good to waive the right to restitution (Matt. 18:22–27). But in many cases, making restitution is beneficial *even for the offender*. Doing so demonstrates remorse, sincerity, and a new attitude, which can help speed reconciliation (Luke 19:8–9). At the same time, it serves to ingrain lessons that will help the offender avoid similar wrongdoing in the future (see Ps. 119:67, 71; Prov. 19:19).

Therefore, if you have damaged another person's property or physically harmed someone, God expects you to do all you can to make that person whole. If he or she decides to release you from your responsibility, you should be deeply grateful for such mercy. On the other hand, if you have been harmed or your property has been damaged, you should prayerfully consider how badly you need to be made whole and whether making restitution would benefit or unduly burden the offender. As you pray about it, keep in mind that blending mercy with justice is a powerful way to restore peace and glorify God.

Appendix D

When Is It Right to Go to Court?

First Corinthians 6:1–8 specifically limits a Christian's freedom to sue another Christian in civil court. There is significant confusion regarding the intent of this passage and the extent of its limitation. In this appendix, I will address a few of the central issues in this passage.

Does 1 Corinthians 6 Apply Only to Scandalous Lawsuits?

Some people argue that 1 Corinthians 6 applies only to lawsuits that deal with such scandalous issues that the publicity would necessarily hurt the reputation and witness of the church. I can understand how they draw that inference from verses 6–8, but I think they are missing another important implication of this passage and related teachings in Scripture.

As James 4:1–3 teaches, prolonged, intense conflict is generally caused or aggravated by sinful desires that war in people's hearts. This is as true for lawsuits as it is with most other conflicts. When two Christians lock horns over legal issues, there are almost always sin issues involved. These may include honoring your contracts (Ps. 15:4), telling the truth (Eph. 4:15), shifting responsibility and getting caught up in self-justification (Matt. 7:3–5), harboring bitterness or anger toward someone (Matt. 5:21–22), refusing to repair damage done to someone (Num. 5:5–7), or cheating or otherwise doing wrong to someone (1 Cor. 6:7–8).

Civil courts can make rulings on legal and property issues, but they have no jurisdiction or ability to address sin or other matters of the heart described in James 4:1–3 and Matthew 15:19 (see the discussion below on possible concurrent jurisdiction). Therefore, civil courts are completely powerless to resolve the root causes of a lawsuit or to help people break free from the sin that is fueling their dispute. Only the church can authoritatively carry out the ministry that is needed to thoroughly resolve a lawsuit between believers. Therefore, when two Christians have a legal dispute, it makes no difference whether it involves major issues that may cause a scandal or small issues that are of no interest to outsiders. If the dispute involves matters of the heart, as almost all lawsuits do, God wants it resolved through the one institution he established to minister to the heart, which is the local church.

To Whom Does 1 Corinthians Apply?

There are three common views on the scope of 1 Corinthians 6:1–8 (which I will refer to as 1 Corinthians 6). One view holds that this passage forbids lawsuits against both Christians and non-Christians. This view is difficult to support. The passage talks about "one brother [going] to law against another—and this in front of unbelievers!" (v. 6). It also asks if it is possible "that there is nobody among you wise enough to judge a dispute *between believers?*" (v. 5, emphasis added). Moreover, this passage instructs Christians to submit to the "judgment" of the fellow believers within the context of the church. Paul would have hardly expected unbelievers to submit to the authority of the church. In fact, earlier in the same letter he had specifically warned the church not to judge unbelievers (1 Cor. 5:12). Therefore, 1 Corinthians 6 should be understood to apply only to disputes between Christians.

Another view of this passage is that it forbids any and all lawsuits between people who profess to be Christians. This view is not supported by the express language of the passage, nor is it consistent with the rest of Scripture, which clearly indicates that God has established civil courts and expects his people to respect their authority and cooperate with them in appropriate situations (see Rom. 13:1–7; 1 Peter 2:13–14; cf. Acts 24:2–4; 25:10–11).

The third view of this passage is that it forbids Christians to sue persons who are members in good standing of a Christian church that is faithful to Scripture. I believe this is the most reasonable view of this passage. Paul was upset with the Corinthian Christians because they were suing one another in secular court rather than resolving their disputes with the help of the church. Realizing the terrible witness this was giving to unbelievers (v. 6), he said it would be better to be wronged or cheated than to sue a person who is part of the church—that is, someone who is "among you" (vv. 5, 7). As indicated in 1 Corinthians 5:1–13, however, a person should not be considered to be part of the church if he or she has been removed from the fellowship through official church discipline (see Matt. 18:17). Even if that person claims to be a Christian (1 Cor. 5:11), once he or she has been removed from the protection of the church (v. 5), that person can no longer enjoy the fellowship and privileges that belong to believers (vv. 9–11). Among other things, this means that such an offender no longer qualifies as a "brother" who is "among you." Therefore, I do not believe 1 Corinthians 6 applies to that person, and other Christians are not necessarily forbidden to go to court against him or her.

Exhausting Church Remedies

The view I described in the previous paragraph gives the church a crucial role in resolving conflicts between people who profess to be Christians. If the church obeys Jesus' commands to help resolve disputes between Christians (Matt. 18:15–20), many conflicts will be settled far short of litigation. If your opponent (or you) refuses to listen to the church, and if the church obeys Scripture and removes such a person from fellowship, the dispute can then be resolved legitimately through the civil courts if necessary.

If your opponent's church does not carry out its biblical responsibility, it places you in a difficult position, because your opponent will still be a member in good standing of a Christian church. When this happens, I believe you have at least two alternatives. First, you could drop the matter and suffer loss (1 Cor. 6:7). This course would be appropriate if the issues are not very important and if it is likely that a lawsuit would cause others to think less of Christians and of Christ. Second, you could ask the leaders of your church to meet with the leaders of your opponent's church in an effort to persuade them to fulfill their biblical responsibility to help resolve your dispute. If they respond to that appeal, the two churches could cooperate by appointing a panel of reconcilers from both churches who would carry out the responsibilities described in 1 Corinthians 6, with both churches agreeing that they will support the decision of that panel and, if necessary, enforce it through church discipline.

If your opponent's church rejects the appeal of your church leaders, you could again consider dropping the matter. If that would not be wise, your church could declare that since your opponent's church is not acting in a manner faithful to Scripture, it should not be treated as a true Christian church, at least for the purposes of this conflict. As a result, your opponent need not be considered to be a part of a true Christian church. This would make 1 Corinthians 6 inapplicable and allow you to proceed with litigation if the other two conditions discussed in chapter 9 are satisfied.

Of course, your own church may refuse to work with you and decline to either appeal to your opponent's church or declare that church to be disobedient to Scripture. If your church leaders believe that you do not have a biblical basis to pursue an action against your opponent, in general you should respect that counsel and drop the matter. If, however, your church simply refuses to obey what is taught in Matthew 18:15–20 and 1 Corinthians 6, you should consider moving to a church that is faithful to Scripture.

When you have to stay in your church because there are no Bible-believing churches in your community to which you can move, you should still avoid deciding for yourself whether you should treat your opponent as a believer and proceed with a lawsuit. Such unilateral conduct would violate the spirit of Matthew 18 and 1 Corinthians 6. Instead, you should turn to a few spiritually mature Christians who can objectively evaluate your situation and give you biblical counsel. They may even approach your opponent in one last effort to resolve the conflict biblically. If your opponent still refuses to cooperate, and if these advisors conclude that your opponent is behaving "as a nonbeliever" and that your action is worth pursuing, you may be able to proceed with a lawsuit.

Two Additional Conditions

There are two other conditions you must satisfy before proceeding with a lawsuit against another believer. In addition to exhausting your church remedies, you must be sure that the rights you are seeking to enforce are biblically legitimate. As we saw in chapter 4, some of the legal "rights" and remedies available through civil courts today are contrary to Scripture. For example, some of the actions that employees can legally bring against their employers undermine the authority that God has delegated to employers through Scripture. Conversely, some of the things employers can legally do are biblically wrong. As Justice Scalia has noted, exercising such rights is clearly wrong in the eyes of God. Before proceeding with a lawsuit against anyone, you should make sure that the rights you are about to assert are consistent with Scripture.

The third condition for bringing a lawsuit is to make sure that your action has a righteous purpose. As we have seen from our study of

1 Corinthians 10:31–11:1, never assert your rights if doing so is likely to dishonor God, harm other people, or draw you away from Christ and deplete your ability to serve him. Therefore, do not file a lawsuit unless you are confident that it will somehow (1) advance God's kingdom (e.g., by promoting justice or providing a positive Christian witness to those who observe the action); (2) benefit your opponent (e.g., by invoking the power of the state to force him or her to bear the consequences of wrong behavior, which may help the opponent to behave more responsibly in the future; see Rom. 13:1–7); and (3) enhance your ability to know and serve Christ (e.g., by preserving rights and resources needed to minister to others or to provide for those who depend on you).

When considering this final condition, it is important to realize that litigation often takes a much higher personal toll than most people anticipate. The financial, emotional, and spiritual demands of the adversarial process can be enormous, and they can even outweigh any gains made through a favorable judgment. That is why Abraham Lincoln gave this advice to a class of law students over a century ago: "Discourage litigation. Persuade your neighbors to compromise whenever you can. Point out to them how the nominal winner is often a real loser in fees, expenses, and waste of time."

As this warning indicates, you should be very cautious about filing a lawsuit. If the three conditions described above are satisfied, however, you may appeal to the civil courts to resolve a conflict. Although this is not the preferable way to settle disputes, it is one that God can and does use to restrain wrongdoers, to protect the weak, and to promote justice, all of which are necessary for peace and the preservation of society.

Who Has Jurisdiction?

In certain situations, it may be appropriate to pursue legal remedies at the same time you are pursuing church remedies. This may happen in cases where both the church and the state have jurisdiction over a matter and when irreparable harm might occur if legal action is delayed.

God has given the church jurisdiction over the way Christians respond to the commands set forth in Scripture. (Jurisdiction means the right or authority to interpret and apply the law.) In other words, the church has jurisdiction over sinful acts and attitudes—that is, offenses that are violations of God's revealed will. This is why the church has both the responsibility and the authority to lovingly correct a person who is guilty of sin (Matt. 18:17–20). If a person refuses to respond to the correction of the church, the church may impose a variety of biblically established penalties, the most severe of which is to put that person out of the church and treat him or her as a non-Christian. This penalty essentially removes the person from the jurisdiction (and protection) of the church and exposes him or her to the unfettered attacks of Satan (1 Cor. 5:4–5; 1 Tim. 1:20).

Likewise, God has given civil government jurisdiction over the way people interact with one another in society. Government has jurisdiction over criminal acts—that is, offenses that are violations of society's laws (Rom. 13:1–7; 1 Peter 2:13–14).[1] This is why civil government has both the responsibility and the authority to correct a person who is guilty of criminal behavior. This correction may include a variety of penalties, including fines, imprisonment, loss of property, or even capital punishment.

When a believer's offense is a sin but not a crime (e.g., refusing to be reconciled to another person), it comes under the exclusive jurisdiction of the church. When an offense is a crime (e.g., shoplifting), it is also a sin if the violated law is biblically legitimate; therefore, it comes under the jurisdiction of both the church and government. In other words, there are certain acts over which the church and government share concurrent or overlapping jurisdiction.

First Corinthians 6 indicates that when an offense comes under the jurisdiction of both the church and civil government, those involved should normally turn first to the church for a resolution, especially if there is a possibility that the church may be able to resolve the matter completely. If the church is unable to resolve the matter, those involved may turn to the civil courts for a remedy. For example, if Bob steals a CD player from Betty's store, Betty may postpone filing charges while she enlists the help of Bob's church in an effort to resolve the matter. With the help of the church, Bob may be brought to repentance, at which point there would be no need to involve the civil authorities. But if Bob refuses to repent and make restitution, the church should treat him as an unbeliever, at which point the church's jurisdiction ends and the jurisdiction of the civil courts may be legitimately invoked. Then Bob would have to face criminal penalties.

On the other hand, if an offense is a *dangerous* crime and others may be seriously injured if the offender is not effectively restrained, it may be appropriate to invoke simultaneously the jurisdiction of the church and the civil government. While the church attempts to deal with the sinful heart condition that prompted the act, the civil authorities may deal with the behavior itself and restrain the offender from harming others. For example, in cases of physical or sexual abuse, it would be appropriate to call in the church and the police at the same time, especially when there is an indication that further abuse is likely unless there is effective intervention.

Unusual Situations

Because our society has changed in significant ways since Paul wrote his letter to the Corinthians, there are some situations that do not fit easily into the 1 Corinthians 6 scenario. When this happens, it will be necessary to consider carefully the jurisdictional issue as well as the three conditions for proceeding with a lawsuit. Most of all, it will be important to remember that one of the major concerns behind 1 Corinthians 6 is the potential for a negative witness when Christians sue one another in civil courts.

For example, since the church does not have jurisdiction over civil government or corporate organizations, it is appropriate to resolve disputes with these types of bodies in court, assuming you cannot arrive at a solution through personal and informal means. The same would be true of disputes involving insurance coverage. Since the church does not have jurisdiction over insurance companies, you will need to turn to the courts for a remedy if you are unable to arrive at a settlement. Even so, if the insured person who injured you is a Christian, you need to do all you can to resolve any personal animosity in a biblical manner. Furthermore, it would probably not be appropriate to seek excess damages from that individual (i.e., damages that exceed the coverage of the policy) without involving the church.

There may also be situations in which the only issue in dispute is the interpretation of a point of law. If there is truly no animosity between you and your opponent, and if you both believe that the other person is simply mistaken rather than acting in a sinful manner, it may be appropriate to allow a civil court to resolve relevant legal questions. When going this route, you must both agree that you will accept the court's decision without resentment. Of course, if possible, it would be preferable in many ways for the two of you to submit the legal issue to a respected Christian lawyer or judge who would resolve the matter more informally, perhaps through binding arbitration.

What If Someone Sues You?

The three conditions for filing a lawsuit apply equally well to defending yourself in a lawsuit. If you are sued by a person who professes to be a Christian, you should do all you can to divert the case to a church setting. If your opponent refuses, you should follow the Matthew 18 process, as described in chapter 9. If you exhaust that process (as described earlier in this appendix) and are confident that you are defending biblically legitimate rights and that you have a righteous purpose in defending yourself, you may continue in court with a clear conscience. If you do not satisfy all three conditions, however, you should follow the advice given in Matthew 5:25: "Settle matters quickly with your adversary who is taking you to court."

Summary

Since every conflict is somewhat unique, it is impossible to address every question that might arise when a matter may be headed toward court. Moreover, as Jesus warned, it is important not to get caught up in a multitude of detailed and legalistic rules. Instead, you should pay attention to the basic principles set forth in Scripture and focus on what our Lord called "the more important matters of law—justice, mercy and faithfulness" (Matt. 23:23; cf. Micah 6:8). One way to apply these principles when you are trying to decide whether or not to go to court is to remember that you are a steward of Christ and to ask yourself, "Would my Master be pleased and honored if I use my time and resources to pursue this matter in court?"

Appendix E

Peacemaker Ministries

Peacemaker Ministries was established in 1982 to equip and assist Christians and their churches to respond to conflict biblically. Most of our energy is devoted to training Christian laypeople, church and ministry leaders, and professionals to apply God's peacemaking principles to the conflicts of daily life. At the same time, our international network of trained reconcilers and Certified Christian Conciliators™ handles hundreds of family, church, business, and legal disputes every year. Our ministry is guided by four core convictions:

- *The Centrality of Christ*—We believe that genuine peace between people can be found only through Jesus Christ. Therefore, we encourage people in conflict to believe the gospel and trust in Christ, and to faithfully rely on the promises and obey the commands he has given us in Scripture (see John 14:27; 2 Cor. 5:18–19; Col. 3:15–16; 2 Tim. 3:16).

- *The Responsibility of the Church*—We believe that peacemaking is an essential ministry of the local church, not a task reserved for professional mediators or lawyers. Therefore, we encourage Christians to take unresolved conflicts to their church families, which are called by God to restore peace by promoting biblical justice and reconciliation (see Matt. 18:17; 1 Cor. 6:4; Eph. 3:10; Heb. 13:17).

- *The Necessity of Biblical Counseling*—We believe that destructive conflict comes from desires that battle within people's hearts. Therefore, we do not merely try to resolve surface issues. We also counsel parties to find their fulfillment in Christ, renounce sinful desires and actions that have contributed to conflict, and seek genuine reconciliation with others (see James 4:1–3; Gal. 2:20; Prov. 28:13; Rom. 15:14).

- *The Comprehensiveness of God's Word*—We believe that God's Word is totally authoritative and completely sufficient for all aspects of life and that his peacemaking commands and promises apply to every conflict a Christian can encounter. Therefore, we work across the entire spectrum of conflict, helping people resolve everything from school yard quarrels to family disputes, business conflicts, congregational divisions, and multimillion-dollar lawsuits (see 2 Tim. 3:16–17).

One of our primary activities is helping churches identify and train gifted members to serve as reconcilers in their local congregations. Reconciler training involves seventeen hours of coursework that are available on audio- or videotape and a live two-day practicum that gives students the opportunity to apply reconciliation skills in extended role plays based on actual conciliation cases.

For more information about reconciler training, educational or conciliation services, or Peacemaker Ministries in general, visit www.HisPeace.org; write to P.O. Box 81130, Billings, MT 59108; send an e-mail to mail@HisPeace.org; or call (406) 256–1583.

Appendix F

CULTIVATING A CULTURE OF PEACE IN YOUR CHURCH

A Culture of Peace

Churches all around the world are changing the way they respond to conflict. By God's grace, they are deliberately training their congregations to be peacemakers. As a result, their churches are cultivating a *culture of peace*. In the process, they are discovering the wonderful blessings promised in James 3:18: "Peacemakers who sow in peace raise a harvest of righteousness." This harvest James referred to involves a wide variety of relational fruit.

When a local church teaches its people to live out the gospel in the conflicts of daily life, people are more willing to admit their shortcomings and ask for help before a crisis occurs. Families are better equipped to handle disputes, which makes divorce less likely. Members are encouraged to go to each other to discuss problems instead of letting them fester. The church is protected from division and splits, and offended members are less likely to leave. As a result, church growth is improved.

Pastors and other church leaders can experience many benefits as well. When leaders fulfill their shepherding responsibilities more fully, respect and appreciation for their work grows. As they are taken out of the day-today "complaint loop," they can spend less time dealing with disgruntled members and more time on forward-moving ministry. When members learn to stop gossiping, leaders are subjected to less criticism. As conflict declines in a church, stress on leaders' families is often reduced. And when respectful discussion and reconciliation are the norm, pastors and other staff are less likely to burn out or be forced out of their jobs.

Of course, no church sees all of these benefits at once or all the time. Our sin continually works against a culture of peace. Even Paul and Barnabas had a falling out! (See Acts 15:2.) So we should not be surprised when members forget what they have learned, leaders are inconsistent, or our efforts seem to have been wasted. Even though we stumble, we need not fall, for the Lord upholds us with his hand (Ps. 37:24). As he helps us back to our feet, we can learn from our mistakes, forgive one another, and continue to grow. When we do, God can use both our mistakes and our forgiveness to encourage others.

One of the greatest benefits of resolving conflicts biblically is that outreach and evangelism are enhanced. Conflict is inevitable in a fallen world; Christians and unbelievers alike struggle with disputes and broken relationships. So when unsaved people see Christians admitting their failures and forgiving and reconciling with one another even after intense disputes, they cannot help but take notice. The more our relationships reflect the amazing love and mercy of God, the more people will want to know about the power that is working in us to maintain peace and unity. What a marvelous way to increase the harvest!

Leading a Cultural Transformation

Most of these peacemaking churches had anything but a culture of peace a few years ago. In fact, almost all of them had what might be called a *culture of disbelief*. They did not believe there was much the church could do to help its members deal with conflict. The reason for this disbelief was fairly simple. They did not really understand what the Bible teaches about peacemaking, and they lacked faith that biblical principles would actually work in today's culture.

This disbelief robbed them of the ability to respond to conflict in a constructive and helpful way. They did not provide their members with any practical training on personal conflict resolution, and they were unprepared to assist members who were caught in difficult disputes. As a result, their churches were characterized all too often by gossip, broken relationships, divorce, and a steady turnover in members. Worse yet, they lost much of their ability to give an effective witness to the reconciling love and forgiveness of Jesus Christ.

God graciously led the leaders in these churches to take an honest look at their "peacemaking culture," or their combination of attitudes, traditions, habits, and abilities for resolving conflict. What they saw troubled them. They realized that their church cultures were not conducive to peacemaking. So they asked God to help them change.

The pastors of these churches played a key role in transforming their churches. Their preaching and personal example set the stage for change. At the same time, they wisely delegated most of the day-to-day educational and reconciliation work to elders and other gifted people in their congregations. Together, they transformed their church cultures and steadily raised their level of peacemaking productivity. This process was like nurturing a tree and bringing it to a point of abundant fruitfulness. It usually involved five levels of growth and productivity:

- *Level 1—A Culture of Disbelief:* People lack practical training in resolving conflict and doubt that the church can do much to help them resolve their differences. This church is like a tree that is missing some of its sweetest fruit.
- *Level 2—A Culture of Faith:* People begin to understand God's peacemaking commands and promises and to believe that his ways will work in today's culture. This church is like a tree blossoming in the spring.
- *Level 3—A Culture of Transformation:* People want to put off worldly ways of resolving conflict and are taking steps to learn how to respond to conflict biblically. This church is like a tree that is being pruned and cultivated for greater productivity.
- *Level 4—A Culture of Peace:* People are eager and able to resolve conflict and reconcile relationships in a way that clearly reflects the love and power of Jesus Christ. This church is like a tree producing a rich harvest.
- *Level 5—A Culture of Multiplication:* People delight in expanding God's kingdom by showing other people and churches how they too can be peacemakers. This church is like a tree that is reproducing by spreading its seed.

The Characteristics of a Culture of Peace

A church that has a culture of peace usually has eight essential characteristics:

- *Vision:* The church is eager to bring glory to God by demonstrating the reconciling love and forgiveness of Jesus Christ, and therefore sees peacemaking as an essential part of the Christian life (see Luke 6:27–36; John 13:35; 1 Cor. 10:31; Col. 3:12–14).

- *Training:* The church knows that peacemaking does not come naturally, so it deliberately trains both its leaders and its members to respond to conflict biblically in all areas of life (see Gal. 5:19–21; Luke 6:40; Eph. 4:24–26; 1 Tim. 4:15–16; Titus 2:1–10).

- *Assistance:* When members cannot resolve disputes privately, the church assists them through in-house, trained reconcilers, even when conflicts involve financial, employment, or legal issues (see Matt. 18:16; Rom. 15:14; 1 Cor. 6:1–8; Gal. 6:1–2; Col. 3:16).

- *Perseverance:* Just as God pursues us, the church works long and hard to restore broken relationships, especially when a marriage is at stake, and even when attorneys are involved (see Matt. 18:12–16; Rom. 12:18; Eph. 4:1–3; Matt. 19:1–9; 1 Cor. 7:1–11).

- *Accountability:* If members refuse to listen to private correction, church leaders get directly involved to hold members accountable to Scripture and to promote repentance, justice, and forgiveness. (see Prov. 3:11–12; Matt. 18:15–20; 1 Cor. 5:1–5; James 5:19–20).

- *Restoration:* Wanting to imitate God's amazing mercy and grace, the church gladly forgives and fully restores members who have genuinely repented of serious and embarrassing sins (see Matt. 18:21–35; Eph. 4:32; 2 Cor. 2:5–11).

- *Stability:* Because relationships are valued and protected, leaders serve fruitfully year after year and members see the church as their long-term home (see 1 Tim. 4:15; Heb. 10:25).

- *Witness:* Members are equipped and encouraged to practice peacemaking so openly in their daily lives that others will notice, ask why they do it, and hear about the love of Christ (see Matt. 5:9; John 13:34–35, 17:20–23; 1 Peter 2:12, 3:15–16).

How to Transform a Church Culture

Peacemaking is an attitude expressed through action. The heart of this attitude is the joy and thankfulness that come from fully understanding the gospel of Christ (Phil. 4:4). Jesus died on the cross in our place to release us from the penalty and ongoing slavery of sin. He gave his life to buy our forgiveness, earn our freedom, and bring us back to God. Now he wants us to pass this priceless gift of reconciliation on to others in the form of personal peacemaking: "As God's chosen people, holy and dearly loved, clothe yourselves with compassion, kindness, humility, gentleness and patience. Bear with each other and forgive whatever grievances you may have against one another. Forgive as the Lord forgave you" (Col. 3:12–13; see also Eph. 4:1–3; Gal. 6:1–2; 2 Cor. 5:18).

These attitudes and actions do not come naturally to people. In fact, our instincts usually take us in the opposite direction! Therefore, in order to build a culture of peace, a church must do both pruning and cultivating. It must help its people put off worldly ways of resolving conflict and put on peacemaking attitudes and actions that mirror our reconciliation with God.

Pruning and cultivating takes a lot of work. The good news is that this work does not have to be done by an elite few, but can be shared by gifted people throughout a local church. Senior pastors in particular do not have time to resolve everybody's conflicts. Therefore, they should follow the advice Moses received when he became weary from serving as the sole judge for Israel:

> The work is too heavy for you; you cannot handle it alone. . . . Teach them the decrees and laws, and show them the way to live and the duties they are to perform. But select capable men from all the people. . . . Have them serve as judges for the people at all times, but have them bring every difficult case to you; the simple cases they can decide themselves. That will make your load lighter, because they will share it with you. If you do this and God so commands, you will be able to stand the strain, and all these people will go home satisfied.
>
> Exodus 18:18–23

Like Moses, a senior pastor is responsible before God to make sure that his people have the teaching and assistance they need to respond to conflict biblically. Since a pastor must play a primary educational role from the pulpit and may occasionally have to assist with difficult conflicts, he would be wise to develop a solid understanding of the basic principles of biblical conflict resolution. (*The Peacemaker* and *Guiding People Through Conflict* provide a thorough foundation for personal peacemaking, conflict coaching, and mediation.) At the same time, a pastor can and should entrust most of the educational and reconciliation activities to capable leaders and members of the congregation.

In many situations, God will give a vision for peacemaking first to members of a church and then work through them to bring this vision to the leaders. As leaders and members work together to weave peacemaking into their overall discipleship efforts, their church can cultivate those eight characteristics of a culture of peace: vision, training, assistance, perseverance, accountability, restoration, stability, and witness. This cultivation usually involves five essential activities.

First, gain support from church leadership. Although God often works through lay members of a church to initiate interest in peacemaking, cultural transformation will take place only when church leaders officially support and lead this effort. The most important "tipping point" for seeing major progress is when the senior pastor sees peacemaking not as a helpful side ministry, but as something that is vital to the well-being and fruitfulness of the church.

Second, form a core support group (sometimes known as a "church reconciler team"). This team will be responsible for guiding educational and reconciliation activities within the church. Church leaders should spearhead the team, but it may also include spiritually mature lay members who have gifts for peacemaking.

Third, educate the entire congregation in peacemaking. God's peacemaking principles are like yeast. The more thoroughly they are worked into a congregation, the more good they can do. This requires an ongoing effort to teach peacemaking to every person in the church. The best way to do this is to educate in two stages. Begin by presenting a preaching series that elevates the congregation's interest in and commitment to peacemaking. Then encourage every person in the church to participate in a Sunday school class or small group Bible study where they can learn specific peacemaking principles and discuss how the principles apply to conflicts in their own lives. (Educational resources are available through Peacemaker Ministries.)

Fourth, train gifted people within your congregation to become reconcilers. Reconcilers are gifted church members or leaders who have been trained to help others deal with conflict. This help may be provided through conflict coaching (advising one person how to respond to conflict biblically) or mediation (meeting with both parties to facilitate discussion and agreement). Well-trained church reconcilers can help members respond biblically to a wide variety of personal, family, employment, business, and even legal disputes.

Fifth, upgrade your church's organizational documents to support peacemaking and reduce legal liability. Churches are being sued at an alarming rate for conflict-related activities. Legal actions against churches include negligence, breach of confidentiality, defamation, sexual misconduct, and intentional infliction of emotional distress. Judgments can be extremely costly, with church leaders sometimes being held personally responsible for the award. Upgrading church bylaws and adopting special policies for counseling, confidentiality, conflict resolution, and church accountability can substantially reduce exposure to legal liability. (The *Managing Conflict in Your Church* seminar set contains detailed information.)

Some churches can make substantial progress in all of these areas in two years. Others will take four or five years to overcome deeply engrained attitudes and traditions. Yet even small initial efforts can produce noticeable fruit. A few people going through a Sunday school class on peacemaking can have a ripple effect on their own families and friends. As they use the basic principles in their daily lives and share what they are learning with others, relationships can be improved and a growing interest in peacemaking can be nurtured. These benefits will multiply as cultivation continues.

Peacemaker Ministries has developed comprehensive resources and guidelines that will help your church implement each of these five steps.

The "Level 5 Church"—A Culture of Multiplication

With many blessings comes great responsibility. God has given the church a unique and precious talent: the power and ability to bring peace, unity, and reconciliation to a broken and conflicted world. Sadly, many churches have been afraid to use this talent; like the unfaithful servant, they have hidden and neglected it for years. If they do not repent, they will be ashamed when Jesus calls them to give an account someday (see Matt. 25:24–27; Ezek. 34:1–16).

How much better it will be if your church can say what the faithful servant said: "Master . . . you entrusted me with five talents. See, I have gained five more" (Matt. 25:20). What a joy it would be to hear the answer, "Well done, good and faithful servant! You have been faithful with a few things; I will put you in charge of many things. Come and share your master's happiness!" (v. 21).

How can your church produce the maximum harvest with the peacemaking talents God has given you? Start by weaving peacemaking thoroughly into the fabric of your congregation, as discussed in the previous section. But don't stop there or you may still be hiding part of your talents. Ask God to help you build a culture of peace that is so fruitful that it overflows into your community, other churches, and your denomination. The following are ways that many churches are already doing this:

First, equip and encourage members to carry peacemaking into everyday life. As church members interact with their family, friends, neighbors, or coworkers, they will naturally have opportunities for peacemaking. When they themselves are involved in a conflict, they can ask God for grace to respond with humility. If they see others in conflict, they can ask God for wisdom on how to offer advice or encourage agreement. As word spreads about their ability to resolve conflict effectively, others may seek them out for advice, which can open the way for witnessing and inviting others to church. And when a church gains a reputation for resolving "small" problems, it will have greater credibility when it speaks to "large" issues that impact an entire community.

Second, teach peacemaking to children. Most parents would welcome any program that could teach their children to resolve conflict. Churches can respond to this need by using *The Young Peacemaker* curriculum in Sunday school or vacation Bible school classes that are advertised to people outside the church. As children and their parents benefit from this training, many of them may be drawn to the church and to the Lord.

Third, send peacemakers with mission teams. Churches can strengthen their missions efforts and promote peacemaking overseas by including trained peacemakers on their short-term mission teams. These peacemakers can protect teams from destructive internal conflict by teaching members conflict resolution skills and by serving as reconcilers if conflicts occur on the field. Peacemakers can also teach these principles to pastors in other countries. As those pastors teach and model peacemaking in their own congregations, the benefits will continue to spread.

Fourth, develop a church-based reconciliation ministry. Once your church reconcilers have gained experience by working within your congregation, they can expand their ministry by making their services available to people outside your church. This kind of practical ministry provides an excellent way to demonstrate the power of the gospel to unchurched or unsaved people who are in conflict, and it could draw them to your church as it helps them make peace.

Fifth, share your experience with other churches in your community or denomination. As God blesses your church with a culture of peace, you can multiply that blessing by sharing what you have learned with other churches. For example, you can host a Peacemaker Seminar in your community or train your reconcilers to assist neighboring churches when they cannot resolve internal conflicts on their own. You can also share your church's testimony by working with your denominational leaders as they seek to promote biblical peacemaking in your district.

Sixth, plant new churches that have peacemaking as part of their original "DNA." As God enables your church to support church planters and give birth to new congregations, you can pass on the spiritual characteristic of peacemaking. This precious gift will increase the new church's ability to survive natural growing pains and thrive as a family of believers who are visibly committed to living out the love of Christ in the natural conflicts of real life.

It Can Start Today, with You

Even if a church is stuck in a culture of disbelief today and sees little peacemaking fruit, by God's grace, it can eventually overflow with a culture of peace that benefits its entire community and brings praise to God. What a wonderful way to fulfill Jesus' command in Matthew 5:14–16: "You are the light of the world. A city on a hill cannot be hidden. Neither do people light a lamp and put it under a bowl. Instead they put it on its stand, and it gives light to everyone in the house. In the same way, let your light shine before men, that they may see your good deeds and praise your Father in heaven."

All it takes is one person who hears the call of God and responds, "Here am I. Send me!" (Isa. 6:8). Perhaps for your church, that person is you. Please pray about it and reflect on the Scriptures given above. Ask God to give you a longing to see a culture of peace in your church that reflects the love and power of his Son. If he gives you that longing, hard work awaits you, but great blessing is also in store, for Jesus' promise in Matthew 5 is absolutely dependable:

Blessed are the peacemakers, for they will be called sons of God.

verse 9

(For comprehensive resources and guidelines that will help your church implement these changes, visit www.HisPeace.org, go to the Culture of Peace page, and click on "Detailed Implementation Plan.")

NOTES

Chapter 1: Conflict Provides Opportunities

1. *The Young Peacemaker,* which was written by my wife, Corlette, is a superb tool for teaching conflict resolution skills to children at an early age. This curriculum may be used with children from third to seventh grade at home, in Sunday school, or in Christian schools. For more information, see www.HisPeace.org.

2. Charles R. Swindoll, *Growing Strong in the Seasons of Life* (Portland: Multnomah Press, 1983), 85–86.

3. I have found that many Christians rely more on their own ideas and feelings than they do on the Bible, especially when Scripture commands them to do difficult things. In particular, many people seem to believe they can be sure they are doing what is right if they pray and feel a sense of "inner peace." Nowhere does the Bible guarantee that a sense of peace is a sure sign that one is on the right course. Many people experience a sense of relief ("inner peace") even when they are on a sinful course, simply because they are getting away from stressful responsibilities. Conversely, doing what is right sometimes generates feelings other than peace, especially when we are required to obey difficult commands, die to our own desires, or put others' needs above our own. Since the Bible alone provides absolutely reliable guidance from God, it should always be our supreme source of truth and direction. As the Spirit works to help us understand and obey Scripture, we can enjoy a sense of confidence that we are indeed walking in God's will, even if we don't have a peaceful feeling about it (Mark 14:32–34; Luke 22:43). For more information on how God guides us, read Garry Friesen's book *Decision Making and the Will of God* (Portland: Multnomah, 1980).

4. For an excellent description of how the Holy Spirit works in our lives, read J. I. Packer's book *Keep in Step with the Spirit* (Grand Rapids: Revell, 1984).

Chapter 2: Live at Peace

1. Tim Hansel, *When I Relax I Feel Guilty* (Elgin, Ill.: David C. Cook, 1979), 93.

2. For a biblical perspective on spiritual warfare, I recommend *Power Encounters: Reclaiming Spiritual Warfare* by David Powlison (Grand Rapids: Baker, 1995).

3. See also Phil. 4:2–9; 2 Thess. 3:11–15; 1 Tim. 6:3–6; 2 Tim. 2:23–26; Titus 3:1–2, 9; Philem. 17–18; Heb. 12:14; James 3:17–18; 1 Peter 3:8–9.

4. Justice Warren Burger, "Annual Report on the State of the Judiciary," *American Bar Association Journal* (March 1982): 68.

5. Justice Antonin Scalia, "Teaching About the Law," *Quarterly* 7, no. 4 (Christian Legal Society, Fall 1987): 8–9.

6. There has been a dramatic increase of interest in secular negotiation, mediation, and arbitration in recent years. Appendix B describes these dispute resolution options and compares them to what can be accomplished through the church.

7. There are a few situations when litigation may be necessary and appropriate for a Christian. Appendix D discusses this issue and provides guidelines for deciding when it is appropriate for a Christian to go to court.

Chapter 3: Trust in the Lord and Do Good

1. John Piper, *Desiring God* (Portland: Multnomah, 1986), 26.

2. J. I. Packer, *Knowing God* (Downers Grove, Ill: InterVarsity, 1973), 37.

3. J. I. Packer, *Hot Tub Religion* (Wheaton: Tyndale, 1988), 35.

4. First Peter was specifically written to encourage Christians who were undergoing severe trials and suffering. If you are presently involved in a difficult conflict, I encourage you to read Peter's letter for its encouragement and guidance.

5. This passage refers to the two dimensions of the will of God. To prevent confusion, I will briefly describe the distinctions between the two. God's sovereign will (also called "decretive will") is the ultimate cause of all things, whether God wills to accomplish them effectively and directly or permits them to occur through the unrestrained actions of people. His sovereign will is not fully revealed to us, but it will always be accomplished (see Isa. 46:9–10). God's revealed will (also called "preceptive will") is the pattern of rules that he commands us to follow in order to glorify him and enjoy fellowship with him. His revealed will is

completely revealed in Scripture, but it is often disobeyed.

6. The more confidence we have that God is both sovereign and good, the meeker we can be. Meekness is an attitude toward God that causes us to accept all his dealings with us as being good, and thus to accept them without resistance or resentment (Rom. 8:28). A meek person is content and thankful no matter what his circumstances (Phil. 4:12–13), because he sees that God has already given him everything he needs in Christ (Matt. 5:5; Rom. 8:31–32). Thus, instead of thinking, "I'm missing out; it's not fair," a meek person thinks about and gives thanks for God's goodness, mercy, power, and provision (Acts 4:23–31; 5:40–42; 7:59–60; John 18:11). Meekness has nothing to do with weakness, for both Moses and Jesus are described in the Bible as being meek (Num. 12:3; Matt. 11:29). In fact, meekness has sometimes been referred to as "power under control." This quality is highly commended throughout Scripture (Ps. 37:11; Matt. 5:5). Meekness has a direct impact on our dealings with other people, especially in the midst of conflict. Knowing that God works for good in all things, a meek person is able to endure mistreatment from others with patience and without resentment or bitterness. Because this attitude does not come to us naturally, we need to pray that the Holy Spirit will work steadily to help us to become meek.

7. Elisabeth Elliot, *Through Gates of Splendor* (Wheaton: Tyndale, 1981), 252–54.

8. Ibid., 268–69, 273.

9. Joni Eareckson Tada, "Is God Really in Control?" (Joni and Friends, 1987), 1.

10. Ibid., 9.

11. Packer, *Knowing God,* 145.

12. Marital conflicts are particularly painful and present many difficult questions. If you are trying to understand biblical options for dealing with a difficult marriage, read Jay E. Adams's *Marriage, Divorce, and Remarriage* (Grand Rapids: Zondervan, 1980). If you are facing a marital separation, read Gary Chapman's *Hope for the Separated* (Chicago: Moody Press, 1982).

Chapter 4: Is This Really Worth Fighting Over?

1. Wayne Mack, *A Homework Manual for Biblical Counseling,* vol. 1 (Phillipsburg, N.J.: Presbyterian and Reformed Publishing, 1979), 12.

2. Scalia, "Teaching About the Law," 9.

3. See Rom. 14:1–15:3, 1 Cor. 8:1–13, and Philemon for three additional examples of when it is appropriate not to exercise rights to their fullest extent.

Chapter 5: Conflict Starts in the Heart

1. I owe John Bettler, Paul Tripp, David Powlison, and Ed Welch of the Christian Counseling and Educational Foundation (www.CCEF.org) a great debt for the many insights they have given to me on this topic through their books and seminars.

2. F. Samuel Janzow, *Luther's Large Catechism: A Contemporary Translation with Study Questions* (St. Louis: Concordia, 1978), 13.

3. *Journal of Biblical Counseling* 16, no. 1, fall 1997, 34.

4. John Piper, *Future Grace* (Portland: Multnomah), 9.

5. If you would like to learn how to delight in God during the ups and downs of daily life, I encourage you to read C. J. Mahaney's superb devotional book, *The Cross Centered Life: Keeping the Gospel the Main Thing* (Sisters, Ore.: Multnomah, 2002).

Chapter 6: Confession Brings Freedom

1. One kind of "tearing down" is beneficial. It involves the work of God's Word and the Holy Spirit in our hearts to convict us of our sins and help us to see our need for God and for change (Matt. 5:3; Acts 2:37). Therefore, when we speak the truth *in love* to people, they may feel broken for a while. This is beneficial if it results in repentance.

2. R. C. Sproul, *The Intimate Marriage* (Wheaton: Tyndale, 1988), 32.

3. In chapter 11, we will look more closely at ways to identify someone else's interests and develop creative ways to help meet those needs and desires in a biblical manner.

4. For a more detailed discussion on how to deal with issues of authority in conflict situations, contact Peacemaker Ministries for an audiotape entitled, "Uneven Playing Field: Conflict with Those in and under Authority."

Chapter 7: Just between the Two of You

1. See Matthew 5:38. Remember that the "eye for an eye" principle was to be applied by judges, not individuals (see, e.g., Exod. 21:22–24). Moreover, the context for this passage is Jesus' teaching on what his followers must be willing to suffer for the sake of the gospel (Matt. 5:11–12).

2. As a general rule, the closer you are to someone, the more latitude you should have in mentioning your concerns. For example, if one of my close friends sees me saying or doing something that may hurt my marriage, irritate others, or make me less useful to the Lord, I would want him to point it out to me, even if it's not a terribly serious sin. This kind of loving and constructive confrontation is one of the privileges and blessings of being part of the body of Christ (Ps. 141:5; Col. 3:16; Heb. 10:24–25).

3. Although space does not permit me to go into further detail on this topic in this book, I am compelled to add a strong word of warning before leaving this subject. Churches have a definite tendency to deny and cover up incidents of abuse, usually to prevent scandal, protect a pastor's career, or avoid the difficult and painful work required to bring healing in these situations. This strategy is blatantly disobedient to God's Word, which commands us to confess sin, not conceal it (Prov. 28:13; 1 John 1:8–9). As national headlines reveal, this approach has also proven to be disastrous for victims, abusers, churches, and entire denominations. God's Word provides a solid track to run on, no matter how terrible the sin or conflict. For

more information on how to apply biblical peacemaking principles to these situations, see "A Better Way to Handle Abuse" at www .HisPeace.org/html/artic26.htm, or contact Peacemaker Ministries directly.

Chapter 8: Speak the Truth in Love

1. One of the best ways to cultivate a gospel-centered life is to read and reread C. J. Mahaney's excellent devotional book, *The Cross Centered Life: Keeping the Gospel the Main Thing.*

2. If you would like to improve your ability to breathe in God's grace, I recommend Donald Whitney's excellent book, *Spiritual Disciplines for the Christian Life* (Colorado Springs: NavPress, 1991).

3. For a more detailed discussion of making charitable judgments, read *Judging Others: The Danger of Playing God,* by Ken Sande, a thirty-page booklet that is available through Peacemaker Ministries.

4. If you would like to learn more about how to help people understand their own hearts and change harmful behavior, you can find no finer guide than Paul Tripp's book, *Instruments in the Redeemer's Hands* (Phillipsburg, N.J.: P & R Publishing, 2002). Paul's earlier book, *War of Words: Getting to the Heart of Your Communication Struggles* (Phillipsburg, N.J.: P & R Publishing, 2002), is equally helpful.

5. When you refer to God's Word as the basis for your concerns, some people may accuse you of *legalism,* a term that is often misunderstood and misused. Legalism is the *abuse* of God's Word, not the *faithful use* of God's Word. It typically involves an effort to earn God's forgiveness and acceptance through obedience to his law. Legalists are overly fascinated with the minute detail of certain laws, to the exclusion of "more important matters of the law" (Matt. 23:23; cf. 5:21–48). They strictly adhere to traditions that are not supported by Scripture (Matt. 15:3–9) and have a pattern of holding others to the strictest legal standard but failing to practice it themselves (Matt. 23:1–4). Unfor-tunately, you may be accused of "legalism" even when you are using the Bible properly. Taking the Bible seriously is not legalism. We are clearly called not only to obey God's commands, but also to encourage and exhort one another to do likewise (Matt. 18:15–20; Gal. 6:1). Doing so with humility, patience, gentleness, and love is not legalism—God calls it obedience.

6. Ron Kraybill, *Conciliation Quarterly,* Mennonite Central Committee (Summer 1987), 7.

Chapter 9: Take One or Two Others Along

1. Some early manuscripts do not have the words "against you" in the first sentence (v. 15). Thus, this passage is not necessarily restricted to addressing sin that was committed against you personally (cf. Luke 17:3).

2. One way to ensure that conflicts related to contract relationships will be resolved in a biblical manner rather than in court is to include a conciliation clause in the contract itself. The Institute for Christian Concilia-tion (a division of Peacemaker Ministries) recommends using this wording: "Any claim or dispute arising from or related to this agreement shall be settled by mediation and, if necessary, legally binding arbitration in accordance with the *Rules of Procedure for Christian Conciliation* of the Institute for Christian Conciliation, a division of Peace-maker® Ministries (complete text of the Rules is available at www.HisPeace.org). Judgment upon an arbitration decision may be entered in any court otherwise having jurisdiction. The parties understand that these methods shall be the sole remedy for any controversy or claim arising out of this agreement and expressly waive their right to file a lawsuit in any civil court against one another for such disputes, except to enforce an arbitration deci-sion." The legal requirements for the wording and style of these clauses vary from state to state, so you should consult an attorney before using such a clause.

3. The Institute for Christian Concilia-tion (a division of Peacemaker Ministries)

has developed a set of forms, guidelines, and procedures that can be used by church leaders and others when they are serving as conciliators or arbitrators. The ICC also provides training resources and opportunities for individuals who would like to enhance their abilities to serve as peacemakers. See appendix E for information on how to obtain this training or these materials.

4. You may have already asked the leaders of your church or churches to be involved as conciliators as part of step three, which would have been an informal process. When you ask them to get involved at the level of step four, you are moving into a formal process that invokes the ecclesiastical authority of the church to instruct believers on how they should live.

5. Although civil courts have historically granted churches great latitude in exercising church discipline, recent court decisions have opened the door for churches to be held liable if they do not carry out discipline carefully. Therefore, it is wise to consult with a knowledgeable attorney, a Certified Christian Conciliator™, or Peacemaker Ministries when carrying out discipline in volatile situations. Exposure to legal liability can be dramatically reduced if your church implements bylaw and membership education changes as set forth in the seminar *Managing Conflict in Your Church,* which is available through Peacemaker Ministries.

6. Note that Matthew 18:15–20 immediately follows Jesus' stern warning to repent of sin (vv. 7–9) and his parable of the lost sheep, which emphasizes the church's responsibility to work diligently to reclaim "wandering" Christians (vv. 10–14). It also is important to note that this passage is immediately followed by a teaching on forgiveness.

7. Dietrich Bonhoeffer, *Life Together,* trans. John W. Doberstein (Harper & Row, 1954), 107.

Chapter 10: Forgive as God Forgave You

1. Some people mistakenly believe that unforgiveness can also cause us to lose our salvation. This belief sometimes results from a misunderstanding of Jesus' words in passages like Matthew 6:14–15, which says: "For if you forgive men when they sin against you, your heavenly Father will also forgive you. But if you do not forgive men their sins, your Father will not forgive your sins" (cf. Matt. 18:35; Mark 11:25; Luke 6:36–37). To understand the true meaning of this passage, we must realize that God forgives us in two different ways, because he relates to us in two different ways. God is first of all our Judge. When we repent of our sins and accept Jesus Christ as our Savior and Lord, God forgives us our sins and declares us "not guilty." This process is called "justification." It takes place by God's grace through faith and does not depend on our works (Eph. 2:8–9; Rom. 3:24–30). Since we are not saved because of our works, we will not lose our salvation by failing to perform certain works. In other words, God's judicial forgiveness (and our salvation) does not depend on whether or not we forgive others.

God also relates to us as our Father, and his parental forgiveness does depend on our forgiveness of others. When we become Christians, God adopts us into his family and treats us as his children. (Note that Matt. 6:14–15 and the related passages are all addressed to believers, because they refer to God as "Father.") And how does a good parent treat a disobedient child? He doesn't kick the child out of the family! He may send a disobedient child to his or her room and isolate the child from the rest of the family until behavior changes. In some cases, the unrepentant child may also receive a spanking or be deprived of certain privileges. God treats us in the same way. He does not disown us by taking away our salvation, but he does discipline us. Thus, when we refuse to forgive others, we may suffer afflictions and feel cut off from a close and joyful relationship with God. As Matthew 6:14–15 warns, God will continue to discipline us until we repent of our sin and forgive others as he forgives us.

2. Patrick H. Morison, *Forgive! As the Lord Forgave You* (Phillipsburg, N.J.: P & R Publishing, 1987), 7.

3. Corrie ten Boom, *The Hiding Place* (New York: Bantam, 1974), 238.

4. C. S. Lewis, *Mere Christianity* (New York: Macmillan, 1960), 116. Behaving contrary to your feelings is not hypocrisy. If it were, Luke 6:27–28 would essentially command us to be hypocrites. Rather, hypocrisy is pretending to be what you are not or pretending to act from one motive when you are actually inspired by another motive (Matt. 23:23–32; cf. Gal. 2:11–14). Thus, if you have negative feelings toward someone, it would be hypocritical to act loving and pretend that you are motivated by genuine fondness for that person. In contrast, it would not be hypocritical to behave in a kind and gracious manner, even if you don't feel like it, while acknowledging through your words or actions that you are motivated by your love for God (1 Peter 2:13–25; cf. Acts 7:59–60).

Chapter 11: Look Also to the Interests of Others

1. W. E. Vine, *An Expository Dictionary of Biblical Words* (Nashville: Thomas Nelson, 1985), 679.

2. For further direction and insight on cooperative negotiation, see Roger Fisher and William Ury, *Getting to Yes* (Boston: Houghton Mifflin, 1981). This highly respected book provides excellent guidance and practical suggestions on how to negotiate agreements.

Chapter 12: Overcome Evil with Good

1. These principles are discussed in greater detail in Jay Adams's book *How to Overcome Evil* (Grand Rapids: Baker, 1979).

2. Alternatively, the "burning coals" expression may refer to a Middle Eastern custom of carrying coals on one's head to someone whose fire had gone out. Doing this to someone who had wronged you would be an unusual act of love that might

soften his heart. The expression could also reflect an Egyptian expiation ritual, in which a guilty person, as a sign of his repentance, carried a basin of glowing coals on his head. The meaning here, then, would be that in returning good for evil, and so being kind to your enemy, you may cause him to repent or change. In any case, God promises to reward you (Prov. 25:22).

3. Ernest Gordon, *To End All Wars* (Grand Rapids: Zondervan, 2002), 197–98.

Appendix B: Alternative Ways to Resolve Disputes

1. Scalia, "Teaching About the Law," 9.

2. The information in this section is derived from *Guidelines for Christian Conciliation*, a booklet published by Peacemaker Ministries. Used by permission.

Appendix C: Principles of Restitution

1. Exodus 22:1 is somewhat difficult to understand. I believe its differing treatment of sheep and oxen shows the need for wisdom and flexibility when determining restitution. Since sheep need only to graze in a pasture to enable them to produce wool, meat, and offspring, they are relatively easy to replace. In contrast, a great deal of training must be invested in an ox before it can perform its draft duties properly. Therefore, replacement involves more than simply buying a new ox and turning it loose in a pasture, as you would with a sheep. Thus, Exodus 22:1 seems to imply that the more difficult something is to replace, the more restitution should be paid to ensure that the owner is in fact made whole.

Appendix D: When Is It Right to Go to Court?

1. As the writers of the Declaration of Independence realized, these laws must have as their purpose the protection of "inalienable rights"—that is, those things that may not be

taken from a person without due process. These things include life (e.g., freedom from assault, battery, rape), liberty (e.g., freedom from unjust imprisonment or intrusions into the raising of one's children), and the pursuit of happiness, which the writers understood to mean primarily the right to own and control private property (e.g., the right to contract, freedom from theft, burglary, and certain torts).

BIBLIOGRAPHY

Counseling and Communication

Fitzpatrick, Elyse. *Idols of the Heart.* Phillipsburg, N.J.: P & R Publishing, 2001.

Kober, Ted. *Confession and Forgiveness.* St. Louis: Concordia, 2002.

Morison, Patrick H. *Forgive! As the Lord Forgave You.* Phillipsburg, N.J.: P & R Publishing, 1987.

Powlison, David. *Seeing with New Eyes.* Phillipsburg, N.J.: P & R Publishing, 2003.

Tripp, Paul. *Instruments in the Redeemer's Hands.* Phillipsburg, N.J.: P & R Publishing, 2002.

———. *War of Words: Getting to the Heart of Your Communication Struggles.* Phillipsburg, N.J.: P & R Publishing, 2002.

Welch, Ed. *When People Are Big and God is Small.* Phillipsburg, N.J.: P & R Publishing, 1997.

———. *Addictions: A Banquet in the Grave.* Phillipsburg, N.J.: P & R Publishing, 2001.

Church Conflict

Adams, Jay E. *Sibling Rivalry in the Household of God.* Denver: Accent Books, 1988.

Dobsen, Edward G., Speed B. Leas, and Marshall Shelley. *Mastering Conflict and Controversy.* Portland: Multnomah Press, 1992.

Fenton, Horace L., Jr. *When Christians Clash*. Downers Grove, Ill.: Inter-Varsity Press, 1987.

Flynn, Leslie B. *When the Saints Come Storming In*. Wheaton: Victor Books, 1988.

Gangel, Kenneth O., and Samuel L. Canine. *Communication and Conflict Management in Churches and Christian Organizations*. Nashville: Broadman Press, 1992.

Haugk, Kenneth C. *Antagonists in the Church*. Minneapolis: Augsburg, 1988.

Huttenlocker, Keith. *Conflict and Caring*. Grand Rapids: Zondervan, 1988.

Kniskern, J. Warren. *Courting Disaster*. Nashville: Broadman and Holman, 1995.

Martin, Frank. *War in the Pews*. Downers Grove, Ill.: InterVarsity Press, 1995.

Thomas, Marlin E. *Resolving Disputes in Christian Groups*. Winnipeg: Windflower Communications, 1994.

Van Yperen, Jim. *Making Peace*. Chicago: Moody Press, 2002.

Wecks, John. *Free to Disagree*. Grand Rapids: Kregel, 1996.

Church Accountability/Discipline

Adams, Jay E. *Handbook on Church Discipline*. Grand Rapids: Zondervan, 1986.

Baker, Don. *Beyond Forgiveness*. Portland: Multnomah Press, 1984.

Buzzard, Lynn, and Thomas Brandon. *Church Discipline and the Courts*. Wheaton: Tyndale, 1987.

Gage, Ken and Joy. *Restoring Fellowship*. Chicago: Moody Press, 1984.

Mack, Wayne and David Swavely. *Life in the Father's House*. Phillipsburg, N.J.: P & R. Publishing, 1996.

MacNair, Donald J. *Restoration God's Way*. Philadelphia: Great Commissions Publications, 1978.

South, Tommy. *That We May Share in His Holiness*. Abilene: Bible Guides, 1997.

White, John and Ken Blue. *Healing the Wounded*. Downers Grove, Ill.: InterVarsity Press, 1985.

Marriage and Family Conflict

Adams, Jay E. *Marriage, Divorce, and Remarriage.* Grand Rapids: Zondervan, 1980.

Chapman, Gary. *Hope for the Separated.* Chicago: Moody Press, 1982.

Kniskern, J. Warren. *When the Vow Breaks.* Nashville: Broadman and Holman, 1993.

Rosberg, Gary. *Do-It-Yourself Relation Mender.* Colorado Springs: Focus on the Family, 1992.

Sande, Ken. *Peacemaking for Families.* Wheaton: Tyndale House Publishers, 2002.

Talley, Jim. *Reconcilable Differences.* Nashville: Thomas Nelson, 1985.

Negotiation/Mediation

Fisher, Roger, and William Ury. *Getting to Yes.* Boston: Houghton Mifflin, 1981.

Lovenheim, Peter. *Mediate, Don't Litigate.* New York: McGraw-Hill, 1989.

Sande, Ken and Ted Kober. *Guiding People Through Conflict.* Billings: Peacemaker Ministries, 1998.

Personal Spiritual Growth

Gordon, Earnest. *To End All Wars.* Grand Rapids: Zondervan, 2002.

Piper, John. *Future Grace.* Sisters, Ore.: Multnomah, 1995.

Mahaney, C.J., *The Cross Centered Life: Keeping the Gospel the Main Thing.* Sisters, Ore.: Multnomah, 2002.

Whitney, Donald. *Spiritual Disciplines for the Christian Life.* Colorado Springs: NavPress, 1991.

Spiritual Guidance

Friesen, Garry. *Decision Making and the Will of God.* Portland: Multnomah Press, 1980.

Petty, Jim. *Step by Step: Divine Guidance for Ordinary Christians.* Phillipsburg, N.J.: P & R Publishing, 1999.

Spiritual Wafare

Powlison, David. *Power Encounters: Reclaiming Spiritual Warfare.* Grand Rapids: Baker, 1995.

INDEX OF TOPICS

Index of Persons

INDEX OF SCRIPTURE
REFERENCES

Attorney **Ken Sande** is president of Peacemaker Ministries. He regularly conciliates business, family, employment, and church disputes and serves as a consultant to pastors and attorneys as they work to resolve conflicts outside the courtroom. Ken conducts seminars throughout the United States and internationally on biblical conflict resolution.

MORE LIFE-CHANGING RESOURCES FROM PEACEMAKER MINISTRIES

Culture of Peace Series

This series of booklets provides practical assistance on many topics related to biblical peacemaking, including:

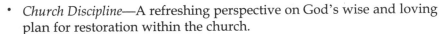

- *Biblical Peacemaking*—Four basic principles you can apply in any relationship (a brief summary of *The Peacemaker*).

- *Judging Others*—Making charitable judgments can transform your relationships.

- *Transforming Your Church*—Learn how to cultivate a culture of peace in your church.

- *Words That Cut*—Learn how to take criticism in light of the gospel.

- *Church Discipline*—A refreshing perspective on God's wise and loving plan for restoration within the church.

The Young Peacemaker

Teach children to be peacemakers with this fun, biblical curriculum. The illustrated parent/teacher manual contains twelve lessons with stories and memory verses. A set of twelve reproducible booklets reinforces the lessons with additional material.

Biblical Peacemaking Adult Sunday School Curriculum

An exciting series designed to teach biblical peacemaking skills in an adult Sunday School setting in six or twelve weeks.

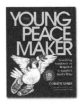

Reconciler Training Program

For those in all walks of life who desire more training in biblical peacemaking, the Reconciler Course offers clear and practical instruction (available in both audio and video versions). After completing this at-home study, you are encouraged to attend a stimulating two-day Reconciler Practicum, where you will learn how to apply the principles in real-life settings.

Please visit our web site at www.HisPeace.org or call us at 406/256-1583 for information about our resources and events.